D1554581

Henry M. Teller

Henry Teller in mid-1870s. Courtesy, Colorado Historical Society.

Henry M. Teller

COLORADO'S GRAND OLD MAN

by Duane A. Smith

University Press of Colorado

© 2002 by the University Press of Colorado

Published by the University Press of Colorado
5589 Arapahoe Avenue, Suite 206C
Boulder, Colorado 80303

The University Press of Colorado is a cooperative publishing enterprise supported, in part, by Adams State College, Colorado State University, Fort Lewis College, Mesa State College, Metropolitan State College of Denver, University of Colorado, University of Northern Colorado, University of Southern Colorado, and Western State College of Colorado.

The paper used in this publication meets the minimum requirements of the American National Standard for Information Sciences—Permanence of Paper for Printed Library Materials. ANSI Z39.48-1992

Library of Congress Cataloging-in-Publication Data

Smith, Duane A.
  Henry M. Teller : Colorado's Grand Old Man / Duane Smith.
    p. cm.
Includes bibliographical references and index.
  ISBN 0-87081-666-7 (hardcover : alk. paper) 1. Teller, Henry Moore, 1830–1914. 2. Legislators—United States—Biography. 3. United States. Congress. Senate—Biography. 4. Colorado—Politics and government—1876-1950. I. Title.
  E664.T27 S65 2001
  328.73'092—dc21

                                                                              2001008021

Design by Laura Furney & Daniel Pratt
Typesetting by David Archer

11   10   09   08   07   06   05   04   03   02   10   9   8   7   6   5   4   3   2   1

For Clark Spence
Friend and mentor for fifty years

Contents

Preface

Although he was easily recognizable a century ago in Colorado, we have generally forgotten Henry Teller today. It reminds one of the words of Charles Kingsley that his contemporary, Horace Tabor, placed on the curtain of his grand opera house in Denver.

So fleet the works of men back to the earth again:
Ancient and holy things fade like a dream.

Teller's career spanned Colorado's history from the pioneering days of the early 1860s to the threshold of World War I. He was the first Coloradan to gain national status, and no one from Colorado has served longer in the U.S. Senate. He was also the first Coloradan to serve in the president's cabinet. He provided and provides Coloradans with a "sense of a personal and possessed past," as Wallace Stegner wrote.

Henry Teller was a transitional leader who took Colorado from the nineteenth century into the twentieth, pointing the way into the future while trying to make the new generation aware of the problems it would have to confront. Water, the environment, Washington's role in the West, America's place on the world scene, and the "new" economy and politics ranked high among the issues that concerned him. Not simply a state or regional leader, Teller was among the first to worry about America's new role as a world power, particularly its involvement in Asia. Today, after World War II, Korea, and Vietnam, his warnings sound hauntingly familiar.

Colorado was fortunate to have Teller as one of its first two senators. He knew the state as well as anyone, represented it carefully and thoroughly in the Senate, and gained the respect of his colleagues with his thoughtful and well-documented positions and presentations. Although he was not a dramatic orator, he was a strong advocate for his state and region. Through the trials and tribulations during his Senate career, he retained the admiration and respect of both his fellow Coloradans and nearly all of his Senate colleagues. Coloradans could ask for no more from their leaders than the intelligence, honorableness, and decency Henry Teller exemplified. A powerful case can be made that Teller was the best and most significant senator who ever represented Colorado in Washington. Few who came after him approached his level of influence and importance; certainly, no one surpassed him.

During his lifetime he saw the old West, as well as the birth of the new West. He did so with a lawyer-businessman-politician-statesman's eye. He did not yearn for a lost Camelot. His life reflected much that had been and foreshadowed much that would come. So come back to an earlier age, the starting point of today's Colorado. Remember the advice of Mark Twain: "To arrive at a just estimate of a renowned man's character one must judge it by the standards of his time, not ours."

"I see you stand like greyhounds in the slips, straining upon the start. The game's afoot," cried Henry V to his troops in Shakespeare's play by that name. It is hoped that readers will proceed in like manner in the pages that follow. Colorado history, and the fascinating people who made it, are the foundation of the modern era.

I owe a deep debt of appreciation to many people who helped make this study possible. Good friend Chris Buys generously shared his Teller material, and Jay Hogan shared some photographs. Listen Leyendecker—longtime friend, Colorado historian, and colleague—enthusiastically contributed material and his knowledge of the era and people involved. Teller descendant Robert Tyler of La Crescenta, California, shared his love for the family and put me in contact with Richard Tyler of Homer, Alaska, who opened his wonderful collection of family photographs that provided new perspective on his Colorado ancestors. My cousins Shirley and Hearold Montgomery took me around Teller's Illinois home, Morrison, and did fieldwork along the way. Charles Smith provided transportation and a cheerful attitude even in the early morning. The national history honorary fraternity, Phi Alpha Theta, honored me with a grant for Teller research expenses.

The staffs of numerous libraries and historical societies provided assistance and insights. The University Archives at the University of Colorado, the Colorado Historical Society, and the Western History Department of the Denver Public Library proved particularly valuable. Their collections are invaluable for those interested in Colorado history.

The staff of the University Press of Colorado showed great patience and professionalism in transforming manuscript to book. My thanks to one and all. My wife, Gay, as she has always done, supported me in so many ways that to recount them would take a page in itself.

Prologue: 1896

St. Louis burned humid and hot, a "boiling sun," one reporter described it. Humidity draped over the city like a fog. Yesterday's rain only made it worse. Visitors and residents alike found no relief. Republicans, attending their national convention, packed the town.

Outside the convention hall the thermometer soared to 86 degrees; inside the muggy auditorium, crowded with 12,000 sweating delegates and visitors, the temperature grew hotter still. Hand fans fluttered everywhere. Tension and turmoil honed the heat and humidity.

The Republican National Convention met in St. Louis that June 18, 1896. The convention, for all practical purposes, had already decided its presidential nominee and thus had offered little excitement until this moment. Except for the rumor that some western states might bolt, the convention was placid and unanimated.

Sweltering, strawhatted delegates, earlier in the day neatly attired in carefully ironed Victorian gentlemen's summer suits and shirts, leaned forward in their wooden chairs to hear the speaker on the platform. A few women listened, too, but this remained principally a man's world. Women had the right to vote in Colorado and neighboring Wyoming, Idaho, and Utah but not elsewhere and not in presidential elections.

The tall, gaunt man, wearing, as it was quaintly described, "the old-fashioned frock coat of the old-time statesman," with only a pink rosebud in his lapel to break his somber appearance, spoke as always with deep

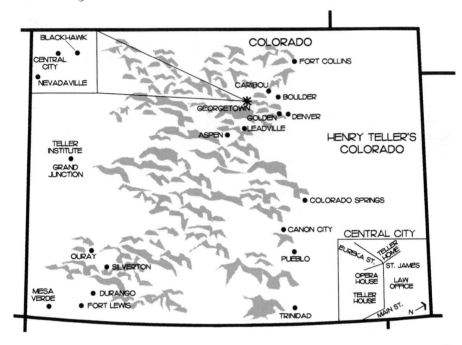

conviction. Looking "worn and weary," the senator spoke from the heart and mind. No poetry, no humor, no stories beguiled his listeners. Still, his "gentle tone" of sadness and regret could be heard throughout the auditorium.

His supporters—waving flags, hats, umbrellas, fans, and handkerchiefs and "shrieking like madmen"—had greeted him as he advanced to the podium. The flags on the ceiling fluttered as cheer after cheer spread across the hall. Then, across the broad floor, a "dead-level calm" fell over the delegates and gallery spectators.

No one that day doubted the sincerity of Colorado's gray-haired senator Henry Teller. Calmly, he spoke for silver, for the West, for a vanishing America. For forty minutes his audience listened, some convinced they were watching history unfold.

> I am vehemently opposed to a gold standard plank, and I believe that if the Republican party takes this course it will depart from its vaunted position as defender of the rights of the people—the masses—and throw itself into the hands of the bond-clippers of Lombard and Wall Streets. This policy is un-American, unpatriotic and opposed to all the best interest of good, safe government and humanity.

Teller, who had been with the Republican Party since its founding, was about to leave it. After reviewing his long party service, he seemed visibly affected: "I must sever my connection with the political party which makes the gold plank one of the principal articles of its faith." He had finished his sincere, temperate valedictory.

Those nearest the platform detected a glimmer of tears in his eyes as he "sank into his seat." A few hisses and a "get out" or two drifted down from the galleries. Then the silver men who had backed him wholeheartedly, engulfed with the emotion of the moment, cheered and applauded. Even some gold delegates and spectators in the galleries cheered the man, although not his cause.

In the Ohio delegation, short, robust Mark Hanna sat fidgeting through Teller's speech, his mouth twitching irritably. He had orchestrated this convention to nominate his friend—Civil War veteran, former congressman, and Ohio governor William McKinley. All had gone well until now. The convention might be getting out of his control; the delegates seemed about to explode.

The issue at hand—the financial plank in the 1896 platform—did not usually stir such emotion, but 1896 proved no ordinary year. Teller championed the minority report advocating a bimetal standard of both gold and silver and the free coinage of silver. Hanna and most of the convention favored the single gold standard. No issue divided the American people more decisively that year.

No attempt was made to answer Teller. Teller's Senate colleague Henry Cabot Lodge from Massachusetts moved quickly to have the minority report laid on the table. If he succeeded, there it would lie, killed forever. Teller countered by demanding a roll call vote on the financial plank issue. The delegates voted nearly 8 to 1 in support of gold. Teller had known this would be the outcome from the beginning, but he had made a "splendid effort on behalf of silver."

Determined to move ahead (it was now around noon), Hanna refused to allow a recess to be called. Utah senator Frank Cannon asked for a personal privilege to address the convention.

Cannon started to read a prepared statement explaining what was about to happen. Both floor delegates and the gallery became increasingly restless and hostile. He spoke in the enemy's camp, and they let Cannon know it. Shouts of "bolt and be damned" interrupted him. A storm of hisses, calls of "throw him out" and "choke him," hoots, and catcalls echoed throughout the hall. Taunting him, several cried "go to Chicago," where the Democrats would meet. Hanna, unable to control himself shouted "go, go." Cannon continued, his strong voice barely heard amid the "Niagara-like" uproar.

A dull convention surged into frenzy. Delegates mounted chairs, waved flags, shook umbrellas. Slowly, deliberately, Cannon announced that the silver people would leave; a reading of their names brought waves of hisses and boos.

At the end, Cannon and Teller shook convention chairman Nebraska senator John Thurston's hand and the hands of others on the platform. Thurston, Hanna's handpicked man, announced dramatically that the convention had nothing to fear from a bolt. It was 1:15 in the afternoon.

Teller and Cannon left the platform and marched down the aisle toward the door joined by twenty-three stern-faced delegates. They were westerners—mostly from Colorado, Utah, Montana, Nevada, and Idaho—not kingmaker states. Hanna worried little about them.

They marched out amid "ear-splitting tumult." People leaped on chairs, shouted, screamed, and threw fans or whatever could be grabbed and pitched. Everything "paled into silence." Torrents of voices roared in mingled rage, admiration, defiance, derision, and loathing: "Let them go and be damned." "Go to Chicago! Take the Democratic train!" The band tried to break into the tumult but was drowned out by the noise. Finally, the musicians and some conventioneers asserted themselves by playing and singing the popular "Columbia, the Gem of the Ocean." Somehow, "three cheers for the red, white, and blue" caught the delegates' attention.

Through the tumult the small group marched among a gauntlet of shouting enemies. Passing beside the bust of former president Ulysses Grant, who had inadvertently started all this twenty-three years before, the silverites left the convention hall. By then many frenzied delegates were singing the chorus of "Good-bye, My Lover, Good-bye." It took another five minutes for the uproar to subside. A pleased Mark Hanna had won the day.

Cheers from friends greeted the men outside. They hustled Teller into a carriage that rapidly carried him to the Southern Hotel, the convention headquarters of the Colorado delegation and, interestingly, of the Republican Party. He was already being talked about as the presidential candidate of a party dedicated to silver. By late afternoon "modest white badges" appeared proclaiming, "We are solid for Teller as Teller is solid for silver."

Covering the convention as a newspaper reporter, well-known free silverite spokesman William Jennings Bryan commented that the silver Republicans "pursued the only manly course left to them." He predicted hundreds of thousands "of the [party] rank and file" would follow Teller out. The number of supporting telegrams the senator received in the next few days suggested that Bryan might be correct.

Thus ended the first day of the first political bolt in the history of the Grand Old Party. More than forty years before, its founders had bolted from the Democrats and the defunct Whig Party to organize their own antislavery crusade. The northern states needed their own political party for sectional and business reasons as well. Deeply concerned about slavery, Teller had joined the Republicans for that reason. Now he had left.

The convention continued on, nominating McKinley and standing by the gold plank in its platform. McKinley had once been a friend of silver. Like other politicians, though, when infected by presidential fever, he had changed his mind. Hanna and other eastern businessmen had convinced him of the error of his ways. Teller and a host of westerners did not agree, believing all the problems of the United States— and it had plenty in 1896—could be traced to the erroneous beliefs of men like Hanna.

McKinley did not stand alone. Many people had changed their minds lately. Now came the time of reckoning. The challenge had been shouted clearly and emphatically to those who followed silver or who disagreed with the Republicans' strongly probusiness outlook. It appeared that the United States had come to a watershed in its history. The 1896 election would decide the issue; a tiger stalked in the hearts of men.[1]

The battle lines were drawn. They had been forming for twenty years: westerner versus easterner; ruralite versus urbanite; borrower versus creditor and investor; radicalism in defense of conservatism versus conservatism in defense of change; farmer, rancher, miner versus banker and big businessman; silverite versus goldbug; the common man versus the elite; "Americans" versus "foreigners"; reform versus status quo. In ways it would prove to be the last stand of the nineteenth century against the onrushing twentieth century.

Silver moved men's minds, inflamed their souls, excited their emotions. Why was silver so significant? What caused it to stir such feelings? Teller would travel a long and fascinating road before he could answer those questions. Henry Teller was well into his forties before he began to study and understand the issue. Then, for the next quarter of a century, it dominated his life.

Henry Teller had never intended to be the lightning rod of this storm. Certainly, there had been no indication he was destined for such a role when he was born on a farm in Allegany County, New York, on May 23, 1830. His boyhood was typical for the time and place in rural America. He would never forget his early years and rural roots in what was then described as a "lively farming center."

Unlike many of his contemporaries, Teller was fortunate to have received advanced schooling, first at Rushford Academy, then at Alfred University. Young Henry started as a teacher and became principal of schools in Angelica, the county seat. In later years he loved to reminisce about his "pedagogic days" and described teaching as a "sacred calling."

Although he enjoyed teaching, from childhood he had dreamed of becoming a lawyer. Soon Martin Grover, one of "New York's most prominent lawyers," accepted him to study law in his office. Grover proved an exacting teacher; thorough, carefully prepared legal briefs and court presentations were Teller's hallmark throughout his career. Another trait also became obvious. A New York friend remarked that "no one ever doubted the sincerity of Teller."

As young men in the exciting 1850s were apt to do, Teller became interested in politics. His father had been a Democrat, and he naturally gravitated in that direction, but the onrushing slavery dispute pushed him into the newly formed Republican Party. During the party's inaugural presidential campaign, the twenty-six-year-old gave his first public speech in the Angelica courthouse, speaking for candidate John C. Fremont. Teller took a road typical for lawyers. Careers in politics and law went together; both were doors to advancement.

His future wife, Harriet Bruce, provided one of the best glimpses of the young Teller. Initially, she was not especially attracted to him. "Not particularly striking" in appearance, his long hair seemed to the young lady to offer whatever character he had. Yet at "first sight I did not like it. He had plenty of it, very black, which he combed back as far as the stiffness of it would permit." Teller enjoyed "nothing more than to run his fingers through his hair" when reading or preoccupied. Harriet laughingly remembered years later her thought that if she and Teller should be introduced, "the first thing I will say to him will be to tell him to cut his hair."

They met in 1856 at the Methodist church both attended in Angelica. Harriet, from Cuba, 20 miles west of the county seat, attended the "young ladies' academy." She soon forgot about the hair and found herself engaged in an "agreeable conversation with a young man who was a close observer and student" of many things: "I liked him from the start and we saw more or less of each other during the time that we both remained at Angelica." Her schooling and his law studies kept them apart much of the time. Nevertheless, romance blossomed.

Henry, meanwhile, taught and worked diligently on his studies, gaining a well-grounded knowledge of law. He was admitted to the New York bar on January 5, 1858.

Approaching thirty, Teller decided his future did not lie in New York or the East. Like many young men he heeded the advice of Horace Greeley: "If you have no family or friends to aid you, and no prospect opened to you there, turn your face to the great West, and there build up a home and fortune."

Harriet and Henry faced a decision. The young couple became engaged, although they lacked the financial resources they believed were needed to start married life. Harriet explained, "Indeed, there was no more money in the purse than was requisite to pay [the] expenses of one to Illinois and insure maintenance there until established in the practice." Harriet and Henry agreed that "he was to come back for me as soon as conditions would justify, and of course he did." Neither imagined how long that would take.

The prairies of Illinois beckoned him. Henry had learned that a young lawyer, Hiram Johnson, practicing in Morrison, wanted a partner. Correspondence between the two produced an agreement, and after passing the bar, Teller prepared to travel west and practice law.[2] Amid the sadness of leaving Harriet and the excitement of new opportunity, he could not have imagined he was taking the first step on a path that would put him in St. Louis on that humid, hot June day in 1896.

NOTES

1.   This composite description of the June 18, 1896, session was taken from the *Evening Star* (Washington), June 19; *Rocky Mountain News* (Denver), June 19; *St. Louis Post-Dispatch,* June 19; *New York Times,* June 19; *Washington Post,* June 19; *St. Louis Globe-Democrat,* June 19; *Weekly Republican* (Denver), June 25; and William Allan White, *Autobiography* (New York: Macmillan, 1946), 77. Various sources estimated the number of people in the convention hall that day to have been between 10,000 and 15,000.

2.   Teller's pre-Illinois life was taken from Harriet Teller interview, "Senator Teller as a Young Man," Colorado Historical Society, 2–3; James Teller, "Henry Teller," Colorado Historical Society, 7; *Denver Daily Tribune,* November 15, 1876; Thomas Dawson, "Scrapbooks," Colorado Historical Society, vol. 61; Thomas Dawson, "The Personal Side of Senator Teller," Colorado Historical Society, 5; unidentified clipping, "Teller Scrapbook," Chris Buys private collection. Horace Greeley's quote is in *Bartlett's Familiar Quotations* (Boston: Little, Brown, 1992), 462.

Henry M. Teller

Prairie Lawyer

The Morrison to which Teller traveled could no longer be said to be part of the frontier West. That region now lay across the Missouri River. Illinois had been a state for well over a generation when he arrived. In fact, Teller had come by train, that new wonder Americans had taken such a liking to in the 1850s.

Located a dozen miles from the Mississippi River, Morrison sat amid some of Illinois's most fertile prairie farmland. It appeared as lush or even richer than any land Henry had seen in New York. The town was situated on the edge of wooded, rolling hills on the north side of the railroad tracks with flat prairie land stretching toward the horizon on the south. Whiteside County was located in the northwest corner of the state and had been one of the last counties to be settled. Nevertheless, it held out great promise for the new, untested lawyer.

Morrison was much less polished than the communities Henry had been accustomed to in New York, but the town showed definite signs of coming maturity. Its newspaper, the *Whiteside Sentinel,* promised in its first issue (·July 23, 1857) to be a "faithful exponent of the interests of the town and county in which it is located." With the enthusiasm of editorial birth, the editor praised the fertility of the soil, the healthiness of the climate, and, last but by no means least, the county's great agricultural and manufacturing resources, all told "unsurpassed by any territory of like extent in the Union." Not bad for a town that was only two years old! The newspaper saluted Henry's new partner, Hiram Johnson, as a lawyer with "business tact and judgement."

Within a year the paper was writing about well-stocked dry goods, grocery, and other shops; well-filled hotels; town incorporation; ordinances written; a new railroad depot; the need to build a sidewalk on Main Street; and, in October 1858, a local census that counted 455 residents. All this occurred despite the "trying times" of the national 1857 crash and depression that would last two or three years. The mainline Protestant churches had arrived—Baptist, Methodist, Presbyterian, and Congregational. Not all proved peaceful and idyllic, as the construction of a new jail revealed; and temperance meetings tried to corral the wayward before it was too late.

On July 4, 1858, on one of "those summer days everybody is glad of," the evening concluded with a "grand supper and ball." At the former, H. A. Johnson, Esq., toasted "Our Country."[1] This was the world to which Teller traveled.

With high hopes after having received some very favorable comments from his bar examiners, the young lawyer arrived. Although his partner Johnson had been there almost from the village's founding, Teller struggled to become established. Hiram Johnson was not the conservative type of lawyer his partner had studied with back home. Undoubtedly popular and capable, Johnson dreamed large dreams and chased the pot of gold at the end of the rainbow. Unlike his new colleague, he rallied to the Democratic Party and supported its leading national spokesman, Illinois senator Stephen Douglas.

The two men got along, however, and they delved into the numerous and varied legal affairs of the day. Their legal card, the only local one in the *Sentinel* on April 14, 1858, announced: "Attorneys and Counsellors at Law and Solicitors in Chancery; [they] will practice at all the Courts of the 22 Judicial Districts and the Supreme and United States District Courts of Illinois."

Plenty of available clients and cases existed, if the November 20, 1860, *Sentinel* gave a typical overview of the variety. Ten prisoners awaited trial at the next Circuit Court term. Four were charged with murder, two with stealing horses, one with breaking into a house, another for stealing a watch, a third for appearing "crazy," and a woman for stealing clothes. To the relief of readers, the sheriff informed the paper that "never" had that many been in jail "at one time before." New communities liked to present the best possible image in their newspapers, and an overcrowded jail did not foster such an image.

The cases gave Teller the background and experience he needed. The firm represented defendant or plaintiff in a host of promissory note cases, including horse trades, land sales, and recovery of wheat, a wagon, and a horse taken by "some one not its owner."

The partners also handled criminal cases. Their client in one rape case lost, but they successfully defended a man in a second case. A burglary suspect was found not guilty, although in the same session another client was convicted of stealing horses.

Teller unsuccessfully defended a man accused of stealing a plow, then won a case involving a father-in-law, a cow, and a bad bargain. The plaintiff received five cents. Several arson cases provided him with further experience.

Cases involving selling adulterated whiskey, engaging in gambling, passing counterfeit coins, "keeping a disorderly and ill-governed house," and committing assault with a deadly weapon gave Teller experience in a wide variety of criminal cases that would prove useful in the future. When he and Johnson defended Thomas Cogglan on a murder charge, they successfully secured a verdict of insanity. Cogglan helped by claiming he desired to make his victim an "angel." Cases involving larceny and "malicious mischief" completed his courtroom experience. All considered, it was a substantial legal docket for the young lawyer to tackle in the span of a little more than two years.[2]

Henry drafted legal documents, advised potential clients, heard complaints and concerns, and considered case strategies. Little free time was left in his busy schedule. Meanwhile, competition grew. By August 1859 the *Sentinel* carried cards of five out-of-town attorneys and four in-town firms. If the number of cases handled in court provide any indication, Johnson and Teller more than held their own.

The community was growing. The Presbyterians completed their new frame building with a "Gothic-style tower," and not a step behind came the Baptists, whereas the Congregationalists took down the church at nearby declining Unionville and rebuilt it in Morrison. A new school, the second in the county, opened with a faculty "acknowledged [as] among the best." Construction of buildings, including one two-story brick structure, belied the depression conditions. Two trains east and two west stopped each day, and the railroad renamed itself the Galena & Chicago. The number of merchants steadily increased, and specialty stores replaced the general stores of only a few years before. Even a "picture gallery" opened so that "all who may be serious of procuring their life like shadows to hand down to posterity and generations unborn" could immortalize themselves.

All this must have reaffirmed Teller's belief that he had made the right decision in coming west to Illinois. Despite his limited time, Henry became involved in his new hometown activities. This was important for him both personally and professionally. In the somewhat unsettled world of a young community, fraternal lodges provided newcomers with access into the community, friends, status, business contacts, and a sense of belonging. Like his contemporaries, Teller joined. He helped organize the Masonic Lodge in May 1859, probably continuing his involvement from New York. The Mount Pleasant Lodge of the Independent Order of the Good Templars gained him as a member. A lifelong supporter of temperance, Teller came from the state that gave birth to the Templars.

Equally important, culture was taking root in Morrison. With great pride the newspaper announced that a lyceum series would meet in the school during winter of 1859–1860, "no way in which an evening each week can more profitably be spent." The topics and programs must have excited the New York lawyer, who remembered a similar series back home. Musical concerts, debates, and speeches highlighted the lyceum series. Participants one evening discussed the recent sensation, "John Brown's Invasion and the slavery question," and another evening debated the question, "Is the acquisition of more territory by the United States detrimental to its interests."

Equally important to Morrison boosters, the town became the site of the county fair. It featured vegetables, fruits, agricultural products, and animal exhibits. Yet visitors could also tour a department of "fine arts" with "mostly oil landscapes." Youngsters no doubt greatly appreciated the appearances of "Antonia Brothers Great Circus" and "DeHaven's Great Union Circus" on other occasions. Town boosters, of which there were many, thankfully realized that Morrison was coming of age as a population and business center if two circuses appeared in one year!

Another sign of "civilization," greatly enjoyed by the young, was the better selection of Christmas toys and other gifts that graced merchants' shelves each year. Churches put on improved programs, as did the school and other groups, although the newspaper announced in its December 29, 1859, issue—after a quiet holiday— that "interest in the day usually lessened when it comes on Sunday!" Santa Claus made his accustomed visit, though, and well-filled stockings "testified" that the "mysterious little old man," friend of the little folks, had once again found Morrison.

The county already had an "Old Settlers' Association." One had to have arrived before July 4, 1840, to be a member and attend the annual meeting and gain the honor of being a real pioneer. Newcomer Teller did not qualify; he was part of the "new" history.[3]

The old settlers well remembered the Winnebagoes who once had lived in the area. When several visited Morrison in November 1859, the paper headlined the news, "LO, THE POOR INDIANS!" Teller had not had the opportunity to observe native people close at hand, and the impression must not have been a good one. The Sentinel reported that they appeared to be in "rather destitute circumstances" and begged for provisions or clothing to help them through the approaching winter.

If the Winnebagoes represented a fleeting heritage, Morrisonians only briefly pondered their fate. More important, Illinois was slowly pulling out of the depression. Further, the heated sectional question over slavery, pitting North and South, was becoming hotter by the month. And politics was never far from the public eye.

Although Teller had arrived in Illinois in time to witness the Abraham Lincoln/ Stephen Douglas debates in the 1858 contest for the U.S. Senate, he never mentioned having done so. One of his neighbors heard Lincoln speak and call Teller "the homeliest man in Illinois." That aside, Teller became a Lincoln man.

Henry had moved from one Republican county to another. The newspaper wholeheartedly backed and most of the people either backed or leaned toward the new party. One branch of the Underground Railroad went through Whiteside County, and the Sentinel after the fact reported that two women had passed through in February 1859.

Teller took an active role in the 1860 political events. In April, after being selected a delegate to the county Republican convention, Henry was appointed to the
committee that drafted resolutions. In addition to supporting Republican principles
and nominees, the resolutions attacked the Dred Scott decision, Democratic president James Buchanan, and the Democratic Party overall. The meeting in July turned
tumultuous when several towns sent contested delegations. Heated debate and shouting filled the room, and the frustrated chairman—unable to keep order—finally
resigned, as did one of the secretaries. Teller supported the majority, but they failed to
regain harmony when the losing delegates walked out.

According to his brother James, Henry went to the state convention that year but
was not chosen a delegate to the national Republican convention in Chicago. He
traveled to Chicago, however, and attended as a visitor the convention that nominated Lincoln, an experience Henry never forgot. Returning home, he campaigned
for "Honest Abe."

On Saturday evening, August 25, Teller addressed the Morrison Republican
Club. Despite his youth and relative inexperience in public speaking, the "plain
common sense speech" was vintage Teller. He fortressed it with history and quotes
from Washington, Jackson, Clay, and others. The local newspaper reporter stressed
that Teller clearly proved that "the Republican is now the only party contending for
the true principles of government as laid down in the constitution and adopted by the
'fathers of the Republic.'" Presidential candidate Lincoln entertained the same views,
according to Henry, as had every "pure patriot and statesman from Washington's
time down to the present day." Democratic candidate Douglas, on the other hand,
favored the "extension of slavery as much as Jeff Davis or any other fire eater Southerner." Caught up in the emotion of the hour, Teller concluded ringingly, "Are northern
freemen prepared to see slavery further extended over our free territories?"

At the conclusion of his remarks the club formed a company of "Wide Awakes."
Sixty-three men signed up to help ensure Lincoln's election. It ended successfully:
"The Republicans have achieved a glorious triumph in 'Old Whiteside.'" Lincoln's
more than two-to-one landslide showed the town's and county's loyalty to the party.[4]

Teller's increased prominence within Morrison and the Republican Party was
shown by the fact that he was one of five members of the Republican Central
Committee. As the country was falling apart, with southern states seceding after
Lincoln's election, the committee called for Whiteside Republicans to meet "to confer upon our duty in this great peril as a Nation. Come, let us council together, and
renew our devotion to the great principles of the founders of our Republic." They
did meet, but news of Lincoln's inauguration and the organization of the new government overshadowed their deliberations.

Morrison readers had been kept well-informed on national issues over the past
three years. The *Sentinel* had been objective initially, considering its political leanings. As
the news became more ominous, however, the paper became more pro-Northern in
its interpretations of events. By 1861 the *Sentinel* was providing excellent summaries

of events ranging from seceding states, organization of the Confederate government, and Fort Sumter. In mid-April it cheered as Morrison raised a company of light infantry to quell "the southern rebellion."[5]

By that time, events in Morrison had receded in importance for Henry. Something had occurred in 1858–1859 that would change his life forever—the Pike's Peak gold rush.

The hard times in the late 1850s made Midwesterners particularly suspectible to the lure of western mining. Only ten years before, California had been the golden land of opportunity. In that wonderful year 1849, dreams became reality in the gold-ribbed streams of the Sierra Nevadas. It appeared that all that was needed to start a second rush was news of another California.

The *Sentinel* seemed never remiss in reporting rumors and news about such a hope. The Frazer River excitement in 1858 did not pan out, nor did the rumor of gold in Texas. Then in the September 16, 1858, issue, the paper reported a "pretty well-established fact" that gold had been found in western Kansas. Even more encouraging, it had the "true California look," and those who "go there are said to run no risk at all." If the rushers found no gold, they could turn to farming. Either way, these pioneers would "contribute toward the establishment of an important outpost of civilization." Potential golden wealth combined with being part of America's destiny seemed too good to resist. By January 1859 the newspaper, as well as many of its contemporaries, was carried away in expectation; "the New El Dorado" had been found. Not willing to see Whiteside County "abandoned," however, the editor cautioned that those who "stay at home have more chance" of making money than those who go to Pike's Peak.

For the next six months, reports in the *Sentinel* mirrored developments, or the lack thereof, in the new El Dorado. Reports of wagons passing through and wishes of good luck contrasted sharply with cries of a Pike's Peak "humbug." Complaints about a lack of information were balanced by letters from former residents who had arrived in the Rockies. Then came the return of several "go backers." The Whiteside County Pike's Peakers had experienced little success; at least one person shot himself, and another became too sick to work. Nonetheless, they did report claims that paid well, including one that yielded $500 per day. Considering the few hundred dollars farmers or laborers might earn in a year, that sum seemed unbelievable. The report failed to mention how long this bonanza lasted.[6]

One Whitesider who did not make a fortune still enjoyed the time of his life. "The sight obtained of that wonderful animal the 'elephant' was prodigiously satisfying," he confessed while enthusiastically recounting his adventures to a reporter when he returned in August 1860. He had "seen the elephant," as the expression went, done things he never expected to do, and been a part of history. Now, however, he believed that "Whiteside county is not a bad place to make money in, after all."

All this proved too much for Hiram Johnson. He had to go West. On August 9, 1860, a long letter appeared in the *Sentinel* from an enthusiastic Hiram. After eight weeks of observation and visiting "all places of note in the mining region," he felt qualified to inform his former neighbors about developments. Writing from Nevada City, Colorado, Johnson correctly forecast that the region's future rested with its quartz mines, not the pan-and-shovel placer operations that had started the rush. He complained about the failure of mining and gold-saving machinery; overly optimistic and inexperienced, eastern "artisans know very little" about what was needed.

The failure of the government—caught up in the slavery morass—to help the Rocky Mountain country with territorial organization, mail service, and the extinguishment of Indian titles upset the lawyer. So did the political fanaticism and disunity back home.

Not discouraged, Johnson predicted a great future for Nevada City, Mountain City, and Central City as "trading posts" for miners. Each boasted a "very enterprising class of merchants, mechanics, and professional men." Regardless, Hiram correctly warned his readers, "All who come here are not deserving of success. A man must have capital, work hard, and be exceedingly lucky, or come short of success." What did the Pike's Peak mines need? Not "gentlemen of leisure," but "hard fisted, big hearted, bold, adventuresome men may come here." The cost of living soared to nearly unbelievable heights, crushing the hopes of many rushers who failed to measure up to Johnson's hard work and capital standards. "This is a discriminating country," he concluded.

All told, Hiram presented a fairly objective view of the mining region. Ever optimistic, Johnson ended on a high note: "Allow me to say, however, for the edification of my friends in Whiteside (and I know that I have some), that the subscriber has no fears as to success."

He wanted his partner to come West as well, to this new field of opportunity. Caught up in politics and legal work, not to mention more conservative by nature, Henry hesitated. As Teller later commented, he thought Colorado was "too barbaric and rough." Eventually, he succumbed, and in April 1861 Henry took the train to St. Joseph, Missouri, then spent seven tedious days on a bouncing and swaying stage across the seemingly endless prairies.

Luring Teller West created the strongest effect Hiram Johnson had on his young partner. He had brought him to Illinois; more important, now he took him on to Pike's Peak country. Colorado offered challenges and opportunities Henry could not yet imagine.

Teller left his brother Willard behind in Illinois in charge of the Morrison law practice. Willard had assumed Henry's New York teaching position when the older brother went to Illinois.[7] Willard had followed the same path from the farm to teaching, then into law.

Back in New York, Harriet must have been wondering why her wandering fiancé continued his westward trek to a new, untested promised land. The two had faithfully corresponded, but the young man had not, in his mind, earned enough to support a wife.

His Morrison days receded as Henry crossed the prairies, although he never completely severed his Whiteside ties. He had purchased farmland in the county, and his parents eventually moved there. In November 1866 Henry gave them a "lease for life" on 418 acres. Teller continued to own farmland in Whiteside County into the 1890s, even though his father had died and his mother and sisters lived in town. Henry returned often to visit his parents while they were alive. His mother lived until 1901 when she was hailed as the oldest resident of Morrison. Most of Henry's three brothers and four sisters also resided there. Only Henry, Willard, and eventually James—twenty years younger then Henry—went West.

NOTES

1. *Whiteside Sentinel* (Morrison, Illinois), July 23, 1857, April 28, May 6, June 23, July 8, September 9, 16, October 14, 1858.

2. William W. Davis, *History of Whiteside County, Illinois* (Chicago: Pioneer, 1908), 327; Harriet Teller, "Senator Teller as a Young Man," Colorado Historical Society, 3; *Whiteside Sentinel,* April 14, 1858, January 6, May 26, June 2, October 13, 20, November 3, 1859, January 19, 26, February 2, May 24, 31, June 7, 1860, and February 7, 1861; Clark Spence, *British Investments and the American Mining Frontier* (Ithaca: Cornell University Press, 1958), 29–30, 157.

3. *Whiteside Sentinel,* July 7, 21, August 18, 25, October 6, December 8, 15, 29, 1859, January 5, March 1, June 7, August 2, 23, November 15, 22, 29, and December 27, 1860; Davis, *History of Whiteside County,* 306, 319.

4. James Teller, "Henry Teller," Colorado Historical Society, 8; Dunham Wright, "A Winter in Estes Park with Senator Teller," *The Trail* (July 1920), 9–10; *Whiteside Sentinel,* June 24, 1858, February 17, November 3, 1859, April 26, July 5, 12, August 23, 30, and November 8, 1860.

5. *Whiteside Sentinel,* 1858–1861. The letter of the Central Committee was published February 28, 1861.

6. *Whiteside Sentinel,* May 6, September 16, 1858, January 27, March 10, April 7, May 5, August 4, 18, 25, 1859, January 12, March 22, 1860.

7. *Whiteside Sentinel,* August 23, 1860; Harriet Teller, "Senator Teller as a Young Man," Colorado Historical Society, 3–4; James Teller, "Henry Teller," 8; Davis, *History of Whiteside County,* 327; *Denver Daily Republican,* November 15, 1876; *Denver Post,* May 26, 1911; Whiteside County Township maps, Morrison (Illinois) Public Library.

CHAPTER 2

The Promised Land: Central City

Henry Teller left Illinois and joined the westward migration across the Missouri River. In the words of a popular Methodist hymn, Henry could say in truth, "I am bound for the promised land. Oh who will come and go with me? I am bound for the promised land." He had never taken a trip like this one; nor had Teller ever seen scenery like that which rolled past the stage as it lumbered westward. It proved, he remembered, a "wearisome journey of 700 miles across the plains." Teller's recollections were less dramatic than those of his contemporary Samuel Clemens who, leaving his "military" career behind, took the stage later that summer to Nevada. Sam (later Mark Twain) wrote:

> Our coach was a great swinging and swaying stage, of the most sumptuous description—an imposing cradle on wheels. . . . We stirred them [hard leather letter sacks and bumpy canvas bags] and redisposed them in such a way as to make our bed as level as possible. Whenever the stage stopped to change horses, we would wake up, and try to recollect where we were.

The meals at the stage stations were often a memory savored only later, if then. As Clemens described, "Our breakfast was before us, but our teeth were idle. I tasted and smelt, and said 'I would take coffee.' "

Teller and three other men arrived in Denver on Wednesday morning, April 24, 1861. The Central Overland, California & Pike's Peak stage had not encountered any trouble from the plains tribes, despite rumors to the contrary. All in all, the journey to the two-month-old Colorado territory had been peaceful. The ticket was not cheap—$100.

As Teller journeyed westward, the United States entered the Civil War with the unwarranted belief that it would be a one-battle war. Henry had read the news of firing on Fort Sumter in Charleston harbor before he left Morrison, and he heard a smattering of developments as he traveled. When he reached Denver, he came face to face with the war's repercussions. Editor William Byers told the story in the April 25 issue of the *Rocky Mountain News*. Someone, or a group, hoisted a "small disunion banner" over the Wallingford and Murphy store. Other than it constituting "a rag to disgrace their premises, the event is of no importance." Teller recalled years later that, indignant over the event, he looked up the "marshal, an old-time acquaintance from Illinois," and convinced him to take it down.[1] The "rag" came down, but Byers and other unionists grew excited about "secesh" lurking here and there.

Teller did not stay in Denver long. Arriving in Central City (Central, the locals called it), he beheld a town and a community lifestyle unlike anything he had experienced. Morrison had been a new settlement when Henry arrived, and his experiences there helped prepare him for his Colorado home. He found, though, in many ways it seemed very little.

On its narrow streets the newcomer saw buildings of log and rough frame nestled in the "Y" of two narrow canyons that formed a third canyon; he also saw dirt streets and the hustle and bustle of crowded streets that characterized a booming mining district. High wages might have looked astounding to outsiders, but high prices predominated because of the town's isolation and distance from markets. The people, he saw, were chiefly northern Europeans, many sporting a Midwestern heritage. Mostly men walked the streets; women were in a decided minority in the mining West.

They lived in a community barely two years old, in the midst of its transformation from a rough-hewn, transitory mining camp to an established mining town. Still unsure of the town's future, the residents needed to promote its image and prospects. A year away from having its own newspaper, Central had to rely on Golden and Denver papers to boost the town and its mines. Local letter writers rose to the occasion, and through them the Central of April 1861 and the war years emerges. Combined with visitors' and travelers' accounts of what they saw and experienced, a peek into Teller's home materializes.

The conversion from log and small frame structures to stone, brick, and frame homes and buildings continued at a furious pace; it "seems to be the rage just now." Sensitive about their newness but proud of what was being accomplished, writers went out of their way to praise developments. One "new stone warehouse" would "vie with any other of its kind on this side of the Missouri River," declared an enthusiastic local. "Shops and saloons without number" graced the business district, which was steadily gaining specialty stores such as drug, daguerrean, and book establishments. The town did need a "commodious, first class hotel" and an opera house, both reportedly being considered. Repeated reports of high gold yields and "unbounded" confidence in the coming mining season appeared regularly.

Prices seemed high, even for a mining district. One writer complained that he wished merchants offered supplies "at Christian prices," but the best they could hope for were "Denver prices." Tied to Denver through location, merchants, and transportation, Central faced a fact of life that did not sit well with many locals. They also disliked the weather. The spring that had started out so promisingly turned back to winter, "cold and cheerless weather."

The writers did not speak of the litter, garbage, and trash that could be seen everywhere. A smell wafted into every corner of the town, smoke whirled through it, and noise from the surrounding mines blanketed homes and businesses, making life less enjoyable. The creeks no longer ran clear. These things were not written about because they would not promote Central's image.

In the midst of all this, the residents obviously strove for permanence, and culture was trying to take root. The Jack Langrishe company played to packed houses in the "beauty and chivalry of the Gregory gold region." Balls featuring "gay and graceful mountain maidens and matrons and gallant gentlemen" caught the writers' attention, although one correspondent found no Easter services to attend.

Travelers coming along the popular Golden Gate route found the way "densely dotted with dead oxen and other quadrupeds whose decaying carcasses completely choke the air." The sickening "perfume" did not stop them.[2]

Newcomers found the locals, as writers remarked, full of "spunk," hospitality, and general friendliness. These Coloradans also reflected the attitudes of their eastern brethren. For instance, an African American was informed that a separate school for "colored" children would be started when there were enough of them to warrant such a development.

Peeking behind the houses, one saw the nearby hills denuded of trees in the haste to find wood and dig mines. Traveler and writer Bayard Taylor had little patience with what he encountered in June 1866: "I am already tired of these bald, clumsy shaped, pock-marked mountains; this one long, windy, dusty street, with its perpetual menace of fire." He also did not like the fact that everybody seemed to offer "specimens" to show and "feet" (stock shares) to sell. Taylor further complained about the cost of living: "Central City, I must say, is the most outrageously expensive place in Colorado. You pay more and get less for the money than in any other part of the world." Because of such impressions, which were not infrequent, a Colorado writer warned his readers, "The first impressions of an Easterner, on arriving in Colorado, are not usually very flattering."

Many of the miners came from Cornwall, England. The best in the world, they migrated from their declining homeland with their skills, equipment, saffron breads and cakes, and mining superstitions. "Cousin Jacks," as they were nicknamed, left a mark on all around them. They worked long, labor-intensive, dangerous hours for three dollars a day. Their skills had saved the district, whose future lay in hard rock, or quartz, mining. The simpler placer mining had nearly played out before Teller arrived.

Brown University professor Nathaniel Hill, later a political rival of Teller's, came to Central in 1864 and 1865 to inspect mines. His impressions were less harsh than many others. Riding up the canyons, he gave up trying to describe the scenery to his wife, Alice: "I can give you no conception of the scenery we passed through that day. It was grand and sublime beyond description. . . . I was truly enraptured by the scenery through which we passed." He did note that the gulch "is so narrow that if you go into backyards of houses, you are in danger of falling down the chimney" of a lower neighbor. He met "many very pleasant and sociable gentlemen" and told his worried wife that the people "seem to be disposed to help a stranger on, as much as they can." Hill enjoyed the opportunity mining gave him to form connections with "influential parties."

Hill, too, found the cost of living high. He purchased a house for $3,500, and it cost another $1,800 to repair it. He could rent out part of it for $120 a month. He expected that in a year or two the land would be worth more than he had paid for everything. Nathaniel did not appreciate Colorado hotels. If the ones in which he had stayed were, as advertised, the "best," then "deliver us from the worst." He told his wife, "You may imagine the worst you can."

Central was a town of contrasts. The residents strove to have churches, families, theaters, schools, city government, fraternal groups, stone and brick buildings, and such less definable things as culture, society, refinement, and the latest fads and fashions. Teller understood this, but he had never seen temptations so openly flouted. Gambling halls, saloons, dance halls, cribs, low-class variety theaters, and parlor houses—the red light district—also flourished in this bachelor, male-dominated society. It all reflected part of the mining West. One guidebook author in the Pike's Peak or Bust days warned all who went to the mines, especially the young, to "*yield not to temptation.* Carry your principles with you; leave not your character at home, nor your Bible"; you would need them "to protect you in a community whose god is Mammon, who are wild with excitement, and free from family restraints."

Central folks always hailed the arrival of the popular Jack Langrishe theatrical troupe and flocked to performances, which offered serious drama, melodrama, and olios. They also liked to recreate memories of former homes, particularly at Christmas and on July 4. Like their contemporaries elsewhere, they complained about the weather—snow, cold, wind, rain, and dryness all generated comment.

Central embodied a place of expectations, of dreams, and of stark realities against the backdrop of a fast-paced, rapidly changing life. These were years of fortunes to be made from business houses to mines, of opportunity to start life anew beckoning around every corner, of the chance to seek fresh opportunity. Yet it was also a time when wood haulers protested the low prices they received; when people like William Fletcher simply disappeared, leaving worried friends; and when people such as the popular and friendly Cora Babcock died at age eight. Underneath it all lay an unstable, transitory life. No one knew when the mines might pinch out. They seemed to have done so by 1863, and the new wonder—the "poor man's diggings" of Montana—started drawing people away. In the "grow or die" mentality of the day, that could be fatal.

The Colorado poet Thomas Hornsby Ferril, in his poem "Magenta," captured Central City as the history books cannot. "Magenta" tells the story of the town's women and leaves this vivid impression.

> Then they would look into mirrors and come back,
> They'd look out of the windows and come back,
> They'd walk into the kitchen and come back,
> They'd scratch the curtains with their fingernails,
> As if they were trying to scratch the mountains down,
> And be somewhere where there weren't any mountains.
>
> They could remember coming up to the dryness
> Of the mountain air in wagons, and setting the wheels
> In the river overnight to tighten the spokes;
> But by the time they got to the mountains the wheels
> Were broken and the women wanted the wagons
> To be repaired as soon as possible
> For going away again, but the men would cut
> The wagons into sluice boxes and stay.

How does one describe life in a mining community? In an editorial published in the *Tri-Weekly Miners' Register* (Central City) on April 18, 1863, the writer lamented:

> In settling a new country, the old established habits of the people are, in a great extent, broken up. This is especially true in a country like ours, where loved homes have been left far behind, and everyone is seeking after the almighty dollar; everyone is in a hurry to get rich, and thinks he has no time for anything else.

He had not intended to do so, but the editor provided a fitting epitaph for a transitory mining district. Central City residents planned with determination to make their community permanent, as Henry soon found out.

His new home was "urban," hardly classified as a frontier, but Central was set amid a frontier. Utes arrived in town from their home beyond the "snowy range." As late as 1865, they occasionally appeared. Unsettled miles separated towns, districts, and the territory from "back East in the states." The crude conditions might be improving, but Bayard Taylor held out little hope: "The whole string of four *cities* [Nevada, Central, Mountain, and Black Hawk] has a curious, rickety, temporary air. . . . Everything is odd, grotesque, unusual; but no feature can be called attractive."[3]

That was Central City when exciting tidings arrived in 1861. News of the firing on Fort Sumter reached Central on the morning of April 27 as "a breathless crowd" gathered in front of the *Rocky Mountain News* agent. Central folks had become caught up in the troubles back East.

TELLER WAS GETTING NICELY ESTABLISHED both in Central and with his law practice when he fell seriously ill with what was diagnosed as "mountain fever." This not uncommon ailment had first appeared in summer of 1859 among the fifty-niners. The faster pace of life, the altitude, the poor food, an unsanitary site, and the pressure of getting a practice started may have combined to cause Teller to come down with a mysterious fever that nearly proved fatal. Perhaps it was some malarial type of fever that had been dormant in his body since Illinois, a region well-known for fevers.

The man who nursed him back to health, Dunham Wright, provided a glimpse of Teller at the time. Teller appeared, when Dunham first saw him, "extremely pale, much emaciated." After helping him through the worst stage of the fever, a doctor ordered his patient to go to a lower elevation. Teller, however, improved so much that Dunham took him and several other men up to the park where Joel Estes had a cabin. Here, amid the mountains and winter weather, they spent several months. Roughing it did wonders for Teller's health. His appetite returned, and Henry took increasingly long hikes from their campsite.

Wright remembered that Teller enjoyed nature and found "much pleasure studying trees and shrubs." In the evening the men would gather around a campfire and do "some tall talking."

Teller was often the center of attention, and others grew quiet when he spoke; "we accepted him as the authority on all subjects." Teller had "read much" and was a "close observer" of people and nature. Dunham recalled he had an air about him that "compelled attention and respect." Henry displayed the ability to make even stories about commonplace incidents seem "to take [on] unusual interest." Years later Teller wrote to Wright that "I was not much of a hunter but I enjoyed the trip very much."

When the party walked the 75 miles out of Estes Park, Teller did so with a much firmer step. His friends, Dunham remembered with pleasure, hardly recognized the young lawyer when he arrived back at Central City. His sojourn as one of the first health seekers in Estes Park proved highly beneficial.

Teller returned to Central but did not immediately resume his law practice. Henry had determinedly concluded that the future looked so promising that he could return to New York to marry Harriet. Naturally, she had continued to worry about his going West. Her "Mr. Teller" faithfully maintained his correspondence, however, and Harriet read joyfully about his improved hopes. After "he had arrived in Colorado," he began to write "me about carrying out our plans."

They were married in her home in Cuba, New York, on June 7, 1862. The bride felt it was not a "very joyous occasion." Dunham might have been pleased about Henry's recovery, but Harriet commented that his "recovery had been slow."

He was "thin as a rail and almost without color." Her sister had just died from "galloping consumption," and her own health was "so precarious that it was believed I was coming down with the fatal disease." She remembered, "I was as pale as the bridegroom, and people generally remarked that never had they seen such a hopeless looking couple so far as health was concerned." Their friends thought the stage trip to Colorado was a "desperate undertaking" for two invalids: "Many were the predictions that neither of us would again see New York State."

Henry promised his grieved mother-in-law that he would let her "daughter come back to see her often." He kept that promise even in the days before the railroad reached the Rocky Mountains. Meanwhile, the newlyweds faced a long train and stage trip. Harriet recalled that it was 2,000 miles from Cuba to Central.

They finally reached Colorado. The trip was an ordeal for almost everyone coming west, but especially for the bride with her "wretched health." The country was "all new and strange to me," Harriet reflected. "I should have enjoyed it but for my physical condition."[4] She found the strength to visit her mother in 1864; it was "a hard journey, but I got through with less difficulty than I had on my bridal journey."

The Tellers eventually had three children, including two sons, Henry Bruce and John. The eldest and only daughter, Emma, was born April 14, 1865, the day President Lincoln was assassinated. Pregnancy could be life-threatening for women in the nineteenth century, and Harriet was no exception. She described her health as very bad: "I lingered almost between life and death." A worried Henry consulted physicians who urged him to take his wife to a lower altitude. Fearing the worst for her baby, Harriet protested, but the day after Emma was born, they started back East without, Harriet remembered, much preparation.

After the tiring stage journey to St. Joseph, Missouri, with the new father in "entire charge of his daughter," they found no sleeping car available. A ten-dollar tip to the porter suddenly produced one, and on they went to Morrison and eventually back to Cuba. The trip almost undermined Teller's health, but both mother and daughter flourished at grandmother's home. They stayed there a year while Henry recovered and then journeyed back to Central.

The family's return trip to Colorado in 1866 proved memorable. Danger accompanied them. The stage before theirs had been attacked, and the plains were in a state of upheaval. The Sioux, Cheyenne, and Arapaho—pressured by oncoming settlement—fought to save their homeland while their new neighbors defended their land.

Their party "confidently expected" to be attacked. Harriet Teller recalled, "The driver was armed to the teeth and all the men passengers, including Mr. Teller, carried guns" and were "determined to resist to the utmost." Harriet remembered a long, suspenseful night passing through the region where the attack had occurred. She was the only woman aboard and the only adult "not prepared to fight": "I made my husband promise that in case of our being attacked and overcome he would shoot both me and the child. It was, of course, a trying ordeal for him, but he took the same view of the situation that I did and he gave me his word that he would do as I required."

The new day finally dawned, and the "awful suspense" passed. By morning she was the only one in the stage who was awake. The heavily armed men had all dozed off. The long night might be over, but they never felt "free from danger" until the stage reached Denver.

On another occasion Henry rode abroad a stage with a drunk driver. After first going the wrong way, he turned about and lashed his horses to make up for lost time. The terror-stricken passengers, believing "a crash [was] possible at any moment," breathed a sigh of relief when they reached the next stage station.

The Tellers and all travelers coming and going from Colorado faced the twin problems of isolation and distance. Stages and wagons were only temporary expedients; the answer loomed on the horizon—the railroad.

Harriet and Henry might have been an upper-middle-class couple in the 1860s, but they still faced the same pioneering conditions as their friends in Central. Harriet commented that when they were first married they lived in a light frame building nestled in the windy canyon that actually had to be staked down: "The wind would come up unexpectedly at almost any time and would swirl down the gulch with such ferocity that there always was danger of buildings being toppled over until their owners learned how to make them secure." Henry, in fact, had suffered through that disaster earlier in Central City. The wind carried off the upper story of the house in which he lived and scattered his possessions. The Tellers eventually moved into a beautiful frame house on Eureka Street across from St. James Methodist Church.

In the genteel Victorian manner, proper Harriet always referred to her husband as "Mr. Teller" even years after his death. Her memories from the Central days reveal a loving and devoted marriage and a warm family life. The studious Mr. Teller, she noted, "seldom was found without a book in hand when about the house. Next to books he liked nature. Nothing pleased him more than to get out in the woods with the children Sunday afternoons and tell them about the trees and flowers." Although never known as a "hale fellow well met," his wife defended him: "He was more sociably inclined than he got credit for being, and when we had company gave much attention to guests, relating experiences and telling anecdotes and talking very freely." Robert Sayre, the son of Teller's partner Hal Sayre, left his impression from a boy's view: "I always considered him pretty much of a 'stuffed shirt.' "[5]

The family also must have enjoyed playing cards, as they owned a copy of *Popular Games of Cards: How to Play Them*. Card playing ranked with dancing among the "sins, and nearly as badly as drinking" for some church-going neighbors.

Thomas Dawson, who later served as Teller's private secretary and came to know him as well as anyone outside the family, provided further insight into the man: "He never put self to the front in anything that he did and always seemed absolutely indifferent to adulation—more so than any man I have ever known in public life." Dawson affirmed that Teller did not drink or use profanity or tell "risqué stories," and he "eschewed tobacco in all its forms." Another friend said Teller did not waste time on "those unworthy of cultivation," but he had not the "slightest haughtiness or distance." He treated everyone pleasantly and listened "with respect when they have anything to say." This unidentified individual agreed with Harriet that when he chose to unbend, "no man is more attractive or instructive" than Henry.

Henry's scrawly penmanship left much to be desired. Longtime friend Moses Hallett wrote Teller in January 1878: "I have your letter of [the] 7th but I must confess that I cannot read all of it. I believe it is a struggle [to read your writing]."

Following the dramatic events of Emma's birth and first year, two sons, John Harrison (September 10, 1869) and Henry Bruce (June 6, 1874), joined the Teller family. The Methodist Church played an active role in their lives. Churches were the social centers for respectable families in mining towns. The dinners, festivals, Christmas parties, teas, Sunday school, Bible classes, church programs, and other church-sponsored community events offered social outlets that the entire family could participate in without fear of social reproach. Perhaps as significant, the church offered something besides the materialism that dominated mining communities.

The Tellers went to church regularly, although Emma more clearly remembered going home "joyously" to take a long walk with her father, weather permitting. Because her parents "did not approve of [her] being out in the evening," she missed some social events. Another memory she retained was of the Cornish "being given to long prayers," some very "eloquent," others "inclined to be stubborn and hard to handle." Nevertheless, her parents' house was the "headquarters for Methodist ministers."

To start and maintain a congregation and a church in a mining community took ongoing and unwavering effort. It took the Methodists nearly eight years to finish St. James, which was finally completed in 1872. Henry had been on the initial building committee in 1864, and the cornerstone had been laid in September of that year. When completed, it was the largest church in the territory.

St. James reached out to the community in a variety of ways. It offered acceptable society for all "good" people, and its literary society sponsored concerts and lectures. The church's library was long ranked the best in town; nonmembers could belong to the Library Association and check out books. Occasionally, Methodists ran afoul of local views, as when they pushed for "observance of the Lord's day" and for such reforms as temperance and ending the "nefarious liquor traffic." They could not stop the wide-open Sunday, the best business day of the week. Emma recalled that her parents never talked about issues such as gambling and drinking before the children.

The church, too, provided an array of outlets for women the larger society often did not offer. They could hold leadership positions, be involved in a variety of issues, and express their opinions. Harriet, for instance, was an "ardent worker" in the Methodist Church and the Home Missionary Society and opened her home to teas (Emma did not like the popular saffron cakes) and to prayer and other meetings. She eventually helped establish an orphans' home in Unalaska, Alaska, and both she and Henry "always contributed freely" to Methodist causes. As Irving Stanton, a neighbor and friend, observed, "Mrs. Teller was the leading lady member of the church."

Henry, who served as a church trustee for many years, did not formally join St. James. Although he seldom spoke about his religious views, he came close to explaining his convictions during an 1886 Senate debate: "I am not a churchman myself in the extreme sense of the term." According to Harriet, he never lost interest in Methodism, finally placing his name on the membership roll in 1902. She speculated, "I think he would have done so earlier but for the fear that people would attribute the act to political motives."[6]

During his Central City days, Henry was most active in the Masons, part of his lifelong involvement in that lodge. As the Masonic lodge had done in Morrison, the Masons gave him a meeting place with like-minded individuals, a social and business outlet, and involvement in fraternal activities.

Teller was affiliated with the Chivington Lodge No. 6 of Central City, named for Colorado's first grand master, John Chivington. As part of the eventual fallout following Chivington's Sand Creek debacle, the name was changed to Central Lodge in 1869. Henry eventually held virtually every office in the lodge and served as grand master for Colorado seven times. This gave him the opportunity to travel around the territory and meet fellow Masons at lodge meetings and at the annual Grand Lodge meeting. The Masonic order grew steadily during these years, surpassing the territorial growth rate.

As grand master, Henry refused to allow several lodges to be chartered because of their sparse population and the corresponding strong possibility that they would fall into debt. Despite accusations that he was too conservative and slow in establishing lodges, he pointedly defended himself in 1871. Weak and debt-ridden lodges, Teller reminded the Grand Lodge delegates, proved more of a burden than a blessing. As he well knew, mining life was transitory, and it appeared better to wait and see than to leap. The members must have agreed for they reelected him grand master, and he pledged to maintain the order "resting upon its sublime principles of Faith, Hope, and Charity."

Teller also helped build Central's Masonic Hall and organize the city's Knights Templar Lodge (a Christian-based order of Masonry). He served as the first grand commander of the Grand Commandery of Knights Templar in 1876. He became a member of the Scottish Rite and was designated a Thirty-Third Degree Mason. "No man," according to a Masonic historian, "before or since has achieved the accomplishments" of Teller over his fifty-four years of active involvement. The history of Colorado Masonry "is his history."

The twice-monthly meetings at Central not only involved Masonic activities but provided a social outlet for members. The Masons also reached out to the larger community. The successful 1863 Masonic festival was rated as "decidedly the gayest ever gotten up in the mountains, at least so say those who attended." *The Tri-Weekly Miners' Register* (February 23, 1863) went on to praise the superb supper and did not overlook the ladies, "such an array of beauty and dress has never before been witnessed in these mountains." Harriet, well into her first pregnancy, chaired one of the committees for the 1865 festival, which was even larger and grander than the one in 1863.[7]

Teller maintained his involvement with the Good Templars. He supported temperance, as he always had, despite living in a world where temperance, let alone prohibition, seemed highly foreign to many of his contemporaries.

He also helped organize a literary club, allowed his office to be used for school board meetings, and spoke at various events. The young lawyer helped raise funds for the 1864 flood victims in Denver and that same year raised money to help several counties with the costs they incurred "hunting down and killing" the Espinosa brothers who had terrorized several southern counties. Elected to the Central City Council during that busy year, Teller presented a resolution to establish a Masonic cemetery.

Henry served as one of the two aldermen from the First Ward from 1864–1866. Having sampled local politics, he turned his attention to territorial politics while keeping his political base in Gilpin County.

Politics and civic service were fine, but Teller had come west to fashion his stake in life. One way to make money in a mining community was to purchase real estate. Teller did not hesitate, carefully adding to his holdings on occasion or as a specific need arose.

All the camps and towns within Gilpin County had faced each other as rivals at some time or another. Then in 1872 Central, Black Hawk, and several nearby towns in the "Little Kingdom of Gilpin" organized a Board of Trade for the county; the "spirit manifested has rarely been equaled in any public meeting held here for years," proclaimed a *Daily Register* reporter. In the dog-eat-dog world of urban mining, Gilpin communities needed a spokesman and defender. Henry served on the board as one of the four representatives from Central. The board's grand idea did not pan out as hoped and soon disappeared. The need did not disappear because Central was becoming "long in the tooth" for a mining town by the early 1870s and needed to promote itself.[8]

As befit a man of his stature, Teller served as president of the Rocky Mountain National Bank. He also became president of Rocky Mountain Telegraph Company and of a railroad he hoped eventually would reach Central.

The telegraph company, organized in 1874 to meet the need to extend rapid communication, went northward to Caribou, Boulder, and beyond and also to Georgetown. Telegraph lines had tied Central to Denver for a decade. The larger Western Union did not want a competitor in the mountains and purchased the aggressive rival within a year. Central now had better communication than at any time in its history.

The railroad, the Colorado Central, it was hoped, would end the problems of isolation and poor transportation. The railroad had reached Denver in 1870, and plans had already been discussed and routes planned into the mountains.

Ambition, reality, optimism, and desperation fueled Coloradans' desire for a railroad connection. The transcontinental line was being built by the Central Pacific eastward and the Union Pacific westward, eventually to link the nation. Shockingly, it only touched Colorado's extreme northeast corner at Julesburg. Finding themselves bypassed, and with a Union Pacific rival established in Cheyenne, Denverites and others pushed successfully for a railroad link. Considering the economic doldrums in which the territory languished during the second half of the 1860s and the problems the Union Pacific faced building its line, this took courage. They succeeded in their effort.

Denver had gained its connection; now the mountain communities wanted theirs. The idea had come from Golden's chief booster, William Loveland. It grew out of urban rivalry. Loveland and his friends did not want to see Denver become the sole railroad hub in the territory, thereby gaining the upper hand in many areas. Loveland had chartered a railroad as early as 1865 with the dream of going into the mountains. The name was changed to the Colorado Central two years later. He planned standard gauge to Denver, narrow gauge into the mountains. The 3-foot-wide narrow gauge proved an excellent choice for mountain railroading. It could go up steep grades and around sharp curves, and it cost less to build. Ground breaking was scheduled for New Year's Day 1868. It took two years before rails finally reached from Golden to Denver, and by then Loveland had to ally with the Union Pacific to circumvent problems and Denver's jealousy.

Laying track into the mountains did not prove easy. By now, Teller had become involved and helped draft the charter. He well understood the importance of a railroad, having crossed the plains and endured mountain travel by stage. As early as 1868 he reassured his neighbors that the railroad would "come directly to us as fast as it can be built." He went on to say that "railroad matters are questions of the most vital interest to us, and the sooner they are built the better." Before the year was out, he took abuse from Denver. Henry denied the charge that he had opposed granting land to the Denver Pacific Denver's leaders were building to connect with the transcontinental Union Pacific.[9]

The *Rocky Mountain News,* "no admirer of Mr. Teller," admitted that "he is a Colorado man, that he is largely interested in the growth and prosperity of the mountain communities, and that he will do all in his power to hasten the construction of a [rail]road to the mines." He assuredly planned to do just that. Regarding the railroad, Teller served on the board of directors, as president, sometimes as attorney, and often as spokesman. A host of problems delayed construction. Disagreements over where the route should be placed and even over where it was to stop aroused emotions. At an August 1871 meeting in Black Hawk, for instance, Teller aggressively defended himself against charges that he had shared the "spoils" with other directors, that the coming of the railroad would reduce miners' wages, and that county bonds were needed for construction. Teller resolutely pointed out that freight rates would be reduced and wages would not go down, and he emphatically refuted charges of "spoils."

The bond issue did not go away. Some voters in Gilpin County were upset, as were eastern investors—particularly those of the Union Pacific, which slowly gained more influence over Loveland's road. Teller went to Philadelphia in August 1871 to try to find an "amicable adjustment to existing difficulties." A resolution was reached, and the Union Pacific management promised that if the people voted for the bonds, they would "no doubt have a railroad to Nevada by the middle of 1872." The voters approved $250,000 in bonds if the railroad reached Black Hawk by May 1872. No train puffed into Black Hawk until December, and suspicious Gilpin County officials reduced the offer to $100,000 in bonds.

Teller stood trapped between Union Pacific's New England investors and his upset Gilpin County neighbors. Frank Hall, editor of the *Register,* complained to Teller in July 1872 that "we are suffering all the evils of a prostrate community." He also thought the Colorado Central should "compensate" the paper for its support in "time of need" over the past year. The *Rocky Mountain News* did not let up either. In a stinging editorial in April, the paper stated emphatically "that Denver has no connection with Clear Creek, and Gilpin mines is chargeable to Henry M. Teller and his Colorado Central." The rails reached Black Hawk and there they stayed as the county, territory, and country dropped into the 1873 crash and depression. Railroad building came to an abrupt halt.

In the years of Teller's presidency, he also had to contend with springtime floods, derailments, accidents to workers, requests for passes, passenger complaints, and other matters. Miers Fisher, for instance, complained that a grass fire started by "one of your locomotives burnt down" his barn. He wanted compensation. The Woeber brothers wanted a spur line to their coal mine. They asked the railroad to pay for rails, switches, and so forth; they would "pay you by our personal notes." Railroads needed coal for fuel, and coal provided a profitable freight item. Coal offered a natural linkage for mine and train. Teller learned another fact of railroad life: any cow that had the misfortune to encounter an engine with dire results immediately gained the label of a prize bovine.[10]

The Colorado Central did eventually reach Central City in May 1878. The engineering achievement required to surmount those last few climbing, snaking miles warranted the accolades it received, but Teller was no longer an official. The great dreams of what the coming of the railroad would bring failed to be fulfilled. The cost of living did go down, access became easier, low-grade ore could be profitably shipped, and people did come. Central Citian Frank Young was among those who were not happy about it: "Our mountain retreat, we feel, is now no longer on—or indeed beyond—the frontier, as in the past." He feared an invasion of travelers, tourists ("of all sort and conditions"), commercial drummers, scientific bug hunters, pleasure seekers, and "possibly capitalists now and then."

The history of the Colorado Central offered a classic example of reality not living up to expectations. The financially starved, mineral-rich West, desperately needing capital for development, turned to outside investors. The marriage turned bitter as both sides anticipated more than they received. Investors did not receive profits, and westerners seemed to lose control of their destiny, as shown by the fact that the deficit-running Colorado Central was leased to the Union Pacific in 1879 for fifty years. Railroads had been a mixed blessing for Coloradans; nonetheless, without the outside investments the region would not have developed as fast as it did. In the end, though, Colorado became a virtual economic colony—railroads, mines, industries, and almost everything else fell under outside control.

Teller had gained invaluable experience with railroading, eastern business-men, and investment dangers. He also understood the depth of Denver's mistrust of him, which reflected local and territorial politics more than railroad rivalries. A few bouquets came his way, as when he was invited to join tours of Colorado with the Russian imperial party, the Grand Duke Alexis, and to join author Grace Greenwood.[11]

CENTRAL HAD A WELL-ESTABLISHED REPUTATION for theater, and according to one of its residents it was "nothing if not musical." The Cornish, with their well-established musical heritage, can be given credit for much of the culture. Long interested in legitimate theater, Henry was one of the "movers and shakers" to bring it to Central. He helped finance construction of the Belvidere Theater in 1875 and subscribed to fifty shares (13 percent) to build the opera house. When completed in 1878, it glistened as the crown jewel of Central and as one of the best opera houses in the state. The building, its architect claimed, "would be in harmony with the great mountains surrounding it."

Teller's greatest personal heritage to Central City, though, was the Teller House, built while he served on the Board of Trade. Every town wanted a "fancy" hotel that would entice visitors to stay, investors to invest, and newcomers to remain and would serve as the "elite" community social center. In late 1870 Teller offered to build a $60,000 hotel provided "the people of Central will take twenty thousand of the stock." The *Daily Register,* which had been agitating for such a structure, advised its readers that "we trust there will be no delay in taking the stocks." Six months passed while discussions took place and money was raised. By May 1871 a hotel committee was canvasing the town. Success crowned their efforts, although they raised only $10,000, and the hotel—jointly owned by Henry and Willard—shifted from dream to near reality.

Construction started in July on a site that had previously housed Teller's law office and a bowling alley. A variety of problems plagued construction. The site was flooded in August, lack of material slowed progress in October, snow piled up in November, and then winter clamped down. Even with these struggles, by the end of 1871 the five stories and roof were completed on the exterior, with every brick laid. Flaring torches had allowed workers to work longer hours, as well as providing a community diversion. In the evening, interested residents watched the construction.

Work on the interior seemed to take an eternity, causing the impatient *Daily Register* (March 22, 1872) and Coloradans "at home and abroad" to ask, "When will the new hotel be finished and ready for occupancy?" Three more months passed before the great day arrived. By mid-June "immense" loads of furniture crowded Eureka Street, carpet was being laid, a "car load of assistants, mostly feminine," had arrived, and invitations were sent out for the grand opening.

The *Register* was beside itself: "The importance to the city of this public resort should be constantly borne in mind." The June 26 issue trumpeted, "It is an ornament to the city, and the pride of the people. May it 'live long and prosper.'" More than $107,000 had been spent to build and furnish the Teller House, with the new lessees paying for the furniture ($20,000). Guests could lounge in the parlors, "perfect marvels of elegance." The 150 sleeping rooms were "tastefully fitted up," with each door having a "patent safety lock" and no transoms, allowing guests "to lie down to peaceful slumbers undisturbed." There were "water closets" and "pure soft water" on each floor and bathrooms on the second and third floors. A reading room, with its "well-filled library"; a billiard room and bar; and the business office, with its "splendid selection of minerals and geological specimens," completed the hotel.

"The Triumph of the Season," a magnificent inaugural ball and supper, officially opened the Teller House. Gaiety and pride ruled, and the *Daily Register* reporter called the supper "the finest we have seen in the Territory." A few minor additions, consisting of a "croquet ground" for the convenience of guests, among other things, completed the project.

Visitors were impressed. Denver newspaperman William Byers wrote, "Central City at last has a really fine hotel—the Teller House." Central Citian Frank Young thought from an "aesthetic point [of] view" the hotel's exterior "might easily be taken for a New England factory." That did not matter; it was the most "pretentious structure yet erected" in Central and reflected "our deep satisfaction at possessing at last a building adapted to our needs." The Teller House emerged as the social hub of the town. Those "closely associated with the brightest side" of Central came to "club parties, afternoon teas, dressy evening receptions," and other gatherings. Some "good folks" without "roofs of their own" made it their home.[12]

The "elegantly furnished" Teller House received national attention when President Ulysses Grant visited Central in April 1873. Henry was among the party that accompanied him from Denver. The highlight of the trip came when the group walked into the hotel over a sidewalk of silver bricks brought from neighboring Boulder County's leading mining camp, Caribou, as a publicity exhibit. The "silent hero" seemed "quite incredulous when told that the slabs were genuine silver, but had finally to accept the truth." A grand dinner and reception followed, then the Grants bid Central good-bye and rode the stage to Idaho Springs.

Fortunately, Henry and Willard had built their hotel of brick and stone because on May 21, 1874, fire roared and raced through the community. The two fire companies, plus another from Golden that arrived as soon as it could by train and horse, had little hope of checking the "one vast ocean of fire," as flaming waves leaped from one dried wooden roof to another. Teller lost property but, fortunately, saved the Teller House. Praise came his way.

Under the leadership of Henry M. Teller, who, by the way, was in the thickest of the fight throughout the day, directing and working with the strength and valor of a giant—assisted by William H. Bush [hotel man and leaser of the building], and perhaps a hundred others—mounted the roof and by much hard work prevented ignition there.

Frank Young bemoaned what happened and, more to the point, what had not happened: "We have been predicting it, discussing it, dreading it—doing everything, in fact, but preparing for it—for lo! these ten years." That typical procrastination among mining communities at the time doomed Central to a disastrous fire. Teller heroically helped fight the fire, but among wooden buildings and a raging fire (muddled by a lack of fire-fighting equipment), he was in a rear guard trying to save at least part of the town.

A disastrous fire such as this could spell the end of a mining community, or it could be a form of urban renewal. In Central's case the latter carried the day. Within twenty-four hours a relief committee had been formed to aid "destitute or impoverished" families, and special permission had been granted to erect temporary wooden buildings. People went to work "with renewed energy," and the *Rocky Mountain News* correctly forecast: "Before the summer shall have come and gone, it is likely that Central will Phoenix-like rise up from her ashes, a new and beautiful city." With brick and stone, the city did.

Now a family man and in his mid-forties, Teller—businessman, civic booster, and a leading citizen of Central—could look back on his first decade in Colorado as a success. Henry emerged as a Gilpin County entrepreneur, not unusual for prominent men in the West. With faith, he had invested time and reinvested money to make Central and Gilpin County prosper and improve.

Back on December 19, 1868, the *Daily Register* had pointed out the three "great wants of Central"—a railroad, a hotel, and a schoolhouse. The editor thought that with "judicial management and earnest effort," all of these wants could be secured. He was right, thanks to Henry Teller. The hotel and railroad were major success stories for Henry. And in a small way, he had helped create a better school. He interviewed at least one prospective teacher and supported all efforts to improve the school system. He brought his brother Willard to Central, and in 1869 Willard had been elected to the school board. Willard tried to get children back in school, "as many are known to be loafing on the streets, frequently guilty of petty misdemeanors." By that time, too, Central had a "colored school," a Colorado version of the separate-but-equal doctrine.

If Henry had matured, so had his town. One of the principal communities in Colorado, Central City boasted a population of 3,500, somewhat more than the census takers officially found. A reported 100 businesses graced its main streets. Churches, schools, law and order, and Victorian respectability had taken root, and a less open red light district pushed vices into the mauve background. Central also had reached the zenith of its political power and was still the territory's leading gold producer.

Henry had enjoyed the support of his beloved Harriet. She had successfully given birth to three children, all of whom were still alive—an accomplishment in that era. Harriet had achieved the epitome of the role of middle-class Victorian woman. Active in her church and within the community, she supported her husband, maintained her home, and nurtured her children. The family celebrated Christmas and other holidays, and she opened her home to callers on January 1 to offer good wishes to one and all. The Tellers had become one of the "First Families of Central."

Frank Young remembered the social world of the "Little Kingdom" rather vividly. Although no rigidly drawn "artificial lines" existed, distinctions between one group and another were "clearly established." In this isolated mining town, "a little social community of high intelligence" gradually emerged. The sharp contrast between the "uncouth and dreary outer surroundings of a mining camp" and the "charming interiors of its five or six score of homes" remained distinct in his mind.

Sadly, Young also pointed out that the golden age of Central City would end by 1880. The "exceptional conditions" that enabled it to "hold its distinctive and envious position" had been superseded. The coming of the railroad to Colorado opened and settled other areas and developed "vast new mineral regions." Rival Denver had triumphed. New faces came to town, and old faces left. Young quoted a familiar saying: "You will find a Gilpin man or men in any mining camp, however distant or obscure, that you may chance to drop into." That, in truth, represented Central's and Gilpin's legacy to Colorado and western mining.

After the fire the community settled into a quiet routine, the wide-open boom days a fading memory. As the Tellers came and went in the years ahead, another generation of prosperous Colorado mining would pass while the town slipped into a quiet, gentle decline.

Harriet and Henry had come to love Central City and its mountainous/mining environment. Years later and in a new century, Harriet would remark, "Central always was 'home.'" Henry continually maintained the town as his legal residence and voted there.[13] Central City never left their hearts, even though they left Central City.

NOTES

1. Two undated clippings, Thomas Dawson, "Scrapbooks," Colorado Historical Society, vol. 80; *Rocky Mountain News,* April 25, 26, May 1 (weekly), 1861, May 9, 1897; Mark Twain, *Roughing It* (Hartford: American Publishing, 1872), 37–38, 45.
2. The section on Central City in April 1861 is taken from the *Rocky Mountain News,* daily and weekly editions, March–May 1861.
3. The composite picture of Central City was drawn from numerous sources, including Bayard Taylor, *Colorado: A Summer Trip* (New York: G. P. Putnam, 1867), 54–60, 68–70; Samuel Bowles, *Our New West* (Hartford: Hartford Publishing, 1869), 97, 181–183; Louis Simonin, *The Rocky Mountain West in 1867* (Lincoln: University of Nebraska Press, 1966), 44; Robert C. Baron et al., *Thomas Hornsby Ferril and the American West* (Golden, Colo.: Fulcrum, 1996), 53–54; *Daily Miners' Register,* August 4, 1863, April 11, 1864, May 21, 26, 1865; *Tri-Weekly Miners' Register,* September 17, 24, October 10, 25,

December 24, 1862, January 30, February 9, March 18, 23, April 18, 25, 30, 1863; *The Rocky Mountain Directory and Colorado Gazeteer* (Denver: S. S. Wallihan, 1870), 253; Nathaniel Hill to wife, June 23, 30, 1864, July 16, 1865, Colorado Historical Society; William Byers and John Kellom, *Hand Book to the Gold Fields of Nebraska and Kansas* (Chicago: D. B. Cooke, 1859), 12, 23–27, 93–98.

4. Harriet Teller, "Senator Teller as a Young Man," Colorado Historical Society, 4–5; Dunham Wright, "A Winter in Estes Park with Senator Teller," *The Trail* (July 1920), 5–11; Henry Teller to Dunham Wright, Henry Teller Collection, Colorado Historical Society.

5. Harriet Teller, "Senator Teller," 5–10; Harriet Teller obituary, *The Trail* (January 1924), 16; Robert Sayre, "Hal Sayre—Fifty-Niner," *Colorado Magazine* (July 1962), 171, 173. The Tellers' home was torn down in 1897 to make way for the Gilpin County Building. *Rocky Mountain News,* May 9, 1897.

6. Emma Teller Tyler, "Personal Reminiscences," University Archives, University of Colorado; Harriet Teller, "Senator Teller," 10; Thomas Dawson, "The Personal Side of Senator Teller," manuscript, Colorado Historical Society, interviews, 1, 4–5; Harriet Teller obituary; St. James Church Records, Central City; Irving Stanton, *Sixty Years in Colorado* (Denver: State Historical Society, 1922), 141; *Congressional Record,* January 21, 1896, 461; unidentified letter in newspaper signed "H.," "Teller Scrapbook," Chris Buys private collection. H. could stand for Harriet, but that appears highly unlikely.

7. Masonic Records, Teller Papers, University of Colorado; *Centennial Celebration: Grand Lodge A.F. and A.M.* (Denver: n.p., 1961), 11, 14, 31; *Proceedings of the Grand Lodge* (Denver: *Rocky Mountain News,* 1861–1875); *Tri-Weekly Miners' Register,* January 2, 1862, February 23, 1863; *Daily Miners' Register,* February 17, 19, 24, 1865; *Rocky Mountain News,* December 24, 1868, September 27, 28, 1871; *Henry M. Teller Lodge No. 144* (Denver: n.p., 1964), 23–24, 28.

8. Central City Government Records; *Tri-Weekly Miners' Register,* October 27, December 26, 1862, July 21, 1863; *Mining Journal,* April 5, 1864; *Daily Miners' Register,* May 16, 1863, May 25, June 5, August 7, 1864, April 11, 14, 1865; *Central City Register,* November 5, 12, December 10, 1872; *Rocky Mountain News* (weekly), July 6, 1864; *Rocky Mountain News,* April 4, June 16, 1874. The various Teller collections contain documents and letters involving real estate.

9. *Central City Register,* December 20, 29, 1868; *Daily Miners' Register,* April 23, 1868; Robert G. Athearn, *Union Pacific Country* (Chicago: Rand McNally, 1971), 214; *The Trail* (March 1914), 27. For the problems railroads faced, see Stephen E. Ambrose, *Nothing Like It in the World* (New York: Simon and Schuster, 2000). For the Rocky Mountain Telegraph, see Frank Hall, *History of the State of Colorado,* vol. 3 (Chicago: Blakely, 1891), 315, 415, 417.

10. *Rocky Mountain News,* 1868–1872; Athearn, *Union Pacific Country,* 214–217; *Rocky Mountain Directory,* 122, 344, 433; *Central City Register,* August 30, 1871; Robert C. Black III, *Railroad Pathfinder: Edward L. Berthoud* (Evergreen, Colo.: Cordillera, 1988), 63–79; "Colorado Central vs. William Odgen," Teller Papers, University of Colorado; Frank Hall to Teller, July 20, 1872; John Titcomb to Teller, December 15, 1873; Miers Fisher to Teller, May 9, 1874; and Woeber Bros. to Teller, August 4, 1874, all in Teller Papers, University of Colorado; Stephen J. Leonard and Thomas J. Noel, *Denver: Mining Camp to Metropolis* (Niwot: University Press of Colorado, 1990), 35–37.

11. Telegram to Teller, no month or day (1872), Teller Collection, University of Colorado; *Rocky Mountain News,* October 22, 1872, November 16, 1881; Frank Young, *Echoes from Acadia* (Denver: Lanning Bros., 1903), 126; L. C. Rockwell to Willard Teller, November 5, 1879, Teller Papers, University of Colorado.

12. Young, Echoes, 32, 34, 127–130, 131–132, 178–180; Byers quoted in *Central City Register,* October 8, 1870–June 28, 1872, November 27, 1872, April 3, May 16, 1873. The Teller House stayed in family ownership into the 1930s. Thomas J. Noel, *Buildings of Colorado* (New York: Oxford University Press, 1997), 194–195.

13. Harriet Teller, "Senator Teller," 4; *Colorado Business Directory for 1875* (Denver: *Rocky Mountain News*), 82–83. For Grant's visit, see *Central City Register,* April 29, 1873, and Duane A. Smith, *Silver Saga: The Story of Caribou, Colorado* (Boulder: Pruett, 1974). For Teller's interest in the theater, see William Bush to Teller, December 19, 1878, Teller Collection, Denver Public Library; *Rocky Mountain News,* July 19, 1879; and H. William Axford, *Gilpin County Gold* (Chicago: Swallow, 1976), 118–120. The story of the fire is found in Young, *Echoes from Acadia,* 140–141; *Rocky Mountain News,* May 23, August 29, 1874 (source of the quotation); and Central City Council Minutes, May 22, 26, June 1, 1874. For Willard and the schools, see Council Minutes, May 3, 1869. For the social scene, see Young, *Echoes,* 15–16, 54, 94, 205–207; *Central City Register,* January 5, 1868, January 1, 1869.

Mountain Lawyer

enry Teller had come to Central City to join his Morrison partner, Hiram Johnson. Well aware of competition, the firm advertised in Central's earliest newspapers. On July 28, 1862, this ad appeared: "Hiram Johnson Henry Teller Attorneys at Law, and Solicitors in Chancery." At that time Central boasted a notable coterie of lawyers including Lewis Rockwell and James Belford, who came to prominence along with Teller.

Johnson had made a good start in a crowded territorial field of around ninety lawyers (at least nine in Central in 1862). Teller again emerged, however, as the pillar in the partnership. The firm became popular, if a survey of lawyers representing clients in the 1862 fall court session can serve as a yardstick. They handled by far the most cases listed in the *Tri-Weekly Miners' Register*. The partners also proudly announced in June 1863 that their new office addition on Eureka Street was nearly completed, and the newspaper bragged: "This will make their office the largest in the Territory; their business requires it." The newspaper worried, however, that although it "makes the most convenient law office in Central City," it was not fireproof: "Their library is too valuable to lose, and yet will be very likely to go in case of fire."

Johnson, as Teller soon found out, had become increasingly enamored with mining promotion and sales. He particularly became excited during the great speculation in Colorado mining stocks from late summer of 1863 into spring of 1864. By summer of 1863 Gilpin County mining desperately needed financial capital, skilled miners, and reduction works for ore that was increasingly becoming what miners termed refractory. Translated, that meant difficult and costly to mill profitably. At the same time, northern investors had money to invest because of the war-stimulated, booming economy. What appeared more secure than a gold mine?

The predictable result, a frenzied speculation in Colorado mining stock, swept over eager investors. Johnson and others raced back to New York City to take advantage of the situation, "so important" to territorial mining interests. Johnson journeyed off with high hopes. He opened an office in the city and never returned to his Colorado law practice. In the years that followed, Johnson—who did not have noticeable success in selling mines and stocks—occasionally wrote to Teller.

Teller once again called on his faithful brother Willard to come to Central to join the firm. Willard was five years younger than Henry and had been admitted to the bar in Buffalo, New York, in 1859. Willard came west in the spring of 1864 and became Henry's partner. Also possessing a "high sense of public and personal honor," Willard was gruffer and more impatient than his brother. He was nearly as capable a lawyer as Henry, though, and they made a formidable team. For several years, however, they continued advertising as Johnson and Teller.[1]

Henry, or H. M. as they called him, dealt with a variety of clients, cases, and legal matters. For example, the firm was hired to collect a note for a St. Louis firm and another for a man in Chicago. The latter wrote "Friend Teller" that the money "reached me at a time when I was just recovering from a severe sickness and entirely out of money and needing many of the necessaries of life." Things did not always work out so well. An old friend from Illinois asked in 1862 why they had not sold his land, because it had been two years since he had given the firm the deeds of trust: "I am very sorry to hear that things have not prospered at the Peak as well as you hoped for and I thought and hoped that you had a sure thing in making some money." Another client needed Teller to collect a note and "look after that butcher shop in Trail Creek." F. F. Digby authorized Johnson and Teller to sell his property and give the money to his creditors.

Teller had several adventures with Gilpin County's legendary miner Pat Casey. One involved a riot by Casey's men after their boss had been arrested for "kicking up a big muss." The combination of whiskey and Irish miners was explosive. Before matters calmed, several people lay battered on the street, and one person had been killed. The miners wanted their boss to be released right away. Teller addressed the mob, appealing for them to go home. At the same time, he urged the marshal not to release Casey. Fortunately, the local militia arrived just in the "nick of time" and broke up the mob. Looking back on the incident years later, Henry reflected, "I think . . . that Central City came nearer witnessing a big fight on that day than at any other time in the history of the town." Another Casey incident involved a mining suit Teller had instigated on behalf of a client. The two men settled it on their own, with Casey promising to pay $1,250. Not trusting Casey, the miner told Teller to "please accept nothing but fine dust with the quicksilver burned out."

There were also divorce actions, ejectment proceedings, a forgery matter, preparing abstracts of title, "drafting papers," foreclosures, mortgage ejectment, trespass cases, and attending court in other towns to defend clients. Occasionally, something exciting happened. In a February 1863 assault case, the crowd favored the defendant, and some rowdies chased the "prosecuting witness" into Teller's office. Another time a contested mine and mill site case involved "blinding sulphur smoke," a suspicion that the judge had been bribed, and Teller almost being arrested. What had gotten him in trouble? Uncharacteristically, Henry sarcastically shouted at the judge, who asked the young attorney to state the difference between himself and the bench: "There is the difference—you are paid by one side in this case and I am paid by the other." The judge ordered that he be arrested, but the sheriff hesitated because the angry crowd sided with Teller. The court adjourned soon after, and Teller did not go to jail. The alarmed judge secretly left for the East at four the next morning and was "never heard of again," according to Teller's recollection in 1897.[2]

Teller and other lawyers had trouble with members of the territorial bench. The western territories often became the dumping ground for political and judicial hacks who had managed to earn some reward from the party controlling patronage in Washington. The situation caused problems in both the courts and the government. Colorado suffered though a few "judicial derelicts."

In August 1861 Teller and others had been admitted to practice before the territorial supreme court. For a while, the honor seemed hollow. In the mid-1870s Teller wrote a friend, "In the early history of this Territory we were cursed with incompetent Judges," a statement he repeated later in Congress. Three members sat on the bench, and they and their successors proved a checkered lot. One was caught in an affair with a married woman, another departed without hearing a case, and a third was so bad a judge that the lawyers organized a boycott against him. None sank lower than the "infamously tyrannical" Charles Armour. The *Daily Miners' Register* (November 17, 1864) said his leaving was "a great satisfaction" for the people of Colorado. Earlier, the same newspaper had blasted: "Seldom has a judiciary been as degraded as ours" because of this "overpoweringly" indolent, ignorant judge. One of Teller's colleagues publicly branded Armour a "liar and a coward." Others as bad included Stephen Harding, whose "venality and incompetence was so odious" that the bar again organized a boycott and forced his resignation. "We consider this the wisest act he ever performed in the territory," commented the relieved *Register*.

Colorado's supreme court was not a complete judicial cesspool; good judges were appointed. Moses Hallett exemplified the best; he was the most "influential justice before statehood" and was known as one of the most skillful judges in handling mining trials. Teller urged his reappointment. Benjamin Hall and Central City neighbor William Gorsline were also excellent appointees.[3] Teller and other lawyers tried to improve the quality of the appointments but were generally ignored.

The court, for all its problems, handed down some significant decisions. The most important for the future, the "first in time, first in right" doctrine for water law, became the foundation for water rights throughout the West. In this edict, Hallett and his court parted ways with hundreds of years of English common law. The court also validated the rules and regulations of mining districts, an important legal milestone for Teller and mining in general.

Being a lawyer in Colorado in those days was tiring, as Teller well knew: "Many a time I have attended court all day in Denver and wound up the day's work with a horseback ride to Central City, in order to be present in the court room the following morning." He rode the circuit much as his hero, Abraham Lincoln, had done in Illinois: "We made horseback rides to Fairplay, Canon City, or Pueblo to attend sessions of court, at times large parties traveling." Add to that trips to Golden, Boulder, and elsewhere as the successful attorney's reputation increased. Teller stated, though, "We were all young then, and thought nothing of the inconveniences of the mountain journey."

With a somewhat critical eye, he contrasted legal affairs in the 1860s with those in the 1890s: "Justice was administered generally with an impartial hand, and I believe the results were even more satisfactory than they are today, with all the complicated machinery of modern practice." Why were the 1860s better? "Arguments and decisions went right at the point, and cases were settled in much less time than under present methods." Maybe he remembered more than had actually happened.

Teller did not always win. James Belford remembered that he once won a case when Teller "attempted to browbeat and ridicule me." He also lost a murder case when the judge overruled his objection and testified against Teller's client. Another case left Henry hanging when the defendant disappeared.

Although usually cool and analytical in the courtroom, at least one client remembered Henry losing his temper. In a mining case in Boulder, Teller "became angry during the trial and took some of the other party's papers, tore them up, and threw them on the floor." He stamped on them and "denounced the whole thing as a blackmailing scheme." Teller won the case.

The reward for all this trial and tribulation was not only an increased reputation, but, as Harriet noted, the firm soon became very prosperous. Their 1863 and 1864 daybooks show what they charged clients: attending a suit of injunction, $5; drafting deed, $2; attending case, $5; drafting sale notices "and advice," $25; trying suit at Black Hawk, $25; retaining fee, $25; obtaining new trial, $50; and abstract of title, $40 and $50. These fees reflect a lawyer's income at a time when miners made $2.50–$4.00 per day, clerks $20 a month, and mechanics $3–$5 per day.

Expenses for the firm were also high: a box of envelopes, $6; bottle of ink, $3; advertising for a year in the *Rocky Mountain News,* $50; $12 to rent a post office box; hiring a horse, $3; $93 for city tax; freight to ship law books from St. Joseph, $16; $14 to rent a team and buggy; a ream of paper, $7; and $18 for one pair of pants, $75 for an overcoat, $13 for two shirts, and $8 for two "pairs of draws." In 1862 Teller's taxable earnings amounted to $1,823; two years later he reported $634.[4]

Clients did not always pay on time or even at all. A Chicago man wrote on behalf of his mining company on August 23, 1875, concerning a $949 bill: "In reply must say at present we have no money in the treasury. For a long time we have expected the property to be sold and expect now that it will be ere long." All the owners "are very hard up," and "I don't see how we can aid you just now."

Although civil cases turned a profit, the route to fortune and fame lay with mining law and cases. Commenting on her husband's early career, Harriet said, "Mr. Teller, sensing the future of the state, specialized on mining law and soon was such a master of its intricacies that he had few if any rivals at the Colorado bar." With pride she concluded, "His reputation spread and it was not long until his practice over-leaped the boundary lines of the Territory."

TELLER WAS FORTUNATE THAT HE WAS IN THE RIGHT PLACE at the right time. Mining law in the West had started as an extralegal effort to solve ownership problems and provide a legal framework for mining operations. Mining districts, mining laws, and miners' courts came out of the California experience. When the fifty-niners came to Pike's Peak country, some experienced forty-niners arrived with them. In a series of meetings in 1859–1860, they established mining districts and laws for Gilpin County. Hiram Johnson helped with the Nevada district. The districts were needed because the Pike's Peak region remained divided among Kansas, Nebraska, Utah, and New Mexico territories. To compound matters, the government had reserved much of that land for the Cheyenne, Arapaho, and Ute tribes. The territorial legislature, as mentioned, recognized the extralegal district laws as legal entities.

Realizing some legal basis for mining had to be created, the federal government set about to develop a federal mining law soon after the Civil War. The results were the 1866 and 1872 laws based primarily on western mining experience and mining district "customs and usages." Miners now had laws on which to base their claims, mines, and operations; but issues only became more complex and complicated. The laws presented a fertile field for mining lawyers.[5]

Teller and other lawyers found mining disputes a bonanza that nearly equaled in fees what successful miners dug out of their mines in gold and silver. A judge commented later, "The flush times of litigation in Colorado furnished a striking illustration of the fact that great causes make great lawyers." In the nineteenth century, the mining lawyer without question starred as the commanding figures among Colorado lawyers because mining was Colorado's chief industry and especially because of the vast sums of money involved in the legal questions concerning ownership and operation. Mining lawyers' prospects were also aided by the rapid decline of placer mining and the corresponding quick rise of deep or lode mining. Technically, lode mining was more difficult, specialized, time-consuming, and costly—balanced by the fact that the rewards could be greater than those from placer mining. From the legal point of view, it promised to be more complicated in the dark recesses of the mines than with surface issues. Little was known in those dark recesses beyond the flickering flame of the miners' candles. Where did the vein go; where were claim boundaries?

Because of these technical and financial problems in Colorado mining, corporations appeared early in the territorial period and dominated every major district that opened throughout the remainder of the nineteenth century. They had the wherewithal and determination to fight complicated, costly, and continuing mining cases and to hire the best legal minds available to argue their side.

A majority of cases Teller and his firm handled involved mining to some degree. Initially, the cases were often simple and routine. William Brown was willing to sell his claims but did not want that to "interfere with my suit" unless the defendant agreed to buy. In Sterling City, James Harlan wanted "your [Teller's] council" concerning mining claims. Drafting incorporation papers and other mining documents provided a steady source of income. Teller often acted as agent in mining sales, a service Francis McGravitt was pleased with, but the latter added, as I "am in need of money [please] send me a draft on some good bank in New York City." Claim jumpers and trespassers brought Teller into court, as did conflicting titles, lost claim markers, and overlapping claims. He even sold a mine for his old partner Hiram Johnson, who advised him in October 1875, "We must make a small fortune out of this property." Johnson did not.

Ore stealing aroused heated feelings, and James Goodman of Chicago urged Teller to "please take strong measures," as he was convinced a neighboring miner was working his vein. One client's New York attorney wanted Teller's advice on evicting a leaser who had "mined very large amounts of ore and is liable" for either royalty payments or some fixed price. The 1872 mining law helped lawyers in yet another way. For a prospector or miner to have complete ownership of a claim, it had to be patented. This involved surveying the claim, preparing and publishing legal notices, and doing development work. Teller's office continually handled patents including one from an old Morrison friend, Edward Warner, who sent Teller his power of attorney and other information on Northup Lode. Like many others before and since, Warner complained in 1874 that "the enterprise already cost me quite $10,000," adding that if any more conflict over the title occurred, he preferred to sell. "Please do the best you can," he pleaded to Teller.[6]

One part of the 1872 mining law, the apex doctrine, bedeviled Henry and a generation of western miners and lawyers. It also turned many dollars for the latter. Congress, in its "wisdom," had hoped this idea would simplify miners' lives; it was intended to "simplify, establish and confirm a clear and unassailable title." Instead, it caused mostly grief, expense, and interminable legal wrangles.

If the apex, defined as the "highest or uppermost" point of a vein, was found on a miner's claim, he could follow the vein beyond the side lines of that claim as far down as it could be mined. Conversely, it could not be followed through the end lines of a claim. In a day and time when geology, mining engineering, and underground surveying languished in their infancy, this clause promised trouble if the apex peaked underground, known as a "blind lode." As the old saying went, "you can't tell beyond the end of a pick in the mine."

Respected mining engineer James D. Hague wrote in 1904 that the apex doctrine "brings forth nothing but confusion and contention with everlasting and costly litigation." Mining Commissioner and reporter Rossiter Raymond put it in a more scriptural manner: "To him that has (the apex) shall more be given; but from him that hath not (the apex), shall be taken away even that which he hath."

Human vultures circled rich mines. Owners of neighboring claims saw profits where none had existed earlier. Mining "experts," mining lawyers, old-timers, and others made a living off the cases. Jury members, even judges, might secretly find money in unusual places. Cases kept courts busy for years.

Teller found himself involved in two classic cases. The first involved the Pelican and Dives properties near Georgetown. Henry had been aware of trouble a year before it broke out with vicious vengeance. Before the case had concluded, guards patrolled mines, shots had been fired, people had been "roughed up" and murdered, reputations were ruined, and both mines sank into near bankruptcy. Teller represented the Pelican people who had struck a valuable ore vein on ground claimed by the Dives. From Central City he tried to follow a confusing crisis that blew up in May 1875. Telegrams raced back and forth. Legal maneuvers were tried, injunctions were issued, yet nothing seemed to work.

Henry told his people to "hold on to what we have got inside our patented lines." Then he received a telegram on May 18 informing him that "all our houses are surrounded by the sheriff and his deputies and others," and they "won't allow our men to go to work." Teller replied to the sheriff that his people were "justified in defending their property" and also, if "compelled, to kill you and your posse." After two murders the Dives people proposed to have the sheriff disarm Pelican men "if we will agree to disarm ours."

The grim situation was not helped by the fact that the townspeople took sides—even, apparently, the sheriff. One of Henry's informants telegraphed him that one of the murderers had left the Dives Mine armed with six revolvers, a rifle, and a shotgun, adding: "Our sheriff don't want to catch him." Understandable, perhaps. The informant concluded in the fourth telegram, sent on May 20, "our sheriff don't amount to anything."

One of Teller's friends at the scene pleaded: "To save more bloodshed see what arrangement you can make with the opposing counsel and come over tomorrow." The opposing faction appeared none too happy with Teller. William Hamill wrote him that his people should stop making excuses, adding "we insist on possession being given at once."

This murderous turn of events shocked Georgetown. It did not help the community's image or reputation. Finally, the parties arranged a truce that eventually led to the consolidation of the two properties. Several years would pass, however, until calm prevailed. Unfortunately for all concerned, production never again equaled its level in the 1870s.

Teller also had to try to keep some British investors informed as to what was happening to their Georgetown property. "All we want is the money and be done with the whole affair," one wrote forlornly in August 1875. They owned 50 feet of the Dives and were not about to give it up. They were "obliged by your continued attention to the business [and] for your letters and advice." It took months, but apparently everything was satisfactorily resolved from London's viewpoint.[7]

An even more famous trial nationally, the *Hyman v. Wheeler* apex case, involved richer mines near Aspen and more prominent people. The litigation dragged on for three years before finally being decided in Denver in 1886. Although the case was less violent than the Pelican-Dives case, it was far more costly, with experts, witnesses, exhibits, and a host of top attorneys on each side. Teller served as one of the attorneys for David Hyman and his colleagues. They won the case, and the apex doctrine was upheld. This finally led to a compromise Teller helped arrange by pointing out the obvious: it seemed a shame to spend a fortune on lawyers' fees when the mines appeared rich enough to satisfy everybody.

Hyman, also a lawyer, stated his opinion of mining litigation: "I can say truthfully that no litigation equals a mining litigation in its intensity and bitterness." The successful party, he observed, looked a fortune in the face, and the losers hated to give it up.

Teller emerged from this litigation with a reputation as one of the "greatest legal authorities" of the day. These two cases and other apex litigation highlighted the changes that were coming to Colorado mining. Outside investors generally stood aligned against Coloradans in both cases. Money played the major role, not experience or long standing in the community. Law and a good stable of lawyers meant as much as a rich claim. Original discoverers found themselves forced out by wealthy corporations, usually from the East. Also, profits disappeared rapidly in this type of litigation with a very detrimental effect on the local industry and owners' pocketbooks.[8] Complications, frustrations, violence, high expenses, and legal maneuvering ended the dream of the promised land. The poor man's mining West had become the playground of the rich and politically powerful.

Because Colorado concentrated on lode mining relatively early, lawyers quickly comprehended that mining law was tremendously lucrative. Although their courtroom appearances attracted the most attention, Teller and his colleagues served as more than simply advocates in court; they often helped as advisers, counselors, and managers. Securing patents on mining claims, preparing title examinations, drawing up deeds and leases, and negotiating the lease or sale of mining properties claimed the largest share of their workload.

Despite Teller's specialization in one aspect of law, he, like other Colorado lawyers, resisted devoting his full attention to mining. He continued to be involved in railroad law, general practice, and other legal work. The trend in both Colorado and the nation in the years near the end of the century was toward the specialization that came to dominate the twentieth century. In this, Colorado appeared in the forefront.

Another example of the changing times sadly came to the fore: the fact that injured miners had little legal success against companies. Court decisions generally found them at fault for accidents, thereby relieving the company of any responsibility. In 1881 a Teller client, Patrick Regan, sued the Winnebago and O.K. Mining Company for $20,000 in damages after being injured by falling rock. As the *Rocky Mountain News* noted on May 7 a "great many suits" were pending on similar issues.

In the 1870s his practice outside of mining was similar to his practice in Morrison, except he had become more prominent. He drew up corporation papers—something new—but he tried to collect an amazing number of debts for himself and others, settled estates, and dealt with a wide variety of cases including assault, larceny, gambling, ejectment, trespass, divorce, and sale of real estate. Not everything went well. Henry fielded complaints from clients about various matters, including one who said he had "never had a scratch of [a] pen from you." And another complained when some of his Central property was sold: "This without notice to me which I consider rather shabby."

Teller rarely became involved in those sensational murder trials the public loved to read and speculate about. The *Rocky Mountain News* (June 21, 1873) reported one in which Henry successfully defended his client. The newspaper praised his concluding speech, with its "eloquent appeal in behalf of his client" and his "close analysis of the evidence." Even the district attorney congratulated him, saying "it was with considerable embarrassment that he entered upon his argument, having to follow the very eloquent gentleman for the defense." The jury took only an hour to find the defendant not guilty.

Sometimes, even in civil matters, legal action took time. The firm of Duncan and Waller, collection agents, of Dubuque, Iowa, wrote Teller in June 1872 that "one James Chapline, formerly of this city," owed a note of fifty dollars. Four months later they wondered what had happened because they had "not heard one word." Chapline was found, but as Duncan and Waller wrote in January 1873, he "has promised time and time again to pay, but fails to do so." If Teller thought Chapline would pay the note plus interest, they would grant an extension; otherwise they planned to seek a judgment against him. Matters dragged on until July 1874 when, "with pleasure," they acknowledged the receipt of fifty dollars and "hereby extend to you our sincere thanks."

As he had before, Teller traveled to Denver, Cañon City, Evans, and elsewhere practicing in county, state, and national courts. He also still received inquiries about Colorado. A fellow Mason, Dr. G. W. Cox of Cornersville, Tennessee, wrote him in 1873 about relocating because of his invalid wife's health. Cox wanted a town with "good" society, churches, schools, and a Masonic lodge: "I am a member of the church and I think strictly a sober man and I try to be a zealous Mason." Teller replied and received thanks for providing the "desired information," but Cox requested additionally: "I wish to know what effect the climate in Colorado has on delicate females that are of a scrofulous constitution."[9]

Throughout the territorial days Central City was hailed for "the number and brilliancy of its lawyers[, which] gave it the first rank in legal circles." Its prominence began to slip, however, as statehood neared and the community's position declined. Teller, meanwhile, emerged as one of Central's most able lawyers, specializing "in real estate suits" under which "come those complicated disputes over mines." The *Denver Daily Tribune* (November 15, 1876) congratulated him for "a most enviable eminence as a lawyer" who was engaged in almost all important civil suits. He possessed, the article went on to say, "rare qualifications of the profession." At the same time, Teller, blessed with a "mind of a critical character," was one of the best workers and ablest advocates who gathered all points in the case "by unexcelled tact."

In concluding, the reporter gave an excellent verdict of Teller's Colorado legal days and the man himself: "He has a splendid reputation among his fellow lawyers as a man of fair dealing and generosity."[10] Teller could not have asked for a better summation of his career since he arrived in 1861.

During this period of Teller's most active involvement in legal affairs (although he handled legal matters well into the 1890s, his main work as a lawyer ended with his election to the U.S. Senate in 1876), the Colorado bench and bar had been conservative, mirroring legal development in the rest of the country. Business interests and stimulating the economy remained paramount. The law materially aided the economic growth and development of the territory, both desired results for Coloradans. The social costs remained hidden to all but the most perceptive or concerned observer. Teller reflected these trends, although he also displayed a growing social awareness that would emerge more clearly later in his life.

NOTES

1. *Tri-Weekly Miners' Register,* August 15, 23, 1862, March 11, April 14, June 11, July 23, August 20, 1863; *Daily Miners' Register,* July 28, 1865; Thomas Dawson, "The Personal Side of Senator Teller," Colorado Historical Society, 2; Clark Spence, *British Investments and the American Mining Frontier* (Ithaca: Cornell University Press, 1958), 29–30, 153–158; W. B. Vickers, *History of the City of Denver* (Chicago: O. L. Baskin, 1880), 609.

2. Docket Book 1861 and Day Book 1863, Teller Papers, University of Colorado; *Tri-Weekly Miners' Register,* February 11, 1863; N. Bliss, January 18, 1862, Allen Hersh, August 15, 1862, Robert Booth, September 18, 1862, F. F. Digby, November 15, 1862, B. Burroughs, November 21, 1862, December 6, 1862, January 27, 1863, Bridge, Beach, and Co., May 1864, George Ingersoll, January 9, 1865, and George Goodwin, undated, all in Teller Collection, University of Colorado; *Rocky Mountain News,* May 9, 1897. For more on Casey, see Duane A. Smith, *The Birth of Colorado* (Norman: University of Oklahoma Press, 1989).

3. *Daily Miners' Register,* September 20, November 17, 1864, June 1, 1865; *Rocky Mountain News,* August 7, 1874, June 16, 1882; John Guice, "Colorado's Territorial Courts," *Colorado Magazine* (summer 1968), 204–205, 215, 217–219, 222–224; John Guice, *The*

Rocky Mountain Bench (New Haven:Yale University Press, 1872), 78–79, 100; John Guice, "Moses Hallett, Chief Justice," *Colorado Magazine* (spring 1971), 147; Robert Murray,"The Supreme Court of Colorado Territory," *Colorado Magazine* (winter 1967), 22–24.

4. Day Books 1863 and 1864, Income Tax Returns, Bills and Receipts, Teller Collection, University of Colorado; *Denver Republican,* June 23, 1904; *Tri-Weekly Miners' Register,* June 30, 1863; *Rocky Mountain News,* May 9, 1897; Belford quoted in *La Plata Miner* (Silverton), December 25, 1885; Alice Polk Hill, *Tales of the Colorado Pioneers* (Denver: Pierson and Gardner, 1884), 240; Murray,"Supreme Court," 33–34.

5. J. Ross Browne, *Report on the Mineral Resources* (Washington, D.C.: Government Printing Office, 1868), 351, 355–356; Rossiter Raymond, *Statistics of Mines and Mining* (Washington, D.C.: Government Printing Office, 1873), 453–459; Harriet Teller, "Senator Teller as a Young Man," Colorado Historical Society, 4.

6. Wm. Brown to Johnson & Teller, September 28, 1862, James A. Harlan to Johnson, April 7, 1863, Elias Baker, January 18, 1862, Henry Woods, October 1, 1862, Francis McGravitt, December 12, 1864, January 20, 1865, Cornelius Walker, May 2, 1873, James Goodman, March 13, 1874, E. Warner, August 19, 1874, F. M Denny, July 7, 1875, Foster & Thomason, March 1, 1875, Hiram Johnson, October 27, 1875, A. Stewart, July 1, 1876, all to Teller, all in Teller Papers, University of Colorado. See also *Mining Journal,* April 8, 1864; *Rocky Mountain News,* March 17, 1868.

7. James D. Hague,"Mining Engineering and Mining Law," *Engineering and Mining Journal* (October 20, 1904), reprint pages 3–8; Raymond quote in Hague,"Mining Engineering," p. 6; Liston E. Leyendecker,"The Pelican-Dives Feud," *Essays and Monographs in Colorado History* (1985, no. 1), 6–7, 36–38, 49–50, 53, 59–61, 63; Jacob Snider, May 18, 20, 1875, ; B. Napheys, May 20, 1875 (four telegrams), E. Naylor, May 20, 1875, W. Hamill, May 20, 25, 1875, all to Teller, Teller to Jacob Snider, May 19, 1875, E. Naylor to Teller, May 24, 1875, for British involvement, see J. P. Lowerby, June 26, July 12, August 7, 27, November 8, 1875, all in Teller Collection, University of Colorado.

8. Leyendecker, "Pelican-Dives," 67–69, 86; Malcom J. Rohbrough, *Aspen* (New York: Oxford University Press, 1986), 101–107; Lee Scamehorn, *Albert Eugene Reynolds* (Norman: University of Oklahoma Press, 1995), 15, 93–94; David M. Hyman, "The Romance of a Mining Venture," American History Center, University of Wyoming.

9. Teller Case Book 1870, Record Book 1871, Teller Collection, University of Colorado; *Central City Register,* May 16, 1873; *Rocky Mountain News,* June 17, 1873; James & Co., April 8, August 5, 1872, Duncan & Waller, June 27, October 21, December 7, 1872, January 10, 1873, July 25, 1874, G. W. Cox, October 7, 1873, January 2, 1874, Jones & Miller, May 29, 1874, R. P. Weibrec, November 10, 1874, Miles Paton, January 10, 1875, John F. Wilson, April 16, 1875, George Lechner, October 10, 12, 19, 28, 1876, George Bates, October 11, 1878, all to Teller, Teller to Dawson, April 27, 1891, all in Teller Collection, Colorado Historical Society; Barry Hoffman, "The Mining Lawyer in Colorado," unpublished paper, author's possession.

10. Frank Hall, *History of the State of Colorado* (Chicago: Blakely, 1890), vol. 3, 409; *Denver Sun*(?), December 11, 1892, Thomas Dawson,"Scrapbooks," Colorado Historical Society, vol. 22; *Denver Daily Tribune,* November 15, 1876; Gordon M. Bakken, "The Development of Law in Colorado, 1861–1912," *Colorado Magazine* (winter 1976), 77.

Mining Man

"Tell the miners for me that I shall promote their interests to the utmost of my ability, because their prosperity is the prosperity of the nation," promised President Abraham Lincoln. Or at least Schuyler Colfax, in a speech at Central City, recalled Lincoln having said that to him on the fateful Friday, April 14, 1865. Regardless of its veracity, Central miners believed the statement, and so did many of their contemporaries.

Two districts may have influenced such a statement: Nevada's silver Comstock, which had boomed spectacularly during the Civil War, aiding the Union effort; and Colorado's golden heart, Gilpin County. Less spectacular and with less production, Colorado, in locals' eyes at least, seemed just as valuable.

Even visitors felt it. French traveler and mining engineer Louis Simonin, after visiting Central City and neighboring mining districts, was moved to say he received very "favorable impressions of the activity and the intelligence everywhere demonstrated by Colorado pioneers."

Even with the territorial mining decline at the end of the war, optimism remained high. Mining reporter James W. Taylor praised Coloradans in his 1867 report for convincing "anyone of the true value and countless and inexhaustible veins." "We may," he concluded, "reasonably expect in the succeeding few years to see a more rapid and successful advance." The struggling territory cheered his belief that "Colorado gold veins invariably are found richer the deeper they are sunk upon."

Six years later, U.S. mining commissioner Rossiter Raymond complimented the progressive nature of Gilpin County's mining, and the next year he praised the "very active mining" led by the "old and standard mines that have done exceptionally well." In the nation's centennial year the *Daily Register* could gush that "flush times" had returned and "everything is booming."

Central City writer and booster Frank Fossett enthusiastically proclaimed in 1879 that the town reigned as the center of the great gold mines that underlay the hills and gulches of Gilpin County. Even with Leadville unfolding before his eyes, he believed those hills contained "the deepest and most productive mines in Colorado."

The *Register-Call* agreed. Its editor observed in the special year's-end summary, December 31, 1880: "To give an exact review of the industries of Gilpin county, her immense wealth, and the stores of hidden and undiscovered riches, still bound up in the bowels of her sun-burnt and rock-ribbed mountains, would require the intuitive perception of a seer or the boundless knowledge of a prophet." The editor summarized, "The present prosperity of Gilpin county is not due to foreign or outside capital; but it is due to her enterprising and energetic citizens, who, in the dull times of ten years ago, saw foreshadowed that it remained with them to demonstrate whether mining was a genuine industry or not." It had been an amazing time for the region, and in Gilpinites' estimation no question remained as to whether mining exemplified a "genuine industry."

Henry arrived in Central City at the end of the beginning of Central's and Gilpin's greatest mining era. Placer diggings had given out, replaced by hard rock mining. Gilpin County through 1873 reigned as the territory's unchallenged number-one mining county. Then for the next decade the county averaged a steady production of more than $2 million in gold plus $150,000 in silver per year to keep it in the forefront. It was, insightful and longtime resident Frank Young wrote, "the golden age of Central."

Even if they did not own or operate a mine, mining lawyers like Teller naturally gravitated into the industry. As Chapter 3 discussed, Teller advised owners on how to sell their properties and performed other duties for them. A New York investor, for instance, asked Henry to see that the necessary assessment work on his claim was completed so he could maintain his ownership. Willard and Henry also looked after a coal mine for a Kansas City owner.[1]

Teller's reputation, knowledge of mining, legal training, and familiarity with Colorado soon made him a central figure within the industry. His mining involvement did not end when he moved from Central. Until the day he died, Henry Teller remained a mining man.

Teller soon learned, however, that mining did not always produce boom days. Colorado's mining fortunes went up, went down, rallied, slipped down, then finally went back up—all during Henry's first dozen years in the territory. A variety of factors caused this turmoil, including the "refractory ore" discussed in Chapter 3, plus the waste of capital in trying to resolve that problem. Poor management, overly anticipated "magnificent" profits, stock speculation, underestimation of expenses, and lack of good judgment nearly ruined Colorado's mining reputation and image. All this forced Taylor to conclude (1866 report) that "quartz mining [in] Colorado has hitherto been unsuccessful." The wanton destruction of timber, which Raymond called one of the "worst abuses" of western settlement, also hurt Central mining. The cost of a cord of wood jumped to ten dollars in 1869—five times what it had been a few years earlier.

The 1871 *Rocky Mountain Directory* provides a glimpse of Teller's mining activities in Gilpin County, the core of his early mining investments. He was listed as a partner in (Willard was a frequent one) or sole owner of thirteen mines, several with stamp mills on the grounds. None of these proved large producers of gold, but several were well developed. His papers show involvement in other claims as well. Beyond Gilpin County, Teller had mines and claims in neighboring Clear Creek and Boulder Counties and in Archuleta, Summit, Lake, and Chaffee Counties. He and Willard also owned coal lands up north in Routt County. He never lost his "fever"; as late as 1898 he and some friends were examining Arizona prospects.[2]

Teller either hired miners or leased his properties, but he still learned the trials and tribulations of the industry in the 1860s and 1870s. He paid $34.51 for assessment work on a tunnel in 1877, for example, and in 1904 he paid $20 to Rank and Fowler for a resurvey and setting of corner markers. Taxes had to be paid and miners employed at the standard early wage of $3 a day, which decreased as the years passed.

Leasing provided a little income, along with headaches. H. M. Thomas assured Henry that "you and me will have no trouble" as he worked the Redrock Lode near Georgetown. No further correspondence remains. Aaron Jones wrote Teller that he had done the annual assessment of the American Flag. "We have a good mine," he assured Teller, adding, however, "I intend to jump the old millsite and build a mill if you are willing." Henry was not. On another occasion Teller provided legal advice to one of his leasers. Lease payments came late, if at all; work sometimes done poorly; at times, little attention was paid to neighbors' property lines; and assessment papers were not always filed on time. Mines not owned outright (patented) had to be shown, as mentioned earlier, to have "not less than one hundred dollars' worth of labor . . . performed or improvements made during each year." If that figure was not met, the property was forfeited on January 1 of the next year and could be relocated.

Patented claims were owned outright. The prospector/miner had to have much more faith in his property to select this route. The claim needed to be surveyed; a notice had to be put on the land; and a plat, field notes, and affidavits of fulfilling these obligations needed to be deposited with the local land office. A notice of application for a patent had to be published in a local newspaper for sixty days, and a certificate of $500 in labor or improvements needed to be filed. If no adverse claimant appeared, for the sum of five dollars per acre a patent would be issued.

Teller was well versed in the 1872 law, "An Act to Promote the Development of the Mining Resources of the United States." He was trying to do just that. How much money he earned is unknown. One statement from 1873 credited him with $1,176 in mining profits, a good sum for that time. Not enough records remain to indicate whether this was typical.[3]

Teller's roles as a mining lawyer and a miner sometimes merged. Caribou, in neighboring Boulder County, had come into prominence in 1870 as potentially the "new Comstock." Its mines never measured up to that standard; however, the new district did usher in Colorado's silver decade that concluded with Leadville's silver bonanza, which nearly matched the Comstock's bonanza in excitement. Central City miners had opened the Caribou mines, and many of the Cornish miners and their families moved there, so strong ties existed between the two communities.

One early Caribou promoter, Cincinnatian Abel Breed, hired Teller as his lawyer in a case involving the Breed, or Caribou, Tunnel, as did other parties involved in a dispute pitting the No Name and Caribou Mines against each other. They all hoped Teller would "fit this thing in." Both cases involved absentee eastern owners who feared they would lose their property.

New York merchant Levi Bates had purchased the neighboring No Name and Poorman Mines in 1874. Bates's problems developed with the larger and wealthier Caribou Mine. After building a mill and putting the mines into operation, Bates either tired of the speculation, saw lawsuits on the horizon, or seized the opportunity for a quick profit. He sold out in October 1875. Old Caribou debts hounded him, however. His New York lawyers worked with Teller on several cases. One case was scheduled for trial in January 1876, but Bates requested it be "held over to the next term" because it had become involved with a larger issue of claim ownership on Caribou Hill.

Teller's frustration mounted because Bates could not come west to testify, so the case had to be postponed. Bates then offered to settle for a cash payment by the Caribou people, although he believed he "could probably beat" them in a trial. The frustrated Bates wrote Teller in January 1877, "I can't possibly see why after all my letters and telegrams you have failed to send on" testimony. Bates finally had everything straightened out, but the matter clearly showed the continuing problems of absentee ownership.[4]

Breed worried about losing his property because he had not done work on it, which by law he was required to do at least once every six months. He retained Teller to be sure it was done. Two years later the tunnel was "broken" into at night. Miners working a neighboring lease broke the "door down," entered the tunnel, and "went to work." The next morning Breed's men tried to work, only to find the intruders held possession. Ejection papers were served. They held out. This caused a multitude of problems (injunction, evidence gathering, depositions, hearings) for now Senator Teller, who turned the issue over to Willard to sort out.

The intruders were removed, but in March 1878 the tunnel was jumped again by men who said they were going to relocate it. Caribou mining superintendent Eben Smith telegraphed Harper Orahood—they needed to oust the "damned scoundrels who have jumped the tunnel at once." Smith managed to reach an unspecified arrangement in late April, and the parties gave back possession. He concluded, "I think I will have no more trouble with them."[5]

Meanwhile, events at Caribou took an interesting turn. Bates had sold out to, among others, Robert G. Dun of the famous Dun Company in New York. Two of Teller's political friends and business acquaintances, Jerome Chaffee and David Moffat, had purchased the Caribou Mine in 1876. They hired the well-known Eben Smith as their superintendent, and his skillful leadership brought the Caribou back into prominence. Dun and his partners, however, became convinced that the Caribou was stealing ore from his property and took Chaffee and his company to court, with Henry and Willard, among others, as his lawyers.

This presented a problem for Teller because he and Chaffee were Colorado's two newly elected senators and the leaders of the dominant Republican Party. Further, Willard and the law firm had defended the previous Caribou owner, the Mining Company Nederland, in a complex lawsuit filed by Chaffee, among others. To resolve what was becoming a costly entanglement, Chaffee and Moffat sold the Caribou to a company in which Dun was a major stockholder, the Caribou Consolidated Mining Company. This only temporarily calmed the situation. The "long and unhappy war," as newspapers called it, continued. Other lawsuits followed, Caribou stock prices collapsed, and Dun lost more money and purchased more property to protect his interests. Eventually, Dun owned almost all the mines on Caribou Hill whose bonanza days faded behind them.[6]

Teller's involvement at Caribou was complex. His old law partner Hiram Johnson was somehow involved when Breed sold the Caribou Mine to the Dutch investors (Mining Company Nederland) in 1873. Teller was still involved with Johnson, who wrote on December 31, 1872, "Do not fail to give this matter [potential sale] your attention as we must act at once if we desire to make sale in this spring."

Hiram had been having little luck in London selling mining properties because, as he complained in September 1872, the "great mass of the business men are either at the sea shore, touring the continent, or hunting in the uplands of Scotland." Nevertheless, he managed to get in on the Caribou sale. The Dutch went bankrupt within two years. Johnson sued to get his money, along with a host of others, in 1877. Through it all he still held out hope for the future of Colorado "with its mines, its lands, and its Rail Road." Johnson confessed, though, that he found himself "without money" and feeling "too poor and too old." Hiram once again would not profit from the future.[7]

Teller also owned in partnership at least two claims at Caribou and nearby, the Eagle and the Central Lodes. He had purchased them early in the Caribou excitement, but jumping in on the ground floor did not guarantee success this time.

In 1878–1880 the Leadville silver mines surged into the front-page headlines. As writer/artist Mary Hallock Foote wrote, "All roads lead to Leadville," and among those who hurried there were the veteran Colorado speculators Chaffee and Moffat.

Before they arrived, however, fifty-niner miner and businessman Horace Tabor had finally struck his fortune and fame.

Tabor had grubstaked two nondescript prospectors, George Hook and August Rische, in April 1878. As luck would have it, they discovered the Little Pittsburg Mine, and Tabor's fortune took wing. Horace soon epitomized the silver lining of Leadville and Colorado mining. Tabor, who realized what happened when a rich mine was struck, needed a partner with money and experience in mining litigation. Jerome Chaffee fit the bill exactly. One of Colorado's premier mining speculators, bankers, and politicians, Jerome had bought a share of the Little Pittsburg for $50,000 and quickly sold it for $125,000—a "cool profit" of 150 percent in only a few weeks.

Chaffee soon regretted his decision to sell as he saw the possibility of even bigger profits. He bought back in for $262,500, and with him came his friend and banker David Moffat. All this occurred in 1878, at approximately the same time Chaffee and Moffat readied plans to unload the Caribou on Dun and his partners. Henry marched right out of Caribou and into Leadville with them.

Chaffee hired Henry Teller, among others, in 1879, to defend his interests in the Little Pittsburg. The victory of Chaffee, Moffat, and Tabor was worth the time and expense; the Little Pittsburg mined into a high-grade bonanza in 1878–1879. The now incorporated company offered the public a chance to taste the fruits of such a bonanza. The directors placed 200,000 shares of stock on the market. Dividends of $100,000 appeared monthly from the Little Pittsburg Consolidated Mining Company; and stock prices, which started at $20, steadily rose, topping the mid-$30-per-share range. The Little Pittsburg was soon a hit on the New York and London stock markets, as happy stockholders saw visions of a silver future for themselves.[8]

In September 1879 Moffat purchased Tabor's third of the mine, giving him and Chaffee three-quarters control of the property. They now turned to speculation. Chaffee's ill health had forced him to retire from the Senate, so he turned to mining. Jerome, who now lived primarily in New York, had direct contact with stockholders and the important stock market. With 1879 monthly dividends rolling in, Little Pittsburg stock rising in price, and predictions of a $50 value before 1880 was out, stockholders relished what the new year would bring.

Ben Franklin once wrote that "he who lives on hope often dies starving," a prediction that seemed unimportant amid continued reports of bonanza ore in the mine. Then suddenly the Little Pittsburg stock price slipped and by mid-February 1880 had lost more than a third of its value; by the end of the month the stock had plummeted to $13 a share. Equally distressing, the value of silver ore mined in the Little Pittsburg dropped from over $100 to $20 per ton. Then came the final blow: the directors decided to stop paying dividends in early March.

The Little Pittsburg's day as a Leadville star was over. Investors placed most of the blame with Chaffee and Moffat, president and vice president, respectively, of the company. They proved illusive to corner, Chaffee begging ill health and Moffat refusing to be interviewed. Nothing stopped the mounting criticism, and eventually they took their stand to defend their actions.

Moffat charged that the fault was the mine's, not management's, whereas Chaffee admitted that in January he knew the ore reserves were "giving out" but then made the damning statement that he feared a panic might ensue if the information reached the public. He had hoped his miners would find new ore bodies to continue the dividends. Unfortunately for the mine's future, it had not worked out that way. Moffat claimed he had been "grossly deceived," that he knew "nothing" about mining, and that this had been his first stock operation. It did not aid their defense when investigation revealed that on March 13 Chaffee had telegraphed Moffat, imploring him to sell out posthaste.

Not everyone pointed fingers at David and Jerome. Leadvillites blamed naive easterners who "knew no more about what they were buying than a boy five years old."[9]

The few facts that came out for the public to ponder did not present a pretty picture. During February the directors had been busy selling their stock. Chaffee and Moffat were accused of selling the stock they owned, which constituted over a quarter—some estimated as high as half—of all the stock sold. To a man, they blamed management. Moffat changed his alibi to state he had been grossly deceived by management. Chaffee blamed the suspension of monthly dividends on the "unexpected and unforeseen" decrease in ore values and the failure of development work to disclose any new large ore bodies. In May Chaffee gave what amounted to his final statement on the Little Pittsburg. Reviewing the first eleven months of operation, he emphatically stated, "I venture to suggest that in the history of mining few companies have ever been able to make a better showing for their first year's operations, or have better prospects for the future."

The words rang hollow. Despite encouraging news from the mine and promising future forecasts, the stock hit $5 as Jerome pontificated and by the end of 1880 sank to a dismal $2 on a "quiet" market.

Rumors flew, questions went unanswered, denials countered accusations—still, the full story never appeared. Without question, Chaffee and Moffat and others had used inside information to dump their stock on an unsuspecting public. Even some of their partners lost money, as a small inside group seemingly controlled the situation. Colorado and Leadville mining slumped; the state's mining reputation was left holding the deflated bag of Little Pittsburg shenanigans. The Little Pittsburg collapse proved the start of a bad year for Leadville and its mines.[10]

The infectious enthusiasm and optimism of those opening years of Leadville's bonanza vanished. In their place stood a grimy industrial town located at an altitude of 10,200 feet in the heart of the Colorado Rockies tagged with an infamous reputation.

What had caused the collapse? The Little Pittsburg demonstrated a familiar scenario in mining districts throughout the West. The company had been overcapitalized to start with, compounded by the stock prices being highly inflated because of a mirage of high hopes and expectations. The Little Pittsburg had promised too much too soon. To pay the monthly dividends, the company depleted the ore reserves and did not spend time and money on exploration for new deposits. Management, spurred on by company needs, had not developed the mine; they had gutted it. For the sake of quick profits, a high profile, and board desires, the Little Pittsburg had been sacrificed. What the directors planned when the rich ore pockets ran out was unfathomable.

Crucial information had been withheld from the public to benefit insiders. Mining engineers' reports that were not highly laudatory did not find their way into the press or to stockholders. One of the debates over where blame lay for the failure of the Little Pittsburg raged between promoters and engineers. Speculation in stock played a role as well.

Chaffee and Moffat received the most criticism from the fiasco. Chaffee might claim that "his sole desire was to sustain the market to keep people from losing their money," words that did not sound creditable even to most local readers of the *Leadville Democrat* (March 30, 1880). The paper, indeed, blamed Jerome for engineering the stock manipulation. Moffat left the public eye as soon as he could while defending the directors' course as "honest and straight-forward." Mistakes might have been made, he conceded; nevertheless, the managers had "acted throughout in the best judgment."

Were these two men as innocent as they professed? The *Democrat* (May 27, 1880) did not think so and pointed directly at Caribou and several other joint ventures as proof. The Caribou and Little Pittsburg episodes, no matter what the two men might say, provide a pattern of their mine dealings that questions their innocence.

Although some might defend their actions as good business and their practices as condoned, in part, by the business ethics of the day, Moffat and Chaffee without question had taken advantage of both the Caribou and Little Pittsburg opportunities for their benefit and to the disadvantage of others. In each case inside information had aided them, as had the gullibility of eastern investors. In both cases their men directed mining operations, giving them up-to-the-date information not provided to other investors. Having fled the scene before the collapse, they hurried on to other matters.

Other individuals involved in the Little Pittsburg collapse also received a small share of the blame. Mining engineer Rossiter Raymond, who reported on the property, was criticized for being too optimistic and hopeful; at the same time, he was defended for being cautious and reasonable. Horace Tabor was criticized in a general way for being involved with the property. Teller appears not to have been a major player. Nevertheless, his friends and political allies lay scattered across the wreckage left by the Little Pittsburg's failure.[11]

Teller had been involved in mining from the inside out. He had been an owner and understood the problems and possibilities the industry offered. Henry appreciated the intense work and skill it took to be a miner and the danger the men faced every day as they labored underground. Henry had also leased mines and supervised mines for outside investors. Having worked with smelters to process his ore, he had an understanding of that auxiliary industry, its potential and problems. To round off his mining experience, he could point to nearly two decades in all aspects of work as a mining lawyer.

Wherever his career took him, Henry Teller represented the mining industry well. Few people in the state or the nation could claim such varied experience or versatility. The mining years in Central City, Gilpin County, and elsewhere in Colorado stood him well in the decades ahead.

NOTES

1. Material for the preceding section is found in Charles W. Henderson, *Mining in Colorado* (Washington, D.C.: Government Printing Office, 1926), 88–90; James Taylor in J. Ross Browne, *Report* (Washington, D.C.: Government Printing Office, 1867), 8, 12; Louis Simonin, *Rocky Mountain West* (Lincoln: University of Nebraska Press, 1966), 40–41, 56; Rossiter Raymond, *Statistics of Mines and Mining* (Washington, D.C.: Government Printing Office, various dates), reports for 1870–1875; Frank Young, *Echoes from Acadia* (Denver: Lanning Bros., 1903), 205–206; Frank Fossett, *Colorado* (New York: C. G. Crawford, 1879), 90; *Register* quoted in the *Colorado Transcript,* October 25, 1876; *Daily Register-Call,* December 31, 1880: H. B. Dodge to Teller, June 9, 1874, Teller Collection, University of Colorado; Alva Mansur to Willard Teller, July 12, 1875, Harper Orahood Collection, University of Colorado.
2. Raymond, *Statistics* (1870), 342, 347; *Colorado Miner,* May 5, 1877; Taylor in Browne, *Report,* 12; Ovando J. Hollister, *The Mines of Colorado* (Springfield, Mass.: Samuel Bowles, 1867), 195–196; *The Rocky Mountain Directory and Colorado Gazetteer* (Denver: S. S. Wallihan, 1870), 178–185; *Pagosa Springs News,* February 12, 1897; *Rocky Mountain News,* August 26, 1879, June 2, July 6, 1881. Teller Collection, University of Colorado, has numerous brief references to mining operations. See also H. Lee Scamehorn, *Pioneer Steelmaker in the West* (Boulder: Pruett, 1976), 70.
3. George Randolph to Teller, Dec. 3, 1873, William Dickerson to Teller, two letters, 1864, H. M Thomas to Teller, March 26, 1877, Aaron Jones to Teller, February 21, 1878, Harper Orahood to Teller, December 14, 1896, all in Teller Collection, University of Colorado; "An Act to Promote the Development of the Mining Resources of the United States," Forty-Second Congress, Sess. 2, 1872.
4. Davies and Work to Teller, December 28, 1874, March 15, 1876, M. A. Smith to Teller, July 16, 1874, L. Bates to Teller, December 14, 1875, April 2, September 20, December 26, 1876, January 13, 1877, all in Teller Collection, University of Colorado; *La Plata Miner,* December 25, 1885; Duane A. Smith, *Silver Saga: The Story of Caribou, Colorado* (Boulder: Pruett, 1974), 41–43.
5. Harriet Teller, "Senator Teller as a Young Man," Colorado Historical Society, 10; D. B. Miller to Tellers, September 20, November 2, 1875, November 2, 1877, March 26, 1878, A. D. Breed to Willard Teller, February 16, 1877, Herzinger and Harter to Tellers, March 28, 1878, Harter to Harper Orahood, April 9, 1878, Eben Smith to Orahod, April 2, 22, 1878, all in Teller Collection, University of Colorado.
6. *Boulder News and Courier,* May 21, 1880; *Rocky Mountain News,* February 13, 1877, February 27, 1878; *Mining Record* (Georgetown), May 15, 1876; *Central City Register-Call,*

May 7, 30, 1878; *Engineering and Mining Journal* (New York), May 3, 1879; *Hiram A. Johnson v. Mining Company Nederland,* July 11, 1876, District Court, Boulder County, Boulder, Colorado; Smith, *Silver Saga,* 68–80.

7. Hiram Johnson to Teller, August 26, December 30, 1871, January 4, February 19, September 10, November 12, December 12, 16, 31, 1872, all in Henry Teller Collection, University of Colorado.

8. *Engineering and Mining Journal,* February 8, 22, June 14, July 12, October 25, 1879; Mary Foote to Helena, May 12, 1879. Little Pittsburg material, James Hague Collection, Henry E. Huntington Library, San Marino, California; *Rocky Mountain News,* July 24, 1879. See also *Mining Record* (New York), August 16, September 20, October 25, 1879; Duane A. Smith, *Horace Tabor: His Life and the Legend* (Niwot: University Press of Colorado, 1989), 72–75, 109–116.

9. *Democrat,* February 25, March 12, 1880; *Engineering and Mining Journal,* February 21, 28, 1880; *New York Tribune,* January 31, 1880; *Rocky Mountain News,* February 27, 1880; *Inter-Ocean* (New York), April 4, 1880; Smith, *Horace Tabor,* 127–129.

10. *Leadville Democrat,* April 13, 16, May 11, 1880; *Engineering and Mining Journal,* January–December 1880; *Inter-Ocean,* April 4, 1880; R. G. Dill, "History of Lake County," in *History of the Arkansas Valley, Colorado* (Chicago: O. L. Baskin, 1881), 233–234.

11. *Engineering and Mining Journal,* January–December 1880; *Leadville Democrat,* February–April 1880; *Rocky Mountain News,* February–March 1880.

Photographic Essay: The Tellers and Central City

Some physical evidence of the Tellers remains in Central City—his office, the Teller House, St. James Methodist Church, and the opera house—but much has disappeared. To the casual visitor that hardly tells the tale of this family who once lived, laughed, worried, and worked there. Shakespeare caught this truth in *Macbeth* with these familiar words: "Life's but a walking shadow, a poor player that struts and frets his hour upon the stage and then is heard no more."

Fortunately, photography came to Central on the heels of its founding. Thus the shadow has been preserved and even though it's heard no more, it can still be seen.

Morrison, Illinois, where Henry Teller started his legal career and where his parents, brothers, and sisters lived, and several are buried. Courtesy, Illinois State Historical Library.

Harriet Bruce. Hattie is said to have never taken a good picture. Friends described her as a lovely girl with red cheeks. Courtesy, Richard Tyler.

Henry Teller, the young Central City lawyer, photographed in Cuba, New York, in 1864. Courtesy, Richard Tyler.

The Teller house (center) *in mid-1870s. Courtesy, Frank Fossett,* Colorado *(1879).*

Emma Teller, taken in Washington, D.C., while her father was secretary of the interior. Courtesy, Richard Tyler.

The Teller boys: Harrison, age fourteen, and Henry, age nine. Courtesy, Richard Tyler.

Henry Teller, U.S. senator and secretary of the interior. Courtesy, Colorado Historical Society.

Henry Teller, probably on the campaign trail at the turn of the century. Courtesy, Colorado Historical Society.

Henry Teller during the silver fight. Courtesy, Archives, University of Colorado.

Harriet Teller. Courtesy, Archives, University of Colorado.

Trying out one of those newfangled automobiles, Henry (on far right) looks a bit concerned. Courtesy, Richard Tyler.

The distinguished and honored Colorado pioneers, Henry and Harriet Teller, in 1905. Courtesy Richard Tyler.

Teller in Idaho Springs (May 7, 1909) celebrating the fiftieth anniversary of the gold discovery and Pike's Peak rush. Judge Moses Hallett is on Teller's right, and Governor John Shafroth is on his left. Courtesy, Richard Tyler.

Central City before Teller arrived. Courtesy, Denver Public Library, Western History Department.

Like prosperous mining towns throughout the West, Central soon matured. Courtesy, Colorado Historical Society.

The Teller home is in the center of the photo across the street from St. James. Courtesy, Gilpin County Historical Society.

Teller's law office. For over a decade this was one of the legal centers of Gilpin County. Courtesy, Gilpin County Historical Society.

The Teller home became the site of the Gilpin County Courthouse and offices. Courtesy, Richard Tyler.

Central City after the 1874 fire. Teller played a yeoman's role in trying to stop the flames. Courtesy, Duane A. Smith.

Central quickly rebuilt after the fire. This photo, circa 1876, prominently shows the Teller House and St. James (left-center) with the white Teller home peeking around the corner of the church. Courtesy, Archives, University of Colorado.

Territorial Politician

When Henry Teller arrived at Central in April 1861, territorial politics already showed signs of the beliefs and policies that would would dominate the next fifteen years. Colorado had been organized during the first weeks of the Lincoln administration; consequently, political appointments had fallen heir to the new party. In fact, for almost the next three decades the Democrats wandered in the wilderness, awaiting the arrival of a Moses to lead them to the promised land of political dominance. If one desired to get ahead politically, the safe path was the Republican path.

Mining controlled the destiny of the territory, and mining men jockeyed for political control and vied for election to the one national office available—delegate to Congress. When Colorado finally became a state, almost all important offices well into the twentieth century went to these gentlemen.

Despite the dominance of mining, its representatives did not hold their fate in their hands. In the territorial period one man—the president in Washington—aided by his party, controlled most local spoils. Therefore, Colorado Republican leaders tended to fragment into cabals as they vied for the chief executive's favor. During the years 1861–1876 they were all Republicans—Abraham Lincoln, Andrew Johnson, and Ulysses Grant.

Denver, the territorial political heart if not always the actual capital, moved vigorously to command political affairs. With the territory's only newspaper at Colorado's political birth, the *Rocky Mountain News* (an unequaled advantage); an aggressive group of movers and shakers; and a crossroads location, the city garnered a strong head start politically as well as economically. This aroused the jealousy of the mountain towns. They wanted a share of the spoils, maybe even the capital designation, and grew tired of being viewed through Denver's eyes in the press.

To add to this potentially volatile mix, the Civil War aroused flaming passions and patriotism. Little room for compromise existed between Northerners and Southerners. Then, of course, there was the Indian "problem." This had been their land, and they seemed determined to resist the white man's "progress." Because the life-supporting transportation links back to the states ran through their lands, the plains tribes almost held Coloradans hostage. Many thought the future of Colorado rested on this issue. In Coloradans' eyes, civilization—investors, settlers, and growth—had to come over those trails. In the way rode the Cheyenne, Arapaho, and Ute, masters of mountain and prairie.

In the background floated the statehood issue. Additionally, the political aspirations of a host of men who had come west to develop their political futures drove attitudes and actions.

Teller had been involved in politics before, but he had never been involved on the ground floor of an entire territory. He was clearly interested and desired to participate. The question that remained was how he would dissect the situation and plan for the future.

He dealt from a position of strength; Gilpin County climbed to the apex of its political and economic power during these years. A quartet of the era's prominent politicians came from the county, including Jerome Chaffee, Henry Wolcott, James Belford, and Teller. The county and town boldly challenged as Denver's chief political rival.

Having converted to the Republican Party because of the slavery issue, Teller had a perfect entry into the Colorado political arena. As he wrote an admirer in 1896: "I thought then [in the 1850s] that the Democratic Party was the party of the people, but I soon found it was owned and controlled by the slave holders, and I left it, and have never voted a Democratic ticket since 1852." With his law partner Hiram Johnson already established in Central City, Teller quickly gained insights into the situation there that other newcomers would have to learn on their own.[1]

Henry was just getting acclimated to his new home and fighting his case of mountain fever when the inaugural territorial political fight exploded. Coloradans had hailed first territorial governor William Gilpin when he arrived in May 1861. His enthusiasm for the West, his boomer mentality, and his apparent connections to the Lincoln administration all augured well for the young territory. Unfortunately, he arrived just as the Civil War started. Its impact reached far beyond the Rocky Mountains. Federal troops, needed back East, hastened away. Coloradans worried about a possible Confederate invasion trying to seize the mines because the South desperately needed gold. Coloradans saw no friends nearby, and Washington could not pay much attention to the settlers in Pike's Peak country because the government was overextended trying to put down a rebellion.

Gilpin worried endlessly about the invasion threat and tried to arouse Coloradans. Many disgusted Southerners left or stayed silent. Northern loyalists wondered why their governor was so involved in an "arms race" to keep guns from falling into the wrong hands when other matters needed attending to. Then Gilpin acted. With no regular troops available to protect Colorado and its transportation lifelines from its "enemies," Gilpin decided to raise a regiment of Colorado volunteers. In his mind as well as those of others, the territory was surrounded by untrustworthy or disloyal neighbors. To make matters worse, Confederate emissaries had reportedly contacted the Cheyenne, Arapaho, and Sioux.

The governor displayed a further lack of political adroitness and understanding when he gave the territorial printing contract to a Denver rival of the *Rocky Mountain News*. Gilpin would pay for that mistake.

Washington had no time or money to support Gilpin's plans, so he decided to pay his volunteers by issuing drafts on the federal treasury. He may have thought he had authority to do that, but the treasury thought otherwise. When local merchants presented the "Gilpin drafts," they were stunned to have them rejected. They had accepted them in good faith for supplies and other essentials the troops needed. Much of what little capital the territory possessed became tied up in this affair.

The drafts haunted the young lawyer Teller and caused the territory's reputation to decline. A client wrote from Minnesota asking when and if he would be paid. By the end of a contentious year, Gilpin's reputation had sunk to new lows, and the *News* had a field day blasting his ineptness. Although some Coloradans supported him, most wanted him out and the drafts paid.

In the winter of 1862 Gilpin hurried to Washington to defend his action in issuing the drafts, but it was too late. The Lincoln administration removed Gilpin, and Illinois railroad and town booster John Evans replaced the unpopular governor.

Teller's first foray into Colorado politics came with the start of the war. Denver resounded with news of the troubles back in the states as residents discussed the startling events. Wednesday, April 24, 1861, readers of the *Rocky Mountain News* found ardent unionist William Byers defending his language of "treason and robbery": "In God's name, how much longer should the Administration have submitted to the menaces, the open treason, and the violent demonstrations of these rebellious leaders?" Five days before, they had learned that the Confederacy had attacked Fort Sumter.

The Confederate flag had been flown in downtown Denver, which infuriated Byers, Teller, and others. Concern rose about what Colorado's pro-Southerners had in mind for the territory. Only slightly less worrisome was a report that "certain quarters" seemed to have a "disposition to inflame feelings against the Indians." Byers knew that the safety, growth, immigration prospects, and peace of Colorado depended on there being no further trouble.

"Shall the folly and rashness of a few inconsiderate persons, who wish to gain a little personal notoriety, be allowed to embroil us in a war with the Indians? We trust not." On a less crucial matter, the *News* reported that the committee planning the reception for Governor William Gilpin would meet the next evening.

Teller read with pleasure that more "troops are offering than can be accepted at present," although it pained him to note that Virginia had seceded. Like many others, he probably agreed with but feared the forecast that "the prospect is for a brief but terrible conflict."

A month later, now in Central City, Teller wrote Lincoln's overstressed and underachieving secretary of war, Simon Cameron, about the Colorado situation. Henry wanted him to know of the pro-Union sentiment in the mountains. "We have," he declared, "hundreds anxious to contribute to the support of the Government" and to assist in maintaining the integrity of the flag of our country." Henry desired to know if the government would accept companies of volunteers: "If we had the assurance that the volunteers would be accepted there would be no lack of men inured to toil and hardship ready to enlist for the war."

His expression of patriotism never wavered. Nonetheless, he was disappointed by the federal government's response. Cameron replied on June 3, and Teller learned a fact of western life: "I beg leave to say that this Department has no desire at present to raise troops at so great a distance from the scene of action, the pressure from the States nearer home for admission into the Army being so great as to compel us to decline troops every day."[2]

The troops might not be needed for the eastern theater in Cameron's view, and federal forces would also not be stationed in Colorado because of wartime demands. The territory, therefore, found itself on its own.

Having recovered from his fever by summer of 1862, Teller jumped vigorously into territorial politics. His base of support, Gilpin County, gave him his main advantage.

With a year's experience under their belts, a host of would-be politicians, who along with the miners had rushed to the Rocky Mountains looking for their own brand of promise, had organized themselves. Few prizes dangled before their eyes. Only the election of the nonvoting territorial delegate to Congress exceeded the local level. Maine-born lawyer and fifty-niner Hiram Bennet, who had won a one-year term in 1861, stood for reelection to a two-year term. The Republicans, now known as the Union Party, fell to bickering among themselves over the nomination.

The renominated Bennet found himself facing the ever-optimistic William Gilpin, who thought he could redeem himself and his followers. But a vindictive William Byers had been waiting for just this chance. He printed stories about Gilpin and his earlier misadventures throughout the campaign. Coloradans got a taste of the rough-and-tumble politics that would become a territorial and state hallmark. "Groaning down" a speaker became a political sport that season. The Democrats, with no chance whatever, made it a three-man race. The unflappable Gilpin, meanwhile, as the

"People's" candidate for Congress, conducted an extensive "electioneering tour on his [own] behalf."

Teller went to the Union convention as a delegate from Gilpin County. He emerged a Gilpin supporter. Young Denver merchant David Moffat also attended with a much different personal result. Moffat felt Gilpin was "killed dead by bolting. The Gilpin cusses backed out of the Convention."

On Monday, August 11, 1862, Bennet came to Central to speak, wanting to secure his base in the second-largest territorial town. Teller responded for an "hour or more," according to the *Tri-Weekly Miners' Register,* also no friend of Gilpin. The editor jabbed him with faint and damning praise: "Mr. Teller is a very pleasing speaker—a lawyer of fine ability, and a highly respected gentleman. He is an ultra Republican, and supported Mr. Bennet when he ran on the Republican Ticket." According to the newspaper, Henry's attempt to "belittle" Bennet in the eyes of the audience did little good: "Though able and eloquent, [he] resembled throughout the argument . . . a lawyer pleading a desperate case before a jury. His plea, though ingenious, we do not think will secure a favorable verdict."

Bennet replied briefly. Tellingly, he asked Henry why he refused to support him on the ground that there had been no party convention. Yet he supported Gilpin, who "had not been nominated by any convention at all." Teller, fighting a losing battle, doggedly stayed with Gilpin. As a lawyer friend wrote his partner, Hiram Johnson, "Bennet is gaining ground everyday. I think the prospects are flattering."[3]

On September 5 Teller defended Gilpin in Nevada (City) with a "lengthy speech full of fulsome adulation of his pet candidate." He continued "belittling Bennet," who was of "ordinary capacity" and who, while in Congress, "did practically nothing." The next night, he and Gilpin appeared in Black Hawk. The *Tri-Weekly Miners' Register* blasted Henry for being "unjustifiably severe upon Bennet" and said his remarks carried little weight with the audience because they were "overdrawn." The newspaper continued, "All who know Mr. Bennet know that he is not the simpleton Mr. Teller represented him to be; and it is equally clear that Mr. Gilpin is not the tremendously eminent statesman, patriot, pioneer, and explorer Mr. Teller endeavored to paint him."

Election day, October 8, passed quietly, and it was a month before all the returns were in and counted. Gilpin came in an embarrassing third in the voting (26 percent of the total), trailing even the Democratic candidate. The election clearly showed the Union Party's dominance; it gathered a total of 64 percent of the votes.

Teller's efforts came to naught politically that year; nonetheless, he had established himself as an orator of some note. He also participated in his first political bolt. Party lines became blurred, the single issue being union or disunion with the Democrats who, because of their prewar Southern base, were tarred as disunionists. Despite its criticism of Henry for his Gilpin efforts, the *Tri-Weekly Miners' Register* praised him for his "unusually eloquent and effective" speech on August 30 on behalf of recruiting Colorado regiments. "It was equally surprising to hear H. M. Teller—who has always been classed among the ultra Republicans (if not an Abolitionist)—denounce the Phillips, the Garrisons and kindred disunionists of the North." Apparently, the disunionists' high-pressure campaign that pushed the Lincoln administration to abolish slavery had angered Teller, the newspaper editor, and other Coloradans.

Teller had learned much about Colorado politics during the recently concluded campaign. The expanding, under-the-surface split between Denver and the mountain towns peeked around every political corner. Henry slowly emerged as the spokesman for the latter. Issues also surfaced that would chart the territory's destiny for the next few years. Statehood caught the attention of some Coloradans. The Indian "crisis" worried everyone and would not go away. Colorado politics showed a dirty, hard-biting side, with personalities often obscuring issues. Nor did western democracy totally clothe itself in respectability. As Frank Young observed, "Black Hawkers vote in Central, and Centralities, not to be outdone in courtesy, return calls and vote in Black Hawk; and when the results are declared, he must be a rash man indeed who would suggest a contest."[4]

Meanwhile, the war raged back in the states while Coloradans watched with fascination, excitement, and horror. War news in the various Central papers (four came and went during the war) kept Henry on top of developments, as did the Denver papers and national ones such as *Harper's Weekly*. By mid-July 1863 Henry was well aware of the enormous significance of the "great victories" at Vicksburg and Gettysburg. The tide of the battle had turned. He watched with equally great interest as Congress passed a bill for a transcontinental railroad and knew what that could mean for Colorado.

Although Teller did not return east to enlist and fight, he patriotically supported the war. He became a fixture at the popular "war meetings" in 1862–1863 to stir patriotism and "do good." By this time pro-Southerners had departed or wisely kept their opinions to themselves, and Teller's contemporaries hailed his oratory. Such phrases as "brilliant style," "handsome tribute to the Flag," and an "unconditional Union man" saluted his efforts. Further, Henry gave money to fund a bounty paid to patriotic men who volunteered.

Although he did not have a military background, Governor Evans appointed Teller a major general in the militia in 1863, a rank he held until he resigned in 1867, commended for "faithful discharge of his duties." He never assumed a field command, but he recruited and organized troops in the plains tribes/military crisis of 1864.

He got back into the good graces of the local Union Party with his ardent support of the North. With the emotional rhetoric of the time, he spoke at a "grand Union" meeting in Black Hawk on August 27, 1863, paraphrasing Andrew Jackson as his theme: the "Union must and shall be preserved." "We must," he argued, stand by "the Union at all hazards" to crush this "unholy rebellion." Teller supported Lincoln's freeing the slaves and taking such measures as were needed to win the war. In his view, "there was no fear of an undoubted Union man being put in jail for disloyalty." Henry ended by entreating his listeners "not to make a history that would bring discredit on the founders of the territory or upon our brothers in the east fighting to preserve the Union."

By August 1863 Teller was back in full stride with the Union Party, working tirelessly for the ticket that won nearly two-to-one in Central that year. On the territorial level, he was elected to the party's executive committee. Here Henry came into more personal contact with the men who would play a major role in his career in the years and decades ahead—Jerome Chaffee, William Byers, John Chivington, Samuel Elbert, and John Evans.[5]

CHIVINGTON AND EVANS INVOLVED TELLER IN COLORADO'S NEXT GREAT CRISIS, the plains Native American troubles in 1863–1864 and Sand Creek. Simply, the issue evolved into the question of the territory's future. It all started in Minnesota in 1862. The local Sioux—tired of broken treaties, pressured on their own land by the influx of settlers, and confronted with a foreign culture threatening their very existence— killed more than 730 settlers. Federal troops rushed north and drove most of the natives out onto the plains where their fury infected their cousins.

In spring and summer of 1863 and again in 1864, the Sioux, Cheyenne, and Arapaho raided and pillaged—closing overland trails, attacking outlying settlements, and causing general dismay in Colorado. Without access to the trails, supplies and investors languished at the Missouri River, the cost of living rose, settlers were killed (some very near Denver), and stress became a way of life along the foothills and in the mountains.

The respected John Evans found himself in a bind. Washington could not free troops to guard the trails, nor could it pay much attention to the Rocky Mountains while the war rolled brutally along. The governor would have to rely on whatever resources existed in Colorado. The district's military commander—the hero of the battle of Glorieta Pass in which the Texas invaders were turned back—erstwhile Methodist minister John Chivington, was equally acclaimed and concerned. Newspapers hailed him: "His popularity among our citizens has constantly been increasing since first he became a military man. He is a regular 'fighting preacher,' and will do to be on."

The two faced a worsening situation exacerbated by Coloradans' rising anger. The heritages of racism, bigotry, misunderstanding, hatred, cultural baggage, and stereotypes the settlers carried with them, and the former sole inhabitants often displayed as well, were about to sire a tragic legacy.

The plains tribes faced a bleak future, with the buffalo disappearing and the land unable to maintain them as it once had. Part of this dilemma was their own fault, as horses and guns changed everything from land use to the hunt.

By summer of 1864 Coloradans had seen enough raiding and pillaging and demanded something be done and done soon. Evans and Chivington responded by raising the Third Regiment of Colorado Volunteers, 100 day troops. They needed to act quickly before the term of enlistment ran out.

To make matters worse, the crisis became caught up in the general debate over statehood. The Lincoln administration, believing it might need all the votes it could muster in the 1864 national election, offered Nevada, Nebraska, and Colorado the opportunity to become states. The offer reflected national politics, not Colorado's readiness. This fact would haunt statehood supporters.

The offer proved to be all that statehood advocates needed; they felt Washington would pay more attention to a state than to a territory, and the state would have its own senators and a representative. Finally, Coloradans would hold their destiny in their own hands; there would be no more congressional interference. Equally critical, they would have a greater say in the location of the Pacific Railroad.

Henry, joined by a host of others, started down the slippery slope to statehood that would occupy his next four years. At the March 1864 Gilpin County Union convention, Teller supported statehood and was elected a delegate to the territorial convention, where the vote for state organization was "all but unanimous." Byers and his *Rocky Mountain News* enthusiastically backed the idea. Colorado had sufficient population, he gushed, and the people were "earnest for statehood." Almost immediately, something unexpected happened: opposition surfaced in Teller's backyard. Black Hawk's *Mining Journal* emphatically opposed the plan. The paper reasoned that statehood would be too expensive, Colorado had insufficient population, taxes would increase, and the time for such a vote could not have been "more ill-chosen." Infuriated, Byers fired back, and a struggle began. Seeds of doubt had been planted in Coloradans' minds.

Gilpin County chose Henry as a delegate to the constitutional convention in July 1864 in Golden, where he was appointed to two committees—judicial and finance and compensation. Henry discussed and offered various motions and amendments. Delegate Teller signed the constitution that would be voted for on the second Tuesday of September. Supported by the major Central and Denver papers, statehood appeared safely on the way. Byers loved the convention, stating, "We may be charged with egotism in making the assertion, but we honestly believe that there never has been a more creditable assembly of men called together in Colorado than those composing the Constitutional Convention." Of course, the territory was barely three years old!

In their enthusiasm, the pro-state backers called a convention in August to nominate a slate of candidates for the soon-to-be state offices. Teller saw Denver seize the lion's share of the important nominations—Henry D. Towne for governor, Chivington for Congress, and Evans for senator. As a sop to the mountain communities, it seemed "generally understood" that Teller would be the other senator. At this point the scheme started to unravel.[6]

Mountain towns seethed, upset with Denver's ravenous political appetite. Democrats did not feel statehood would benefit them in any way; nor did the Hispanics to the south. Would-be politicians outside of Denver did not like the small patronage crumbs that dropped their way. Fears of increased taxes lurked at every meeting and served as a rallying point for anti-staters. Unable to solve the plains troubles, the increasingly unpopular Chivington and Evans found themselves becoming a liability. As long as the plains tribes raided freely, the two men gathered mounting criticism from all sides. They finally "resigned."

Nonetheless, Teller enthusiastically entered the race. He even went to anti-statehood rallies to present his case. The *Daily Miners' Register* (August 16, 1864) reported one such episode. Henry, called to the front to speak, found that "although the antis bellowed lustily they were at length induced to listen to arguments in favor of the state that not one of them has yet or ever can successfully deny or refute."

He opportunely published a letter to the "people of Colorado," signed by himself as superintendent of the Corydon Gold Mining Company and two dozen other mining men. The letter was meant to show readers why mining men supported statehood—it would encourage investment, improve titles, and place mining laws under local control. All this, he argued, would increase gold production. With Colorado mining in a slump, these were strong appeals.

The *News* applauded Major General Teller's efforts and cheered his speech in Denver, stating "no man in Colorado is more careful of his position." The *Mining Journal* (August 17) simply called it a "desperate" effort and pointed out that many of the oldest, "heaviest mining firms" backed the anti-state cause. The tax issue probably swayed many corporations.

Even out-of-territory individuals joined the debate. Professor Nathaniel Hill, who had visited Colorado on the investigating trip, sent a letter stating that any action against statehood would be "prejudicial to the best interests of the country." For once, Teller and Hill concurred. Both sides made their final appeals in mid-September. The *Register* said:

> A vote for the State is a vote not only to protect our interests, enhance the value of our property, render sale of it easy and prices remunerative, too it's a vote to assume our true position as American citizens, and entitle us to vote in the election of the President and Vice President, and strengthens the union cause as we could do in no other way.

The *Mining Journal* (September 12) encouraged the anti-vote to turn against the "unscrupulous energy" of all class of politicians backed by "cords of greenbacks." The voters gave Teller a verdict he did not want. The votes against statehood totaled 450, 304, and 104 in Central, Black Hawk, and Nevada, respectively. Even Denver voted it down, and it lost more than 3 to 1 throughout the territory. The *Journal* simply said, "We won. The Constitution of the United States is respected, the honesty, good sense, and independence of the people vindicated, the government thieves deservedly rebuked."[7]

Once again, Teller found himself out of step with most of his neighbors. They saw political opportunism, Denver greed, higher local taxes, being subject to conscription (territories were not subject to the draft), and lack of population. The majority of

Coloradans simply were not ready to assume statehood responsibilities. The tax argument swayed many in a time of mining doldrums and general depression. Teller's first bid for political high stakes had failed ingloriously. In a matter of months his political career had suffered two major setbacks, enough to discourage many men.

Another factor interceded. The contest had also been a personal vendetta, this time against Chivington and Evans, who seemed unable to solve existing problems. Fritz-John Porter, in Colorado after being court-martialed from the army, commented in private what many said in public. He described Chivington in a letter as a "preacher and pretended soldier" and Evans as a weak coward, fond of bombastic dispatches. Evans and Chivington suffered additional political blows with Sand Creek. Teller was not the recipient of such personal animosity.

In June, as tensions and excitement mounted, Evans ordered Teller to organize all militia immediately. The *Daily Miners' Register* (June 17, 1864) cheered "keep the ball rolling, til the redskins are wiped out." The previous evening Teller had spoken at a meeting at which a volunteer company was organized. Drill was ordered for 8 A.M. Friday, and the new recruits were told to "hold themselves in readiness upon a moment's notice to march." Major General Teller would inspect them at the drill.

Two months passed before Evans notified Teller that he had asked for the authority to "raise and mount" a regiment of 100 day men. These troops would become the infamous Third Colorado. Willard Teller, who had also helped with the statehood fight, addressed a war meeting in Nevada that raised more than $1,200 to be divided among those who enlisted. Meanwhile, Teller proudly announced that the Third Colorado was being rapidly organized and warned his friends in Central, "There is no time to be lost." An Indian war of "unprecedented dimensions is upon us," exhorted a newspaper. When the mountain troops arrived in Denver, Major General Teller and "other prominent public spirited men" came with them.[8]

Colorado faced seemingly endless horrors. With travel cut off, residents faced potential shortages of food and supplies, rising costs, possible closings of mines, and abandoned farms on the prairies and in the valleys. Coloradans had been killed and women captured, labor shortages were threatened as men rode off to war, and with winter nearing the *Daily Miners' Register* (August 18) feared, "if our supplies are cut off we must starve." They did not starve, but Chivington—facing pressure from home to do something militarily—took to the field. The result was the Sand Creek massacre on November 29, 1864. The December 8, 1864, *Daily Miners' Register* called it a "brilliant affair." The true policy, the editor went on, "is to give them no quarter. Kill male and female, young and old, until none are left to tell the tale." Reflecting the attitude of many of his readers, the editor concluded that we have "talked enough, we now want action, just such as they have given us a sample of."

Sand Creek did not turn out to be "brilliant." Quite the contrary; the massacre led to Chivington resigning his commission, his political future shattered, and to Evans's removal as governor. The issue became political; as Denverite George Kassler wrote to his wife, that "bug bear politics must have something to do" with it. Congress rather blunderingly investigated the events, and Colorado's image—already damaged by its mining misfortunes—slumped further. Additionally, Sand Creek did not end the plains warfare. It continued on in Colorado for another four years and on the plains for a decade. Militarily, the attack had only shown that the tribes were vulnerable to winter campaigns.

Although Sand Creek was a controversial event throughout Teller's lifetime, he did not suffer because of it personally or politically. Fortunately for him, he had not been directly involved in Chivington's final campaign, although he, like almost all Coloradans, had demanded that something be done. Later, during an 1882 congressional debate, Henry defended the troops who fought there. Many had been his friends, and although he did not deny that atrocities had occurred, Teller, as mentioned earlier, asked his listeners to understand the events leading up to the battle.[9]

POLITICALLY, COLORADO HEATED UP AS THE FURIOUS AND VENGEFUL PLAINS tribes made 1865 a miserable year. As a side show to the main event, Central, Golden, and Denver all wanted to become the territorial capital. In an amazing turn of events, the statehood issue resurfaced, with people unblushingly changing sides with alacrity.

Using the 1864 enabling act again, statehood advocates tried to reenergize the voters to accept their proposition. Jerome Chaffee had been a late joiner to the bandwagon; now the polished, urbane mining man headed the campaign. Colorado's consummate politician of the era, Chaffee, came to lead what became known as the "Denver crowd." John Evans, who remained interested in the Senate even as the storm of Sand Creek crashed over him, joined Jerome again.

In Chaffee, Teller found an ambitious political opponent who kept his eye steadfastly on the Senate. Eventually, Henry became the recognized leader of the "Golden crowd," or the mountain communities. This split within Republican ranks lasted for nearly a decade and directly affected Teller's political ambitions.

As statehood percolated in late winter and early spring of 1865, Colorado received the wonderful news of Lee's surrender at Appomattox, which was followed abruptly by the shocking news of Lincoln's assassination. Teller long remembered the day of Lincoln's death. A Central City southerner reportedly remarked that he was glad it had happened. A mob quickly gathered to lynch him, but Teller managed to calm them and have the man sent to Denver. His courage in the face of such anger impressed onlookers.

Coloradans had not always appreciated Lincoln, but his tragic death and attitude toward mining made him a hero. In the melancholy aftermath of the assassination and with the multitude of troubles facing Coloradans, his alleged words to Schuyler Colfax, cited earlier, that miners held the hope of the country offered a silver lining. Would Washington pay heed?[10]

The pro-staters called for another constitutional convention. Teller stayed on the sidelines this time. The convention produced a constitution almost the same as that of the previous year, but they advanced no candidate slate of state officers. Amid charges of fraud and "questionable practices," the constitution barely passed by 200 votes. A companion vote found Coloradans rejecting "Negro suffrage."

Waiting might have been prudent at this point, but the pro-state backers fearlessly organized a "state" election, and personalities jumped back into the fray. Chaffee and Evans were determined to ensure that the legislative members would favor their senatorial aspirations. Chaffee gained control of the renamed Republican Party and successfully defeated Teller supporters in county after county. Teller continued to be a favorite in the mountain counties, a letter from Empire stating, "Two names find favor with our miners for the Senate, and those are Evans and Teller. I hear of no opposition to Mr. Teller, while Gov. Evans has a host of friends and but few enemies."

Editor Byers saw trouble coming and in a November 3 editorial pleaded, "The worst fears of those who have the success of the Union cause at heart are being realized in the personal contest in Gilpin County between the partisans of Messrs. Teller and Chaffee." He concluded, "We ask the friends of Messrs. Teller and Chaffee, can you by your divisions afford to let either one or both of your respective friends bear the blame of defeating the union party?"

Teller held Chaffee off in Gilpin County, but he had every right to be infuriated that Chaffee would challenge him in his home county. The election results put William Gilpin back in the governor's chair, and the new "state legislature" chose Chaffee and Evans as senators. Teller had refused to run for the House of Representatives, and that office went to southern Colorado's George Chilcott to help "balance" the ticket. The pro-staters proclaimed that at last, Colorado stood ready to assume its rightful place among the states.[11] Washington, however, had not approved of statehood. Until it did, the election held no meaning.

In 1866 pro-staters smashed into a Washington roadblock. The new Colorado governor, Alexander Cummings, opposed the constitution and took pains to point out that African Americans had been denied the vote. That angered congressional Radicals who emotionally supported the idea and were lining up to fight President Andrew Johnson on this and other issues. Eastern senators also challenged whether Colorado contained a large enough population (it did not) and questioned the legality of the election. Western senators supported Colorado, but their numbers were too small to carry the day. Henry gained no points with the statehood advocates by hurrying to Washington to testify against statehood.

Johnson refused to proclaim statehood on the grounds that the enabling legislation was no longer valid. Again, the hopes of many recently victorious officeholders had been dashed.

Their hopes revived, however, when the Radicals, believing they needed another state for additional support, passed a second enabling act for Colorado with an eye to having it in the union before the 1866 off-year congressional elections. Johnson promptly vetoed the bill on the grounds that Colorado lacked sufficient population for statehood. An attempt to override the veto failed; the two-thirds vote could not be mustered. Now a three-time loser, Colorado seemed destined to remain a disappointed territory. It soon became a four-time loser when an 1867 attempt by the Radicals failed with another veto and lack of override votes.

The territorial fallout proved significant. Chaffee and Evans still controlled the remnants of the unrecognized and nonfunctioning 1865 "state" government. Their diligent efforts to gain statehood had failed and had antagonized a great many Coloradans. Yet all they needed was national approval and recognition and the prize would be theirs.

Golden and the mountain towns, led by Teller, stalwartly fought the Denver faction. More than statehood and political spoils stood in the balance. Commercial competition, the site of the capital, rivalry over railroads, and desire for investment brought both sides to verbal blows. Denver won one round in 1867 by being named permanent territorial capital, which angered Golden and Central even more.

Teller, meanwhile, kept his stronghold in Central and Gilpin County, although mining woes had somewhat weakened their political and economic muscle. An angry Byers attacked Henry during the 1867 Gilpin County convention, snarling that if Teller wanted to drop "all personal strife between himself and Chaffee," it would not require the endorsement of the convention, adding: "The Convention is not Teller or Teller the convention." After accusing him of "manipulating" the meeting, Byers ended by saying "the principles of Teller sink into insignificance when compared to the great principles" he opposed. Why, Byers asked later, would Teller support a pro-state tax argument in 1864 and stand against it in 1867?[12]

Another statehood effort was launched in 1868. The statehood faction had at least one stronger argument—the revolving door of political appointments. In 1867 Alexander Hunt had replaced the controversial and quarrelsome Cummings after only seventeen months in office. The territory would suffer through five governors in ten years. A cynical Mark Twain, who had experience with them in Nevada, claimed, "Territorial governors are nothing but politicians who go out to the outskirts of countries and suffer the privations there in order to build up stakes and come back as United States senators."

The Denver crowd again attempted to gain statehood under the 1865 constitution with Evans and Chaffee angling for the senatorships. In an opening salvo, in December 1867 Henry and Willard got into a newspaper spat between Central and Black Hawk over statehood. The *Central City Register* continued its pro-state position; the Tellers stood in opposition. That aroused Byers and his *News,* which blasted Teller and his anti-state views right from the start of the New Year while questioning his loyalty to the Republican Party. In a January 2, 1868, article and editorial, he attacked the brothers: "The reckless and miscolored statements of the Tellers have been met by Mr. [Frank] Hollister [*Register* editor] with truth and candor, and his caustic criticisms on the disappointed aspirant for senatorial honors are" timely and well put.

Byers accused Henry and Willard of three cardinal sins—standing alone while the rest of the Republican Party favored statehood, supporting Cheyenne against Denver, and belittling Colorado. He let his anger fly unchecked. He asserted the

Tellers "by the most unscrupulous statements" turn "popular sentiment against the admission of the state, they then boast of it as a work of merit. . . . If we do not mistake, they will learn in the long run that popular leaders must be possessed of some disinterested public spirit." Among other things, the *News* charged Henry with having distorted the facts, having a groundless imagination, being inconsistent, and making "base attempts to deceive our people."

Teller went to Washington to present the anti-state case, but he arrived too late. He therefore wrote a "Memorial Remonstrating Against the Admission of Colorado as a State" to counter the Chaffee and Evans "Memorial." Although written for Congress, it aroused passions at home. Vicious personal attacks forced him to answer with a second pamphlet. The pro-state faction was beside itself with anger and loathing. Teller, meanwhile, used his time to lobby New York senator Roscoe Conkling and other prominent Republicans.

Henry's basic arguments were familiar. First and foremost, Colorado did not have enough people to become a state. Second, Coloradans were more opposed to statehood than they had been in 1864 when they defeated it. Third, the people should have the right to express their current wishes. Finally, with the "industrial pursuit of the country steadily decreasing, what inducement have the people of Colorado to assume the burdens of state government?"

Evans and Chaffee submitted statements maintaining, among other things, that Colorado's population had exceeded 75,000 and that the majority of residents were "eager" for state status. Teller denied it, saying a population of around 30,000 was more probable. He was right, as the next census showed.

In his second pamphlet he responded to the "disgraceful" personal attacks launched through newspaper editorials. He had not advocated the present movement for state government, nor had he been a candidate for senator under "this constitution." Henry demonstrated he could fire shot for shot: "If I have made statements not true let Messrs. Evans and Chaffee prove them false and not shirk the responsibility by persistent misrepresentation of the facts." He hit on a further fear: "I have repeatedly declared that if Colorado becomes a state at this time it will be a Democratic one." Can, he asked, "the Republican Party afford to disregard the wish of the people?"[13]

The *News* replied on March 13, with editor Byers claiming no "interest in the admission" except to promote the general prosperity "of our adopted home." The four-column article went on to "refute" and "correct" nineteen points on which Teller had erred. Byers fell back on the charges of "unfairness, erroneous statements, and misrepresentation," all "calculated to do injury to the future of Colorado." Teller's course, he said, conflicted with the wishes of the party and the people of Colorado, who are "generally anxious for statehood."

The next day Byers topped that effort, discussing Henry's "crime against Colorado"—opposing statehood—for which "Colorado will hold him to an account of it." Byers lambasted Teller. He "has reviled Colorado, let Colorado revile him. Let the curse of every citizen be upon him. Let him be a dead man among us, so vile, so corrupt, so offensive, that the very mention of his name will excite loathing." The newspaper war carried on for weeks with much acrimonious debate and little changing of minds. "Nobly," Chaffee and Evans offered to "resign" their never sanctioned offices. It did their cause no good.

The battle would not be won or lost in Colorado; Washington would decide. Colorado statehood was not the issue that spring. The dominant Republicans busied themselves with the impeachment trial of President Andrew Johnson, which they lost by one vote in May. Johnson had been right in questioning all along Chaffee's and Evans's loyalty to his administration. There seems little reason to doubt they would have voted for impeachment had they been seated. The population question, the legality of the 1865 vote, the threatened Democratic territorial majority, and the anti-state faction's forceful arguments about a revote swayed the day.[14]

Teller challenged the Evans and Chaffee group to submit the statehood issue to the voters. They declined. Henry had been right: Coloradans had lost interest in becoming a state.

Henry spent the rest of the year trying to strengthen the Republican Party in Gilpin County, the county with the largest number of Democratic voters. Byers applauded his move toward county "harmony and good feelings" but, nonetheless, kept hammering away. Teller did not let up either, accusing Denver politicians of constituting a "secret cabal" to try to "supervise political conduct of Republicans" throughout the territory: "The disorganized condition and want of harmony in the Republican Party of Colorado today is wholly due to the unauthorized action of such irresponsible secret caucuses."

Byers fired back on November 24, 1868: "Upon what principle, we should like to ask, do they [Teller and his supporters], as politicians, assume the right to 'rule or ruin' the party and the county, when they can't carry one vote in four in their own county."

Henry also defended, albeit weakly, embattled governor Hunt against accusations coming out of Denver that he had "betray[ed] the party" during the 1867 congressional delegate campaign. Rather backhandedly, Teller commented, "I do not approve of the appointment of Governor Hunt as the best that could be made, but as the best that is likely to be made." Even that weak endorsement brought charges that he had "prostituted" himself and was a "political renegade." Despite all of this, Teller spoke at various rallies that fall to help Republicans.

The *News* gleefully pointed out that "before their day" the Republican Party had carried Gilpin County by "tremendous majorities." Since Teller and his "lackeys" had gained control, the county had "always gone" Democratic. That, concluded Byers, "is proof either that they have little strength or have not exerted it on behalf of Republican principles." Byers further failed to appreciate the fact that the Teller men ignored the central committee now "that it is not under their control."[15]

Teller would succeed in bringing Gilpin County back into the Republican column and would also strengthen his base there. After his initial fight on the statehood question, he learned that it did not help one's cause to be out of step with the opinions of constituents. From then on he listened more thoughtfully, discussed issues with them more thoroughly, pursued his own political education more diligently, and tried to represent their views more carefully. Although his first years in Colorado politics had not been particularly successful, Teller had gained invaluable experience in local and territorial politics, emerged as a known, forceful speaker, and understood how to withstand being pilloried by the opposition press and hold his ground.

In 1870 Teller's friend Irving Stanton went to see him in his Central City law office after the Republican convention had just nominated Chaffee as territorial delegate. Stanton hoped to bring the party together in "peace and harmony," a hope Teller dashed even after Stanton made "every reasonable argument for that goal." The latter admitted that "I soon discovered I had undertaken a difficult matter." Teller agreed "to make three Republican speeches in the campaign, but I will not mention Chaffee's name."

Byers, too, had tried to smooth divisive feelings by suggesting Teller, among others, as a potential delegate candidate with energy, an unquestionable political record, and the moral character to command respect. When Teller spoke in Central in September 1870, the *News* fairly gushed with favorable comments. Although "suffering severely from a cold," Teller held the "immense" gathering "spell-bound by the power of his eloquence for nearly two hours."

Henry had an exciting experience the next March. The second floor of the building where the Central City Republicans were meeting gave way. The building caught fire, but amid the "wildest excitement everyone made a miraculous escape."[16]

The old struggle boiled over again in 1872. Part of the problem involved the carpetbaggism that had plagued Colorado. After his inauguration in 1869, President Ulysses Grant had replaced Hunt with his friend and fellow Civil War officer Edward McCook. A fifty-niner who had briefly practiced in Central City, McCook traveled back to the territory. Unfortunately, he managed to alienate many people over the next few years while diligently playing the now customary game of spoils. Agitation and disgust soon grew within the ranks of restless Colorado Republicans.

On the national scene, the scandals of the Grant administration and his vindictive policy toward the South caused a splinter liberal Republican vote to support the 1872 Democratic presidential nominee, longtime Colorado favorite Horace Greeley, who until recently had been a Republican. In Colorado, similarly, the Tellers and others bolted to support former governor Hunt against Chaffee for delegate. Chaffee won, and the Teller faction found itself banished again. Grant also won; the Tellers had lost again.

The Denver faction, wanting to remove McCook, uncovered some local scandals Chaffee soon reported in Washington. Petitions circulated in Colorado's capital city and elsewhere demanding the governor's removal and promoting Evans's son-in-law, Samuel Elbert, for the position. Elbert had been territorial secretary and occasionally acted as governor in the 1860s.

Teller defended McCook and once more found himself vilified in the press while Elbert received praise and endorsements. Grant removed McCook, who promptly raced back to Washington with corruption charges of his own. Elbert became governor, then the pot boiled over when Grant renominated McCook. The problem from Teller's viewpoint, as a friend observed, meant "concentrating too much on one faction."

Chaffee led the fight to prevent McCook's confirmation and, failing to do so, turned his efforts to arousing Coloradans. As Byers harped, "To reappoint McCook adds insult to injury." Nonetheless, in 1874 back came McCook amid charges that competent local men were being passed over for "crippled and superannuated henchmen" of eastern politicians. Teller defended Grant and McCook and blamed all the trouble on Chaffee.

Another election for the territorial delegate was held in 1874. The infuriated Chaffee/Elbert/Evans faction attacked Grant, McCook's reappointment, and Teller, whom they now accused of wanting to move the capital from Denver.

The *News* tore into the "enemy of Denver" again on January 30, 1874, accusing Henry of, among other "sins," trying to cut Denver off from railway communication and "laboring hard to prevent the location of the capital at Denver." Having dredged up the past, Byers now accused Teller of working with "might and main" to have the capital taken away.

Byers's attack came after Teller had spoken at a meeting about the governor's situation. Realizing the great diversity of sentiment among the audience, he nevertheless plainly yet forcefully defended his views. Elbert's administration had not been officially approved in Washington, and Colorado voters did not approve of the way he was handling his job because "since he has been in office, he has governed the territory for the benefit of the few." Teller reasoned that when the removal came, Governor Elbert must not object to it, "for all officials are subject to removal when their stewardship has been found wanting. The governor has been recreant to his oath." Henry would "not bow down to the ring headed by the Evanses."

The deplorable state of Colorado politics in 1874 was shown that evening. Others tried to speak, only to be so loudly interrupted and harassed that the chairman had to adjourn the meeting. Byers blamed McCook's "reprehensible hoodlums."

By the time the Republicans met for their convention in Denver in August, the Chaffee/Elbert faction had lost favor in Washington and sat on the sidelines. Teller addressed the meeting after being asked to do so. He had intended not to participate as a "matter of policy" and explained why:

> Gentlemen of the convention I know that to some gentlemen, members of our party, I am very repugnant, but I was not willing [that] any personal quarrels, any personal antagonism, any disagreements should be carried into the convention. I understand very well that if I ever exercised the ordinary activity that I have been in the habit for twenty years of exhibiting in convention, my motives would be misconstrued and misunderstood. (*Rocky Mountain News*, August 7, 1874)

He understood how deep the antagonism went, but he stayed loyal to the party. Teller went out on the campaign trail with his usual vigor. His themes included the old and the new. In a 135-minute oration in Denver, Henry discussed tariffs, banking, and the records of the two parties; attacked the Democrats; and called the Republicans the party of the "poor man and laborer."

To the Republicans' dismay, following a bitter campaign the Democrats elected Thomas Patterson territorial delegate. The Republicans should have seen it coming; the Colorado party had fallen into disarray, highlighted by personal vindictiveness.[17]

Without question, egos, ambitions, and feelings caused the debacle. Chaffee had held the advantage until the McCook dispute because his daughter had married Grant's son. Teller had stayed out of Washington issues for that reason until he used McCook to attack Chaffee and his Denver backers. Not since 1868 had Chaffee's power and prestige slipped so low.

BOSS CHAFFEE AGAIN ROSE TO THE OCCASION. He portrayed himself as defending Colorado against carpetbaggers, upholding right against McCook's dealings, and being an underdog in the fight for the governorship. He lost the 1874 battle, but he won the war eventually. Coloradans, meanwhile, were appalled that McCook had returned. The governor seemingly had not learned his lesson and fell into a familiar pattern, something Chaffee skillfully used to his own advantage. Henry was unable to stop his rival, who seized the political reigns again.

Chaffee promptly championed statehood again as the only way Coloradans would be able to choose their own leaders. Skillfully, he played on fears of Colorado and Washington Republicans. The price they had paid for their actions, he claimed, was a Democratic victory in what had been a solid Republican territory. McCook's unpopularity and renewed accusations of his corruption helped Chaffee's campaign. The territorial press played McCook as a persistent theme. Grant would have to find another man before disaster overtook the party and its position in the territory. Changes would have to be made among Colorado Republicans as well.

For all this to occur, the two warring factions desperately needed to put aside their animosities and work together for a common cause. When this happened is not known, but the why is obvious. Irving Stanton felt Chaffee and Teller had always been on "friendly terms," personally, but others doubted that. Georgetown politician William Hamill credited Chaffee with taking the initiative in healing the breach. Frank Hall, Central City editor and historian, talked of a meeting in 1877 in which Chaffee commented, "Teller and I have settled most of our differences." The two men now worked toward a common goal: statehood.[18]

The idea that politics make strange bedfellows goes back to Shakespeare's day, although he called it misery. Both terms are applicable. Colorado had never seen such a political shotgun marriage as this. Amazingly, it worked.

Chaffee and Teller might have reconciled, but their followers took longer to unite. Stanton remembered that one heard little but "the pros and cons" of the feud and that feelings were "particularly intense in the Kingdom of Gilpin." A Chaffee supporter, he mentioned little about the feud when he talked with Teller on many occasions in the early 1870s.

Washington got the message. Grant removed McCook, and another Civil War friend of the president, John Routt, was sent west. Three governors in three years, plus a general overturn of other territorial appointees, created a "great sensation for a small western territory, which attributed the president's action to the results of a game of poker between himself and Delegate Chaffee." Whatever the reason, it worked well; Routt proved a good appointment, and Coloradans rallied behind statehood.

Routt had the personality needed to calm matters and to be the conciliatory governor Colorado craved. Out of necessity, matters calmed down. With Chaffee in the lead, the statehood movement again gained momentum. Republicans nationally looked with favor on the somewhat wayward territory. With a presidential election looming around the corner in 1876 and scandals racing through the Grant administration in Washington, they might need Colorado's three electoral votes. On the last day of the congressional session, March 3, 1875, Congress again approved an enabling act.

The procedure was familiar to Coloradans—the call for a constitutional convention, the election of delegates, writing the constitution, submitting it to the people to vote on, and sending it to Washington for final approval. Reunited Republicans again assumed control, electing twenty-four of the thirty-nine delegates. After eighty-four days of steady work, with sometimes acrimonious debate, the delegates (a large percentage of whom were lawyers) produced a constitution. On July 1, 1876, Coloradans overwhelmingly approved it by well over a three to one majority.

Coloradans did not have to wait long to be welcomed into the Union. Republican votes were needed. On August 1, 1876, Colorado became the thirty-eighth state, the Centennial State in honor of the nation's centennial. The long fight was over.

Teller's role in all this remained secondary to that of Chaffee, who earned well-deserved praise for his efforts and emerged the leading candidate for one of the cherished Senate seats. During the critical fall campaign, Teller rode the mountain circuit as well as traveling to Pueblo, Boulder, and Denver. He gave speeches "unobjectionable in tone and temper, and more soundly argumentative than any merely partisan effort," and took part in the popular torchlight parades. His outline had grown orthodox: praise the Republicans, bash the Democrats; praise the common man; "wealth is made by labor," however, "your preacher and your lawyer, and all men who only work with their mouth, don't create any wealth. They are only a circulating medium."

At stake that year were all state offices and control of the legislature, which would select the senators. Willard joined the campaign and proved a pleasant surprise to Byers for his calm, quiet manner and the depth and force of his arguments. The *News* simply said, "VICTORY."

A friend from Fairplay wrote Henry, "Well, we have scooped the enemy. The Republicans of this county are giving the Teller Bros. a good deal of credit."[19]

Colorado was back in the Republican column; the next question became who would be chosen senator, or rather, who besides Jerome Chaffee would be elected. The field looked familiar and crowded; besides Teller, John Evans, George Chilcott, Samuel Elbert, and a host of lesser-known individuals vied for the honor. It appeared, as Golden's *Colorado Transcript* observed on October 4, a "family affair." Nevertheless, Denver would not get the second seat; either southern Colorado or the mountain towns would.

Teller stood out as the favorite for the mountains, whereas southern Colorado had several favored candidates. Henry's major drawback was the fact that some elected legislative members had never forgiven him for his anti-statehood activities in the 1860s or his Republican mavericism. In addition, some resented the fact that Teller had not taken a more active role in the final 1876 canvass.

On November 14 the majority Republicans selected Chaffee and Teller to be Colorado's first senators. The failure of the southern delegates to unify behind one man and the loyalty of the mountain delegates toward Teller produced his victory on the tenth ballot. It had not been easy, but Teller's totals had slowly mounted as the ballots dragged on and votes were counted. The *Denver Daily Tribune* observed on November 15, 1876, "This result seems to give quite universal satisfaction, and even the southern members accept their defeat with the best of grace, and consider that no better man could have been selected than Mr. Teller—were he from their section of the country."

In the same edition the *Tribune* praised the new senator's "eminent qualifications, both intellectual and moral, for the position to which he has been chosen. His ability is universally recognized." The newspaper concluded that with Teller, Chaffee, and Representative James Belford, the new state would be "well represented" in the Forty-fifth Congress. The editor sang Teller's praises: "In the United States Senate he will honor his State even more than she can honor him. He will take even rank with the first-class members of that body."

The *Tribune* had been right about two of the three men. Belford eventually lost the seat to Democrat Patterson. That was the only seat the Republicans lost in the election, and new governor John Routt presided over a GOP legislature. The singular danger for the Republicans in the years ahead remained the old bugaboo of a party split over the loaves and fishes or personal ambition.[20]

The lone matter that remained was who would get the short term and who the long one to produce staggered senatorial terms. The short term would be for only three months, although the incumbent would be reelected by the same legislators who had sent him to Washington in the first place. His next term would last the regulation six years. The long term in 1876 entailed two years in Washington. Then the senator would stand for reelection, facing a new legislature. Both men obviously wanted the former. Chaffee forecast, "Teller will get it. His luck will carry him through." Lots were drawn, and Jerome proved a good prophet: Henry got the short term. The Colorado legislative Republicans promptly elected him to a full six-year term starting in March 1877.

Despite Chaffee's disappointment, their friendship grew as they served in Washington in the years ahead. Teller leaned on his more experienced colleague whose background as territorial delegate made him more skilled in congressional matters and more knowledgeable about the Washington scene. Jerome further possessed an aggressive political personality, something Henry lacked. Their talents balanced each other well. If the national Democratic Party had hoped Colorado would support it in 1876, it had badly misjudged history. Colorado returned to the Republican column and remained there for nearly two decades.

For Henry Teller it had been a long, tortuous fifteen years in Colorado politics before reaching the goal he had yearned to achieve. He had succeeded in his "early love" of politics, as one of his admirers wrote him. Despite splits with local Republicans, Henry had held true to his definition of Republican principles. He had not been as showy or aggressive as some of his contemporaries, but he received plaudits for his honest, studious approach to issues, his carefully constructed speeches, and his untiring advocacy of Colorado. His patriotism and his belief in the common people could not be questioned. Henry had made mistakes and misjudgments along the way, but he had learned and profited from them. Suffering through slander and vilification, he emerged not unruffled but unbowed. Having matured over the years, Teller showed that the *Tribune's* enthusiasm was not misplaced.[21]

NOTES

1. Frank Young, *Echoes from Acadia* (Denver: Lanning Bros., 1903), 205–207; Elliott West, "Jerome B. Chaffee and the McCook-Elbert Fight," *Colorado Magazine* (spring 1969), 148; Henry Teller to William Van Nostrand, September 3, 1896, Colorado Historical Society; James Wright, *The Politics of Populism: Dissent in Colorado* (New Haven: Yale University Press, 1974), 51–52.

2. *Rocky Mountain News*, April 24, 1861; *The Trail* (September 1910), 13; Teller and Cameron letters in *War of the Rebellion* (Washington, D.C.: Government Printing Office, 1899), 3rd ser., vol. 1, 232, 246; G. W. DeGroodt to Johnson and Teller, May 9, 1862, Teller Collection, University of Colorado.

3. David Moffat to Friend Stanton, August 7, 1862, George Kassler Letters, Colorado Historical Society; *Tri-Weekly Miners' Register* (Central City), August 11, 13, 1862; Moses Hallett to Johnson, August 29, 1862, Teller Collection, University of Colorado; *Rocky Mountain News* (weekly), August–October 1862; Frank Hall, *History of the State of Colorado* (Chicago: Blakely, 1891), vol. 1, 289–292.

4. *Tri-Weekly Miners' Register,* September 1, 5, October 8, 10, 1862; *Rocky Mountain News* (weekly), October–November 1862; Young, *Echoes,* 29, 31–32.

5. *Tri-Weekly Miners' Register,* September 1862–August 1863; *Daily Miners' Register,* August 3, 29, September 2, 1863; *Rocky Mountain News,* February 2, 1867; *Grand Junction Sentinel,* February 23, 1914.

6. *Tri-Weekly Miners' Register,* June 27, 1863; *Daily Miners' Register,* March 9, 12, May 26, 27, July 8, 9, 29, August 2, 3, 4, 1864; *Rocky Mountain News* (weekly), March 13, July 6, 13, 20, 1864; *Mining Journal,* April 6, 8, 1864.

7. *Mining Journal,* August–September 1864; *Rocky Mountain News,* August–September 1864; *Daily Miners' Register,* August–September 1864; Elmer Ellis, "Colorado's First Fight for Statehood, 1865–68," *Colorado Magazine* (January 1930), 23–25.

8. *Daily Miners' Register,* June 16, 17, August 12, 17, 18, 26, September 1, 9 (citing Hill), 15, December 8, 1864; *Rocky Mountain News,* August 20, 1864; James Willard, "The Tyler Rangers: The Black Hawk Company and the Indian Uprising of 1864," *Colorado Magazine* (July 1930), 147–148. See also Duane A. Smith, *The Birth of Colorado* (Norman: University of Oklahoma Press, 1989), chapters 11–12.

9. George Kassler to Maria Kassler, January 1, February 2, 1865, George Kassler Letters, Colorado Historical Society; Teller speech, March 31, 1882, in the *Congressional Record,* December 31, 1882, 2456.

10. Kassler to Maria, January 1, February 2, March 7, 1865, George Kassler Letters, Colorado Historical Society; *Denver Post,* December 13, 1903; Alice Hill, *Tales of the Colorado Pioneers* (Denver: Pierson and Gardner, 1884), 106–110; *Daily Miners' Register,* April 16, 1865; Louis Simonin, *The Rocky Mountain West* (Lincoln: University of Nebraska Press, 1966), 56.

11. Ellis, "Colorado's First Fight," 26–27; *Daily Miners' Register,* July 30, 1867; *Rocky Mountain News,* September 26, November 3, 1865; Harry E. Kelsey Jr., *Frontier Capitalist: The Life of John Evans* (Boulder: Pruett, 1969), 164–167; Evans and Chaffee to Edward Cooper, May 12, 1866, microfilm, Territorial Papers of Colorado, National Archives.

12. *Rocky Mountain News,* July 25, 26, 1867, January 2, 1868; *Daily Miners' Register,* July 21, 23, November–December 1867; Kelsey, *Frontier Capitalist,* 165–168; Ellis, "Colorado's First Fight," 26–29; Thomas Dawson, "Teller and Wolcott," Colorado Historical Society, 2.

13. Mark Twain, *Wit and Wisecracks* (White Plains, N.Y.: Peter Pauper Press, 1961), 39; Henry Teller, "Memorial Remonstrating Against the Admission of Colorado as a State" (n.c., n.p., February 1868), 1–10; Henry Teller, "Statehood Question" (n.c., n.p., February 1868), 1–9.

14. *Rocky Mountain News,* March 13, 14, 1868; Harry Kelsey, *Evans* (Boulder: Pruett, 1969), 168; Ellis, "Colorado's First Fight," 28–30.

15. *Rocky Mountain News,* July 2, 8, 9, 18, 26, August 24, 29, November 24, 27, 1868; *Central City Register,* September 4, 1868; *Daily Miners' Register,* July–August 1868.

16. Irving W. Stanton, *Sixty Years in Colorado* (Denver: State Historical Society, 1922), 150–151; *Rocky Mountain News,* June 6, September 13, 1870, March 19, 1871.

17. *Colorado Transcript,* May 28, 1872; *Rocky Mountain News,* May 28, 1872, January 28, February 3, 1873, January 28, 30, August 6, 7, September 2, 8, 1874; West, "Chaffee," 147–148; Wm. Jackson to Teller, December 13, 1872, Teller Collection, University of Colorado; Robert E. Smith, "The Antiimperialist Crusade of Thomas M. Patterson," *Colorado Magazine* (winter 1974), 55; Stanton, *Sixty Years,* 153–154; *The Trail* (March 1914), 27; Wright, *Politics,* 53.

18. C. C. Davis to Teller, January 29, 1874, Teller Papers, University of Colorado; Dawson, "Teller and Wolcott," 3; West, "Chaffee," 145–146, 148, 159–160, 162–165; Stanton, *Sixty Years,* 140–141, 143–144, 153–154; Hamill cited in R. G. Dill, *The Political Campaigns of Colorado* (Denver: Arapaho, 1895), 22; Hall cited in *Denver Post,* November 3, 1902; John Simon to author, June 24, 1998.

19. Stanton, *Sixty Years,* 146; George Lechner to Teller, October 10, 1876, Teller Collection, University of Colorado; Young, *Echoes,* 176; *Colorado Transcript,* May 24, July 5, October 4, 1876; *Rocky Mountain News* (weekly), September 27, October 4, 1876; *Colorado Miner* (Georgetown), September 30, October 7, 1876.

20. Dill, *Political Campaigns,* 20–22; *Denver Daily Tribune,* November 15, 1876; Dawson, "Teller and Wolcott," 3; *Denver Post,* November 3, 1902; E. S. Randall to William Jackson, September 4, 1876, J. S. Wolfe to W. S. Jackson, September 8, 1876, Teller to William Jackson, October 24, 1876, all in William Jackson Papers, Special Collections, Colorado College; Hall, *Colorado,* vol. 2, 358–359.

21. Thomas Dawson, "Scrapbooks," Colorado Historical Society, vols. 61, 80; Dill, *Political Campaigns,* 23; Dawson, "Teller and Wolcott," 3, 9; Robert E. Smith, "Thomas M. Patterson, Colorado Statehood, and the Presidential Election of 1876," *Colorado Magazine* (spring 1976), 162; *History of Clear Creek and Boulder Valleys, Colorado* (Chicago: O. L. Baskin, 1880), 487–488; Eb. Warner to Teller, August 14, 1876, Teller Papers, Denver Public Library.

The Young Senator

On February 1, 1877, Jerome Chaffee presented to the Senate the credentials of Henry M. Teller for his term beginning March 4. This
was Henry's initial six-year term. It would not be as exciting as the
short term just ending, with the electrifying contested Tilden/Hayes election. That contest would not be resolved for almost another month.

Neither Samuel Tilden nor Rutherford Hayes had gained a majority in the electoral college; twenty votes were being contested. Eventually, a committee composed of senators, representatives, and Supreme
Court justices gave all of the votes to Hayes, who thereupon won by
one vote (185 to 184). The significance of Colorado's popular and electoral college vote was obvious; without it, Democrat Tilden would have
won outright. The Democratic press later charged that the wealth of the
leading Colorado Republicans, mostly mining men, overwhelmed the state
Democrats. Chaffee and Teller headed the list of the prominent men who
"played such an important part in the matter of the presidential succes-
sion." At no time since has Colorado played as significant a role in a presidential election.

The junior senator from Colorado was appointed to the committees
on pensions, claims, elections, and—especially important for his state—the
military and railroads. He was also appointed later to a "select committee"
on the violation of rights of U.S. citizens in the 1878 congressional
elections.

The select committee brought Teller briefly into national prominence when he was elected chairman. The committee, which constituted a political effort by the Republicans to find ammunition to use against the Democrats in 1880, traveled to the southern states. Teller and other members visited New Orleans, took testimony, and held further hearings in Washington. They found fraud and violence had been used to intimidate voters, white and black, who opposed the Democratic Party in Louisiana and South Carolina. Despite the partisan nature of the committee, Teller conducted fair hearings. Minority Democrats nonetheless refused to sign the report that recommended national legislation to prevent such happenings in the future.[1]

As a junior member of the Senate, Teller rarely took an active role in deliberations. He did speak on such issues as Indian and military appropriations, and he supported the Chinese exclusion bill and the incorporation of various railroads—topics that interested Coloradans. Farther afield, he supported establishing a "permanent form of government" for the District of Columbia and employing temporary clerks to help government agencies. In the 1880 congressional session, Teller became much more active, no doubt because of the Ute removal fight.

Between 1877 and 1880 Henry did introduce various bills, resolutions, and petitions and enter into debates. He presented resolutions for "prohibiting the several states from disfranchising United States citizens on account of their sex" and for instituting an appropriation for the state agricultural college to build buildings and "purchase suitable machinery for a small sugar refinery." Two joint resolutions from the Colorado legislature were introduced in February 1879: the first proposed to construct a military wagon road in the southwestern part of the state, and the second involved the sale of land for public schools. Several petitions prayed for the "enforcement of the anti-polygamy law of 1862." He also presented a resolution from the First Congregational Church of Falmouth, Massachusetts, involving the "liquor traffic."

The "Boys in Blue" and their widows needed more assistance, and Teller, like other senators, spent a great deal of time on pensions. Coloradans' resolutions and petitions took most of his time, however. Ownership and use of the Pagosa hot springs came into dispute, apparently revolving around Ute claims. A bill to resolve the matter was "postponed indefinitely." The only suggestion made by the committee to which it had been referred was "to adopt some system of disarming the Indians"! Other issues involved selling timber on public lands, providing terms and circuits for district courts, and regulating passenger fares and freight traffic on the Denver Pacific and Kansas Pacific railways.

Claims individuals held against the government also surfaced. The old stagecoach king Ben Holladay, for instance, was still trying to collect money for "certain mail service alleged to have been performed by him." Horace Tabor asked for reimbursement for personal expenses (hiring extra clerks) in running the overwhelmed Leadville post office in 1877–1878. Despite a nearly six-month effort to resolve Tabor's request in 1880, Teller got nowhere. The bill became bogged down in committee, never to reappear. Henry finally exploded on the Senate floor: "There seems an unusual anxiety on the part of one or two members of the Committee on Post Office and Post Roads that this case should not get out of their hands."[2]

As representative of the only state in the Rocky Mountain region, Teller served as spokesman for the interests and concerns of neighboring territories in addition to those of Colorado. He looked into issues involving Wyoming territorial judges. In a debate over appointments, Henry challenged some eastern colleagues on the topic of easterners trying to save the West from itself: "So when anybody says to me now that these people have a remedy, I say theoretically they have, but practically they do not have it. I have seen in Colorado and other territories justice dealt out by the dollar." A particularly incompetent judge and the Senate's treatment of Wyoming caught his ire: "But in fact he [the judge] is incompetent to conduct the business of that new country. The Legislature, knowing it, appealed here. We treated them with the utmost disrespect and discourtesy when we refused to hear their protest."

He tried continually to educate his colleagues about the West. After Congress niggardly refused to print more copies of a study on Rocky Mountain Locust then voted abundant funds for "eastern rivers and harbors," Teller took the floor. Westerners, he pointed out, "voted liberally for eastern rivers and harbors" from which "we get very little direct benefit." His next observation drew laughter: "Whenever there is an appropriation that directly benefits our people, we get it very economically." Senators, he observed, do not realize the "vast magnitude of the West." East was a relative term; for a person from the Rockies, going east meant to Nebraska: "If they criticize my calling it 'East,' they ought to remember that a man may be twenty-four hours on a railroad before he gets to what they call the extreme West."

His experience in mining paid dividends for his constituents. Teller shepherded a bill through Congress that aided miners, and the president signed it in 1880. Required work done on unpatented mining claims would date from January 1 each year, which made things easier for everyone involved from government officials to the claim owner. No more random dates were scattered throughout calendars depending on the filing date.[3]

Members of Congress always hear from their constituents about a wide variety of concerns and issues, not to mention being presented with plenty of free advice. Henry Teller did not escape such counsel. The best remaining examples of constituents' concerns and "wisdom" conveyed to Teller come from his first years in Washington.

Some complained about the federal government or about Teller personally. A hard-up Charles Welch told Henry he was sorry "to hear that you have not plenty of cash to spare for us poor fellows out here." Washington, he sarcastically supposed, "had all the ready cash it wanted at all times." Another writer spoke out on a familiar subject—federal appointments in the territories: "You also know how the people of [the] Territories have suffered from the federal practice of sending incompetent ambitious fools to fill our offices. Pray use your influence to stop such practice." Colorado secretary of state William Clark wrote that he had met some men from the southwest corner of the state who "were a little sore that you, Chaffee, and Belford did not visit them last summer."

Others wanted help. For example, the U.S. marshal for Colorado wanted a pay raise, and a father wanted to send his son "either to West Point or Annapolis." The president of the Denver Board of Trade desired assistance in promoting the "commercial and agricultural interests of our city and state" by securing a federal purchasing agency. Teller heard from the postmaster of that "marvelous camp and . . . very stirring town" of Leadville, Horace Tabor, who wished to be consulted if a new site for the post office or a new postmaster were about to be selected. Another man worried over the importation of foreign assay supplies that threatened to wipe out U.S. manufacturers. The low pay for the "pauper labor of Europe" was the "chief cause" of his concern because "we have to pay such a high price" for labor. Some form of an agreement on duties was needed.

Old Central City friend Bella Buell, now of Massachusetts and in need of money to "pay my debts," wanted help. He would like some federal office in Colorado to "get out of the woods" and work on selling his mining property. A writer wanted fellow Mason Teller to lend him $100. Mrs. S. V. Bryant presented a sadder story. She had been dismissed from an unspecified government position: "I have made every apology for my indiscretion [making statements about a superior?] that I could and have committed no crime." Her family languished in want, and she desired "a letter or recommendation for reinstatement. Do not run a deaf ear to my plea." To err was human, she reminded Teller, to forgive divine. After two months she had "sunk into debt" and asked Teller if she might teach his children "or I would gladly go into your kitchen to work for my board." Unfortunately, Teller's response was not preserved.

In April 1878 James Belford, who had just left Congress, wanted Chaffee and Teller to look after some unspecified claims of his against the government: "When the appropriation bill reaches the Senate, I want you and Chaffee to make my claims as large as possible as I am quite poor and need the money." One-time Colorado newspaper man S. S. Wallihan, now living in Burlington, Vermont, wondered if "you and Chaffee could chuck me into a committee clerkship. I don't want an office." Governor John Routt recommended a man for the Fairplay land office, and Teller's cousin Isaac asked about a position as surveyor of public lands. A man from the San Juans wanted Teller to intercede on some land cases because if something was not done "the New York parties will abandon the project."[4]

Constituents gave the new senator plenty of unsolicited advice and recommendations. In January 1878 well-known mining man Richard Irwin from Rosita offered advice on a variety of topics including giving women the right to vote, something he preferred to see tried in Colorado and some older states before attempting to implement it nationally. Coloradans had just rejected suffrage in 1877; Irwin wondered, "Can the question be submitted to the people again?" Teller had helped in that campaign, but to no avail. Coloradans had not agreed that "suffrage is all right because it is right and truth is mighty and must prevail."

A Gold Hill miner wrote with a specific concern about the federal mining law requiring yearly improvements on mining properties until they were patented. He advised Teller that the requirement hurt mining and was not a "good policy." If the vein proved valuable from the "grassroots," the policy was not bad; however, the fact "is but a small percentage" pay with several hundred feet of development, and "they are of *no permanent value, however expensive,*" unless the mine eventually pays well enough "*to reimburse them all.*" The writer also did not appreciate the expense of "procuring mineral patents." He wanted Teller to look into reducing costs and modifying the law. To John Hitching, "The burden of civilization is very onerous upon miners compared with the farmer as regards his investments and titles."

In response to the nomination of a particular person as chief justice of Dakota Territory, Teller received this bit of advice: "From the good lord deliver us—you know him to be unfit for the place." His former partner Hiram Johnson telegraphed Henry from Salt Late City in support of retaining an "upright judge." From Pueblo came the exhortation not to appoint two nominees as railroad route agents because "they are not fit for it and drink too much whiskey." Another correspondent offered some advice on that "undoubtedly knotty question" of a direct vote for president.

Some constituents thanked him for his efforts, but they were few in number. William Bush of the Teller House thanked him for voting against confirmation of "the custom house appointee. You are a bully fellow." The territorial governor of Wyoming praised him for his support in a Senate debate: "The people of Wyoming fully appreciate your able and manly vindication of them." Routt also wrote him occasionally to thank him for helping the state.[5]

The former teacher took special interest in education-related requests. University of Colorado president Joseph Sewall mentioned some of that school's needs in a November 1877 letter. The state had appropriated "barely enough to pay instructors," so there was little money for equipment. Sewall was attempting to raise $2,500 to "put into a laboratory" because in "the all important department of chemistry and metallurgy" the university "had nothing to offer the student but the bald textbook." The president could "not advise a student to remain here to pursue these branches when he could do so much better elsewhere." Teller obviously did something because Sewall thanked him for his help and also for sending government publications. Henry continued to send maps and government books throughout his first term.

Meanwhile, he got caught up in a donor squeeze. He received a letter from the University Literary Society, which had founded a library "named the Teller Library, but neglected to inform you of the fact." But prominent Boulder merchant Charles Buckingham one of the prime movers in establishing the university, offered $1,000 in cash and $200 a year for five years if the "society would change the name to Buckingham Library." The president of the society, E. S. Howard, informed Teller that Sewall and several others had arrived at a meeting to promote the suggestion; the way they did it, he confessed, "would have done credit to a politician, but they did carry their point." The name was changed.

Howard promised to fight on if Teller wished. Teller had strong support in the society, he affirmed: "I think we can beat the Board of Regents, President, Professors and all. We will do our best for you if it is your wish to have the Library named after you." Teller did not so wish.

A Denver mining engineer wished to organize an "Academy of Sciences" in Colorado for the "advancement of scientific knowledge." Among the men interested or invited to join, he claimed, was a roster of the state's movers and shakers—Chaffee, Hill, Gilpin, Evans, Teller, smelter man Richard Pearce, and others. The well-received idea emerged as the Colorado Scientific Society in 1882.[6]

One topic that consistently aroused Teller's constituents became known as the "silver issue." For reasons discussed later, the government had stopped coining silver dollars in 1873, placing the United States for all practical purposes on the gold standard. That did not trouble miners because the price the government paid for silver had been less than the world price. The price of silver declined steadily during the 1870s, however, while Colorado's production marched upward, even before Leadville burst on the scene in 1878–1879.

Coloradans worried about what the future might bring. Georgetown's *Colorado Miner* (October 7, 1876), for example, complained in an editorial that the ending of silver purchases had caused the stagnation of business, inadequate employment, and "enforced idleness" and had benefited eastern and foreign creditors. The editor blamed this development partly on England because it supported the single gold standard and "forced" the United States to play a "second part." Emotionalism became reality, and Georgetown—which in pre-Leadville days ranked as Colorado's silver queen—led the charge.

Cries for federal assistance from the various western silver mining states and territories reached Washington and received a sympathetic hearing. A bill emerged fairly quickly, the Bland-Allison Act, authorizing the government to resume purchasing silver and coining silver. President Rutherford Hayes promptly vetoed it then watched as his veto was overridden.

His legal friend Moses Hallett supported the idea and encouraged him to stick with the bill, "even to the extent of passing it over the president's veto. . . . Colorado needs it more than the rest of the country I suppose but it will be a good measure for the whole country." Richard Irwin concurred: "It is the most important question I think of the day." He worried that Senator Chaffee "seems to favor the gold view" on the financial question, adding, "I can hardly think he would advocate such injustice to his constituency." Irwin even forecast that the issue would drive the "better portion of both parties" to form a new one "that would outgrow both of the old ones in a short time. At least that is the way it looks to me."

Two months after his earlier comments a disgusted Hallett told Teller on February 6, 1878: "I am half inclined to think that most of them ['gold chaps'] are first class rascals." His Uncle Henry Teller, from Pennsylvania, wrote the senator about the issue: "I think that the act of 1873 destroying the double standard was a mistake and perhaps a misfortune." Irwin, Hallett, and the others who corresponded with Teller on this issue sketched out the future of Colorado politics more correctly than they may have realized. Henry began assiduously studying the financial issues of the day as they related to silver.[7]

Not all Coloradans agreed with the need for government help for silver. Boulder resident Joseph Wolff surely did not. In several of the most eloquently written letters Teller received, Wolff argued to have more greenbacks, or paper money, placed into circulation to ease what he perceived to be the country's impending financial woes.

Wolff, chairman of the Colorado greenback executive committee, wanted Teller's support to make the greenback full legal tender: "Do not throw this down in disgust." Wolff supported the remonetization of silver, but he questioned the plan to have the government buy the bullion: "Why should the government *buy* the silver bullion when tons of it are ready to be coined if it only had the opportunity *without being bought?* Is not our public debt already great enough?"

In a January 3, 1878, letter, Wolff exploded over "the encroachments of the money power to beggar the masses in the interest of the few in the attempt to subvert our republican form of government." Wolff wished to "strike down at one blow both Shylock and his gold and create such a just, sound national system of finance as shall not only restore and perpetuate national prosperity, but at the same time give a death blow to all the monarchies of the earth." Yet he realized Teller's views differed from his: "I hold you in grateful personal remembrance, no matter how widely we may differ in the future over national political measures."

Most Coloradans did not concur with Wolff. James Belford warned Teller in 1878 about the growing influence of the greenbacks, which might disrupt the Republican Party. Another writer from Boulder County completely disagreed with Wolff and his politics. Greenback clubs were organizing all over the country, he cautioned his senator: "This country, as usual, [is] leading the way in lunacy."[8]

For the settlers on the Western Slope, a more pressing issue was what to do with the Utes. Coloradans euphemistically called it the "Ute Problem." Most of the land west of the Continental Divide had been guaranteed to the tribe through a series of treaties. This had caused little concern until gold and silver had been discovered in the San Juans and Gunnison Country. Now, with prospectors and miners moving into these two mountainous districts, trouble erupted.

The *Rocky Mountain News* (March 29, 1877) summarized most Coloradans' position: "The Ute reservation took farming land and comprises some of the best coal and mineral lands in the San Juan country, all of little practical value to the Indians." The land should be opened to whites who would develop these resources and "also make a line straight between reservation and settlements." The cry became the "Utes Must Go."

In the 1873 Brunot Agreement, local Ute bands in that region ceded the mineral-rich San Juans but kept lands surrounding them. That temporary expedient did not last; neither side appeared happy with the result, and the two sides did not interpret it the same way. The federal government found itself trapped between a treaty guaranteeing rights for the Utes and angry taxpayers and voters. Nothing new or unusual existed in this situation or in this centuries-old conflict between the native peoples and the Euro-American intruders on their land. The Black Hills embroglio that led to Custer and the Seventh Cavalry riding into the Little Big Horn happened in even less time.

As more settlers and miners arrived in the San Juans after the mid-1870s, the pressure for a solution mounted. The *Denver Tribune* (March 26, 1873), for example, angrily stated that no American pioneers should be denied their rights "in order that a small band of dirty nomads can idly roam over 20 million acres of hunting ground." This, the *News* lamented on March 29, 1877, "is an atrocity no other Government on the face of the earth but our own would be guilty of committing." Rico's *Dolores News* (October 25, 1879) put it equally bluntly, proclaiming the "Utes long have been a curse and a drawback to industrious people."

The same story was repeated to the northeast in Gunnison County. To make matters more tense, the White River Ute band acquired a new agent. Nathan Meeker, fresh from his success establishing the Union Colony and Greeley, was looking for new areas to conquer because the Greeley folks had grown restless under "Father Meeker's" idealism. This dreamer took his ideas to the Ute Agency along the White River. His sincere, if naive, idealism crashed into Ute reality.

Teller played a role in all this. He had lobbied for Meeker's appointment with Commissioner of Indian Affairs Edward A. Hayt. Henry wrote Meeker on January 3, 1878, saying, "I am anxious you should have it [the position] because I feel you should do something that would be of benefit to our people and to the Indians." Teller wanted a "good, honest agent." He would get half of that. He sketched out his yet undeveloped ideas about Indian education for Meeker. They focused on the practical, such as teaching them to raise cattle.[9]

Teller received numerous letters regarding this drama. At the same time Henry wrote Meeker, he received a desperate plea from several residents of Parrott City in La Plata County claiming the Utes had killed "our stock right before our eyes" and burned houses. The settlers needed protection, as "we are not strong enough to protect ourselves." A Ouray correspondent wanted the government to purchase the land north of town because that would be an "important development to the wonderful wealth of the San Juan mines." A Gunnison writer feared they were in a "perfectly defenseless situation." He applauded the fact that a "project is afoot" to remove the Utes to Indian Territory: "We here only too ardently desire it may be done, besides getting rid of a dangerous band—it will open out a fine farming country for the settlement of thousands of families."

Colorado newspapers fed the growing fury. The new *Ouray Times* as early as 1877 questioned why the Ute reservation covered some of the best land in the region. This theme had been repeated for years, and few miners in the San Juans rose to defend the Utes. The *Denver Times* said bluntly, "Either they [the Utes] or we must go, and we are not going."

At the same time, several editors did realize that the Ute bands had grievances. Trespassing whites caused problems, and the government had failed to honor its obligations. They also praised the Ute leader Ouray, whom they conveniently separated from his people, and pointed with pride when a few Utes followed the white man's road by engaging in farming.[10]

A writer touched on the usually unstated racial issue, evident on both sides. The Utes, he wrote from three years' experience among them, feel "all white men are trespassers in their country. That no white man has rights that they should respect. The Ute Indian feels himself superior to all other red men as well as whites." Many Coloradans felt the same way about the Utes. The writer also wanted troops sent in, perhaps from Fort Riley in Kansas because there "are no Indians there."

Governor John Routt kept Teller informed, and both men agreed that part of the problem lay with the government: "I fully agree with you that if the Indians are properly treated and the govt. will fulfill its part of the contract according to treaty stipulations, we will have no trouble with them." The letters give insight into what Teller was trying to do to resolve the issue. The governor had no doubt "but that you will proceed as you are determined to give the officials at Washington no peace until we feel that the government has done its whole duty." Routt, too, was being pressured. He complained to Teller that hardly a "day passes" when someone does not "see me about Indian news." By April 1878 Routt admitted that "matters look threatening." The Utes "feel aggrieved" because miners have violated the treaty, and the miners "are determined to mine upon the reservation." Routt wanted troops moved into the area: "You are well aware of the disposition of our people, and know that it will be very difficult to settle this trouble without U.S. troops." Routt was right, although it was Meeker who caused the explosion.[11]

Not everyone who corresponded with Teller was anti-Ute. In several letters Uriah Curtis, a friend of the Utes, presented their problems, including provisions not arriving, scarce game, and failure of the government to live up to its agreements: "I do not hesitate in saying that under proper management at the agency there would be no difficulty in making it." He defended the Utes, saying "they are deserving a great deal of credit for their sensible and orderly actions in the matter."

Meeker, when he reached the agency, wrote Teller about the poor conditions there. A freighter had defaulted on a contract, and no provisions had appeared. Mice were eating the few goods stored in the warehouse. The whole agency "is in a state of disorganization." Dismayed but not discouraged, Meeker described his plans for his "wards." It seemed to him their last chance to remain in Colorado. They did not understand "what is to be their fate, that is, to be overrun by prospectors and others. It is impossible for them to hold so large a territory especially while they are off it so much of the time." Meeker judged the situation correctly. The Utes faced a severe cultural disruption. Time, culture, and his tactlessness weighed against him, however.

Meeker ingeniously shifted responsibility for the eventual resolution of the Ute question to Senator Teller:"It seems to me that the best interests of the Utes and of the government, as well as of Colorado, are now placed almost wholly in your hands." Meeker had a point, as Henry would find out.[12]

Meeker's vision for the White River Utes did not coincide with their views. He wanted to turn them to farming, reduce their horse herds, stop their gambling, send their youngsters to school, and have them walk the white man's road. His zealousness in transforming a hunting-wandering people into settled "white" farmers did not sit well with the Utes. Ute men did not want to farm, and horses symbolized wealth and prestige. They enjoyed gambling, and hunting had always been a part of life on and off the reservation.

The results were predictable. Tension mounted at the agency, and the Ute leaders journeyed to Denver to complain about Meeker to new governor Frederick Pitkin. By September 1879 a worried Meeker realized that he would need troops to help with his utopian planning and "civilizing" process. He wrote Governor Pitkin that the opposition ringleaders would be arrested when troops arrived:"I think it high time these Indians should be taught to behave themselves equally with white people, and I might as well try [to tame] them as anybody else."

Troops and force arrived too little and too late in a volatile situation at the agency. The alarmed Utes attacked and with rifle fire pinned down the infantry and cavalry coming from Fort Steele, Wyoming. Headlines told the story: "The Milk Creek Massacre; The White River Utes on the Warpath." Troops from Fort Garland and elsewhere relieved the beleaguered troops and went to the agency where they found the bodies of Meeker and eleven other men. The agency's white women were missing. Coloradans cried that the "Ute war" had begun.

Panic spread through Colorado. Governor Pitkin received telegrams asking for troops, arms, and ammunition, as well as expressing fear about impending attacks from such divergent places as Lake City, Carbonateville, Kokomo, Silver Cliff, Alma, and Silverton. Typical was the missive of Mayor Frank Robb of Silver Cliff, who warned the governor that the Utes had been seen within 25 miles of town. He wanted arms and ammunition to protect the 600 families in the valley:"We can raise 500 men to help exterminate the Utes."[13]

Through the rapid and determined work of the respected Ouray and former agent Charles Adams, the women and children seized by the Utes were released, and the "Ute war" was averted. The game shifted to Washington and Congress, where Teller would learn that Meeker's desire had come true in a perverse way.[14]

The legislature sent a memorial to Congress in 1879 wanting the Utes removed and their reservation opened for settlement. Henry had tried to see that the Utes received fair treatment, particularly concerned about payments from the 1873 agreement. Teller had written Routt in December 1877 that he was "doing his best to secure the treatment of the Indians assured them by the treaty and thus [to] prevent war."

The senator complained, not for the first time, that officials in Washington "are slow to take the advice of westerners as to the best method of treating Indians." For example, in early 1878 Chaffee had sponsored—with Teller's support—a bill to extinguish Ute claims to southwestern Colorado. It passed the Senate and House, then nothing came of it. Later (May 7, 1878) Henry forecast in a Senate speech that "unless some change is made in the administration of affairs in regard to these Indians, there will be war." Unlike many of his constituents, Henry wanted something done only "with the consent of the Indians."

When the Meeker tragedy occurred, Teller himself introduced a bill on December 8, 1879, proposing the removal of the Ute people from Colorado. At the same time, he pointed out that a large portion of the monies promised the Utes remained unpaid. Henry became involved in the investigation of the White River Agency, including determining how many of the claimed "numerous mining camps" actually sat on the reservation "in direct violation of the treaty." In this he challenged the secretary of the interior's and commissioner of Indian Affairs's claim that the "miners were crowding the poor Indians uncomfortably."

During the debate that followed, Teller was unfairly accused of wanting the Utes removed regardless of mitigating circumstances. He defended himself: "I am quite as much in favor of protecting Indians in all rights as any man in the Senate." Teller did not think it was fair to have one punishment in place for a white who stole from an Indian (petty larceny) and a harsher one for an Indian who stole a similar article from a white man (felony).[15]

The discussion about what to do with the Utes moved from Colorado to Washington and back again. For Teller, two significant events occurred. His long-standing disagreement with the policies of Secretary of the Interior Carl Schurz led to open warfare. And he opposed his new senatorial colleague, Nathaniel Hill, who had just defeated Chaffee in an acrimonious state contest that left deep personal and political animosities.

Hill promptly proposed a different solution from Henry's, a rift that became public and heated. For the next six years and beyond, the two remained political enemies with ramifications for the Colorado Republican Party far beyond the Ute matter.

Teller's attitude hardened, and he demanded removal. Belford, now back in Congress, joined him. Hill pushed for authorizing the president to treat the Utes with the view of removal and giving them more of a say in their fate. Hill's approach was much more moderate. Teller and Belford, and Hill to a lesser degree, had to fend off easterners' criticism of their stand on the Ute matter. Teller defended himself and his position while criticizing those who failed to see all the ramifications of the problem. Relentlessly, he unmercifully censured Schurz's "liberal" policy. Hill remained calm and dispassionate and supported the bill that finally passed. President Hayes signed it. Rather undiplomatically but typical for Hill, he publicly blamed Teller for delaying the passage of the Ute removal bill until it was too late to accomplish it in 1880.

During the debate over the final bill, Teller offered a series of amendments to no avail, except for one providing funds for irrigating Ute land. He defended Coloradans as "neither blood thirsty nor cruel. That they are bitter against the Indians I do not deny, but it is because of the wrongs they have suffered at their hands." He continued to emphasize that improvement was needed in handling "Indian affairs," as was a "reorganization of the Interior Department's Indian Bureau." The end result was predictable. The government removed the Utes to reservations in eastern Utah. Not all Southern Utes remained on their reservation in southwestern Colorado, thanks to Ouray's efforts and their noninvolvement in the Meeker mess. By September 1881 the rest had departed, and the Western Slope was finally open to settlement.[16]

For most Coloradans, this came none too soon. Ouray's *Solid Muldoon* (May 7, 1880) had complained, "For seven months have we been hemmed in by a few hundred murderous and treacherous Utes . . . for seven long months has Secretary Schurz been dilly-dallying with a tribe of villainous and superstitious Utes, whose only object in life is murder and plunder." Racism, misunderstanding, fear, and greed had trampled understanding, compassion, and justice.

The Meeker troubles continued to press on Teller's time and conscience. The *Weekly Republican* (March 3, 1882) reported that Teller had recently "received a very touching appeal" from one of the widows of the men killed. She had "little or nothing left to raise three children." Teller introduced a relief bill for her and others. Later, as secretary of the interior, he still handled aftermath issues.

Teller was criticized for his actions covering a variety of issues. They involved, for instance, being part of the "Denver crowd" that wanted the reservation opened, being underhanded in his actions on the issue, and being heatedly anti-Ute. His experience with the tribes, however, was unquestionably greater than that of most of his colleagues, as was his understanding of Ute culture. Many of the practical views he expressed were proven correct, and he again showed that he was not "afraid to go ahead alone." For example, he opposed individual Ute ownership of land as against their customs and religious beliefs. Until the Utes became "civilized," land ownership seemed meaningless. That upset eastern reformers. Yet Teller was not blameless. His special plea that the Ute people must go undermined his position. So did his harsh view of Indians, one he believed was pragmatic: "We ought not to forget that we are dealing with savages—brutal, bloody savages."[17] His speeches, experience, and ideas, as well as his criticism of Department of the Interior and Indian Bureau policies and actions, laid the groundwork for his subsequent appointment as secretary of the interior.

Henry and Schurz had not gotten along for years before the Ute issue forced them to face off. The secretary's views on Indians seemed too eastern, impractical, and idealistic for the senator and most Coloradans. Schurz, for his part, saw another westerner with anti-Indian views. As the *Rocky Mountain News* (October 3, 1879) railed, "The Indians have been making 'progress in civilization,' according to humanitarians for 300 years, but the truth is they are as savage and untameable as when Columbus first landed at San Salvador."

Teller confronted Schurz in several stormy interviews. In February 1880 a blisteringly angry Teller "told him he could not talk fast enough nor loud enough nor strong enough to frighten him from doing [what was] best for his constituents." Nor, Teller decried, had the secretary considered the "welfare and safety" of Coloradans in securing an agreement with the Utes. Infuriated, Henry did not accept Schurz's view that he "thought he had done the best he could," adding that the Utes "had beaten him in diplomacy" just as they had beaten the army.

Teller did not stand alone. A Georgetown resident fired off a letter to Schurz accusing him of a multitude of "sins," including giving in to "Eastern Indian lovers." In his opinion the "frontier settlers [had not] irritated" the Utes by trespassing on their reservation. Quite the contrary; the real problem continued to be the Utes trespassing on Coloradans' land, stealing things, scaring people, and generally causing turmoil.

During his last weeks in the Senate before President Arthur contacted him about a cabinet appointment, Teller defended what had happened at Sand Creek. In a debate with Massachusetts senator Henry Dawes, who criticized Coloradans for their attack on the "peaceful" Cheyenne and Arapaho, Teller jumped to the defense, as discussed earlier. The tribes had "terrorized all portions" of the territory, they were not friendly, women as well as men had "engaged in the contest," and materials from "desecrated ranches" were found in the camp. Although admitting that the troops "committed outrages," they did not equal a hundredth of the "barbarities that had been practiced upon our people." Teller wanted his "emphatic denial" that there was any reason to complain about the attack at Sand Creek put on record.

Speaking from "personal and actual knowledge," and having "contributed during that summer of sixty-four a considerable amount of money" to defend the territory, Teller did not want to have Coloradans "traduced and slandered." Henry wondered why those who had participated in the battle were rarely consulted about it. He remembered being "in the field" and sitting "down by smoking fires in the Indians' camps to eat my dinner." Cheered at home for his stand, Colorado's forthright senator received little criticism in the eastern press. Interestingly, these statements did not make the senator a pariah with the Indian reform group or hinder his nomination.[18]

TELLER WAS NEVER FAR FROM HIS LEGAL PRACTICE and other Colorado interests. A gentleman from Cincinnati, for example, wanted him to handle a divorce case for a woman in Denver. Mining clients reminded him about ongoing cases that needed his personal attention. The Georgetown Pelican/Dives mess continued to haunt him; one individual involved decided not to return to Colorado and press his claims until the "bitterness" had subsided. Some of the lawyers' fees from the affair had never been paid. Bella Buell wanted information about local mining. Hiram Johnson fretted about a financial claim Willard made against him. Problems with leases on his mines and claims worried Henry. Again, one of his lessees planned to "jump the old mill site and build a mill if you are willing." Teller was not.

Letters about problems regarding the Colorado Central and other Colorado railroad matters also crossed his desk. Still involved in the Central's affairs, Teller received letters marked "confidential" describing some plan or strategy or asking questions about bonds or court cases. Teller had to be careful to avoid a conflict of interest. It was pleasing, though, to Central City's most famous resident to read that the railroad tracks had finally reached the town and that "we celebrate the 21st" (May 1878).[19]

At one point Henry's law firm almost came to grief over a dispute between his partner, Willard, and Harper Orahood. The problem came to a head in December 1877. Both men had corresponded regularly with Teller. As Henry knew, his brother could be a curmudgeon. Willard once wrote Henry about an opponent in a case: "I would skin him for a demagogue and liar and I would do it boldly. Get ready for it." The thirty-six-year-old Orahood had joined the firm in 1873 after a business career in Central City and Black Hawk. Henry's brother and Orahood sometimes got along well, although occasionally Willard provoked some issue and Henry needed to settle matters. This time, though, it seemed more serious. Willard moved to Denver, and Harper stayed in Central where he was a deputy district attorney for the First Judicial District and active in civic affairs.

Willard, Orahood wrote, had come to Central on December 30, 1877, for the first time in a month, looked over papers, then left all his keys with Harper. He said "he would probably not return again before next summer some time," said he would not be here to attend to the spring-term court, and ordered "for me to look up the cases and take charge of everything." Further, Harper said, "Mrs. Teller said last week she never expected to see Central again unless it should be for a day or two next summer." Willard stated that "he had no desire to continue the partnership any longer."

Harper continued, "I implied from what he said that he had not so written you." Harper hoped to continue with the firm for another year, but he wanted to be recognized as a full partner: "Reputation goes a great ways in our profession as well as in other pursuits and being connected with you in business would be a great present and future advantage to me and I may hope no disadvantage to you." He concluded, "I hope you will not say anything to Willard about my writing what he has said and done about leaving. Although I have certainly said nothing at which he could take offense."

Some agreement about the firm was apparently reached because Willard returned to handling cases in the spring, but he insisted on remaining in Denver. He and his wife purchased a home and told Henry they would have a "spare room or two" in which "you can reciprocate when you come back." Strains still threatened the firm, however. On May 5 Orahood explained to Henry that Willard had been to Central to talk over the partnership matter; however, they could not "arrive at any conclusion without knowing your feelings." Willard remained dissatisfied with the present arrangement, for, among other reasons, he thinks "you should pay my salary or most of it."

Willard sputtered to Henry on May 14 that he could not understand what "kind of partnership we wanted. The fact is law business in Gilpin Co. is played out." Willard's observation proved true, and eventually all three men joined in a partnership in Denver. The *Rocky Mountain News* announced on January 7, 1881, that Harper Orahood was "settling up" his legal business in Central in preparation for his departure for Denver where he would enter the law firm of H. M. and Willard Teller.[20]

Henry, anxious to keep up on news from Central, received a variety of letters from his friends. William Bush, "proprietor" of the Teller House, sent a newsy letter in December 1877, proclaiming that business "is pretty thin in the hotel business just now." He added encouragingly that the "livery is doing well." Mining prospered; the "mines are turning out lots of gold." That encouraging note must have cheered Henry.

Bush related that one of Teller's legal colleagues, Judge William Gorsline, "went on a big spree," the new "theatre will be a credit to Central City," and Tom Roberts "was married and [is] now living in your house." Gorsline had written Teller earlier about the possibility of a judicial position because "times are very hard and money scarce. Of law business there is very little." It did gladden his heart to see that "our opera house approaches completion" and to "know that the muses soon will have a temple of their own."

Another letter told Teller that a house he owned needed repair, and a second discussed extending the $1,000 note Henry owed. The holder agreed. Later, on a more cheery note, a friend commented that the opening of the opera house "went off splendidly" with a "crowded house." On a less cheery note, Henry read about the August 1881 flood; nothing had been so "destructive" since the 1874 fire. The Teller House had water in the basement, his law office had been slightly damaged, and the cellar of his home had flooded, damaging contents stored there.

Henry also received reports from Joseph Andrew—who managed Teller's farm near Valmont—about such matters as the price of wheat, planting time, a new wire fence, a kitchen addition, and troubles with the ditch people over water. Henry never forgot his agricultural and rural heritage and owned several farms during his lifetime. Despite his wishes to the contrary, he would only visit them, not "romantically" return to his roots.[21]

THE BIGGEST NEWS, WITH THE GREATEST IMPLICATION for Teller's future, was the announcement that his fellow senator Jerome Chaffee would not seek another term. Teller was aware of his friend's ill health. "My health is of more importance to me than the Senate," Chaffee asserted, but that alone did not spur him to announce that he would not be a candidate. Chaffee wrote Henry on June 16, 1878: "I have not taken this step because I think any real necessity required it, but I am sick of the whole business. I am sick of it, really disgusted with it and this gives me a good opportunity to get out. I don't think it will hurt the party." He went on to describe his feelings more concisely: "There is no dignity practiced in the Senate, nothing but a scramble for the floor."

Senator Chaffee had not endeared himself to many Coloradans by taking a conservative stance on the silver issue. James Belford exploded to Henry that "Chaffee's letter on absolute money is a damn fool thing and will do him no good here and anywhere else." Furthermore, he seemed more an absentee senator, living in his New York home, than a Colorado man. At least one man wrote Teller that "JB's chances are slight for reelection."

Chaffee's announcement prompted a rush of candidates to take his place. Colorado politics had not changed since Henry went to Washington. The southern and mountain sections and Denver vied for political offices. George Chilcott, Frederick Pitkin, James Belford, William Jackson, Thomas Patterson, Thomas Bowen, Nathaniel Hill, and others had their names bandied about. Republicans and eternally hopeful Democrats, prominent men all, focused their attention on Colorado's most prestigious elective office.

The Republicans again faced disunity, which promised trouble. Teller knew about the squabbling and did not need to be reminded by Richard Irwin that southern Colorado still felt "sore over the division of offices" from the last election. Governor Routt wrote the same thing: "The southern soreheads are beginning to assert their rights." Belford had warned Teller the previous January that "you may commence to grind your war paint for the fight looks to me as inevitable. It will be lively." A doctor in Grand County alerted Teller that the Democrats had nearly seized control: "If we cannot conquer that rebel clique we may as well move out of Grand County and let them have possession."

In the end, the Republicans nominated a ticket of Frederick Pitkin from the south and Horace Tabor from the mountain region and won the election, retaining control of the legislature. The legislative party caucus would thus select the new senator. Hill had become the front runner by generously supporting legislative candidates with his smelter-gained fortune. At this point a rejuvenated and upbeat Chaffee, his health improved, reentered the race. Jerome and some other Colorado Republican leaders were not happy at the prospect of a Hill victory because of his arrogant manner. Teller supported his friend to no avail. The Chaffee forces had sallied forth far too late. The now Democratic *Rocky Mountain News,* which loved to stir up trouble, asserted that Teller had telegraphed from Washington: "I never promised to support Hill." Some sharp exchanges and "indiscreet and heated utterances" did nothing to calm the political water. Hill won the caucus and went to Washington.

Some of Hill's ill feelings went back to 1877. He had asked Teller to help get a $100,000 damage case against him and his Black Hawk smelter (for illegally cutting trees on public land without paying for them) either "withdrawn or postponed." He went to Washington to lobby his cause, failed, and found himself embroiled in a year-long trial. Even when found innocent "by a jury composed of mountain men and intelligent men at that," he savored a long, bitter memory of that and other "slights." Hill never forgave Chaffee, Teller, and those who opposed him.[22]

What had happened to the *Rocky Mountain News*, which since its inception had been loyally and outspokenly Republican? In 1878 Byers sold his paper to William Loveland, who turned it into a Democratic sheet, thereby gaining the state's leading newspaper for his party. Loveland and Teller had been allies in the 1860s. They had fought to keep Denver from dominating the mountain towns and allied themselves to build a railroad. Times and attitudes had changed.

Byers had brought all this about. Embarrassed by his affair with a "grass widow," but more likely tired of publishing or facing financial problems, he ended his era as Colorado's leading newspaper man. The *News* again went on a campaign against Teller.[23]

Hill's victory set the stage for six years of Colorado Republican distress for Henry. The *News* (January 12, 1880), doing its best to stir up continuing trouble, lashed out, stating that Teller's "conduct is being criticized pretty severely" and accusing him of "double dealing." Teller sent a letter to the newspaper (February 9) that discussed Colorado political realities in his generation. First he answered the *News*'s charges of corruption, "lavish expenditures," and betrayal. He called for Republican unity and for the party to forget the "complaints individual members have or think they have against other members." But money and "lavish expenditures of it" to gain a Republican victory endured as the issue. Teller wrote:

> I have always depreciated the excessive use of money in political campaigns, but I am aware that there are certain expenses that must be incurred, and that in a state like ours, difficult to canvas on account of its size, and character of country, these expenses will always be larger than in many other sections of the country.

The *News* patted itself on the back for giving Teller the benefit of "much wider circulation" than he would otherwise have obtained in the Republican press and went on to say, "but in reproducing it we in no wise endorse the sentiments, the exuberant fancy which dictates a document so remarkable."

That comment was typical. The *News* railed against Teller in the no-holds barred partisan political reporting of his generation. Other headlines included: "Teller's Rampage," "A Check on Teller," and "Teller's Tattle." The paper accused him of being in a "Stalwart Ring," a "very ordinary statesman," and said it would be a "novelty" if his speeches contained even a "slight infusion of law, reason, or intelligence." The *News* believed he had tried to secure his seat for life on the "basis of a self-perpetuating Ku Klux Klan," said his speeches fell flat, spoke of the "growing opinion of your incompetency," and finally, accused Teller of "hopeless mediocrity."

The fight between the Teller and Hill, meanwhile, boiled over into all of Colorado. It did not help when his new Senate colleague claimed in October 1879 that "Teller's defeat for reelection is already assured" and jubilantly pledged himself to remove "every Teller and Chaffee man from office." Hill proved overconfident. His attempt to stop the renomination of Belford, whom Teller backed, at the state convention in 1880 was defeated. Open warfare followed the election.

Teller had been one of the Coloradans to advance the third-term presidential ambitions of former President Grant. Teller and Chaffee had been Grant supporters since 1876. After a bitter fight at the Republican national convention, Grant had not been nominated. James Garfield won, and Hill adroitly and quickly swung to support him, as Teller did eventually.

The senior senator went to Leadville for the Republican state convention in August 1880 to restore some of his lost prestige and curb the growing Hill support. Although not expecting to address the group, he did so and vigorously attacked the Democrats. He waved the now familiar "bloody shirt" against the Democratic "rebels" who "were conquered but not converted." He bluntly asserted that "the only hope of saving the country from everlasting destruction or absolute annihilation" was the Republican ticket. According to a reporter, "He sat down in a tempest of applause."

The *News* on August 27 took him to task as usual for being "so economical of the truth as to repeat libel." "The distinguished gentleman," the newspaper blustered, "unfurled the scarlet garment and shook it vigorously, to the apparent delight of his audience. He proved himself a close student of Mrs. Stowe's 'Uncle Tom's Cabin.'" The reporter thought it was difficult to think otherwise than that "the country" was in the "very midst of a great rebellion" and the only hope of "saving the country is to vote Republican."

Teller campaigned on the plains and in his mountain strongholds. He vigorously presented Republican views in, among other places, Windsor, Central City, Pueblo, and Colorado Springs. In Georgetown, Henry spent two hours on the issues of the day "in favor of the Republican Party." He had friends there, who "turned out in goodly numbers." The *Colorado Miner* gushed, "Our citizens are always delighted to hear Mr. Teller, and were never more so than last Thursday evening." Henry appeared at Silverton, too, where the residents liked him for his Ute stand. Teller gave one of his typical speeches. The reporter caught the essence of Henry's approach to public speaking. The lengthy speech was "a careful and studied synopsis of the reasons why, at the coming election, every voter should support the Republican party. Though unimpassioned, his arguments were convincing and most admirably to the point." Belford and the Republican ticket swept the field.[24]

Teller's first years as senator had been exciting in all aspects. He had gained experience in Washington and on the national scene. He was looking ahead to his reelection where he could count on the determined opposition of newcomer Hill. Willard, who had not favored his brother running for office in the 1878 campaign, complained in a letter to Orahood, "his head is so full of his political advancement that I fear he is forgetting everything honorable and praiseworthy in his pursuit of a second term." Teller had matured politically and as an individual by 1880. His experience as a lawyer and his knowledge of the West had stood him well. He had also gotten a glimpse of what the future held for him both personally and politically. In his supporters' eyes, Henry was the "ablest man in the state"; the "greatest complement" that could be paid Teller was to say "he has made *himself* what he is." Denver's *Weekly Republican* (March 2, 1882) called him "one of the hardest workers in the Senate." And his friend and fellow Republican Ben Eaton wrote, "I am proud of your *record*."[25]

NOTES

1.   The *Kansas City Times,* quoted in the *Rocky Mountain News,* August 25, 1880, challenged Teller's 1876 role. *Congressional Record,* February 1, 1877, 1186, October 30, 1877, 39, October 31, 1877, 201, December 6, 1877, 40, April 1, 1878, 2131, December 3, 1878, 12, December 7, 1878, 57, December 19, 1878, 304, *New York Tribune,* December 18–20, 1877, Elmer Ellis, *Henry Moore Teller* (Caldwell, Idaho: Caxton, 1941), 115–117.

2.   *Congressional Record,* January 10, 1878, 250–251, February 18, 1878, 1129, February 27, 1878, 1395, March 6, 1878, 1506, March 14, 1878, 1753, March 18, 1878, 1822, March 19, 1878, 1853, March 20, 1878, 1878, March 27, 1878, 2053, June 5, 1878, 4120, June 13, 1878, 4550, January 29, 1879, 808; February 7, 1879, 1071, February 19, 1879, 996; June 17, 1879, 4698, January 8, 1880, 234, February 16, 1880, 912, May 17, 1880, 3412, March 7, 1882, 1671; *Georgetown Courier,* March 9, 30, 1882; John Hiching to Teller, December 26, 1872, Teller Manuscript Collection, Denver Public Library; Roy Wortman, "Denver's Anti-Chinese Riot, 1880," *Colorado Magazine* (fall 1965), 291.

3.   *Congressional Record,* February 19, 1878, 1171, February 20, 1878, 1201, 1203, 1207, June 14, 1878, 4584, February 18, 1879, 1511, December 4, 1879, 25, January 7, 1880, 225, 230, 317; John Guice, *Rocky Mountain Bench* (New Haven: Yale University Press, 1972), 87, 94.

4.   All letters were sent to Teller: Bella Buell, February 22, 1878, Charles Welch, April 1, 1878, S.V. Bryant, n.d., December 31, 1877, January 27, 1878, William Clark, October 22, 1877, Philip Wilcox, March 7, 1878, H.A.W. Tabor, May 29, 1878, C. H. Tompson?, November 28, 1877, H. C. Sherman, December 18, 1877, E. Burlingame, April 18, 1878, President Denver Board of Trade, May 17, 1878, C. S. Cudebre, December 12, 1877, James Belford, April 4, 1878, S. S. Wallihan, January 5, 1878, John Routt, November 14, 1877, A. A. Smith, December 27, 1877, T. M. Trippe, July 15, 1878, Isaac Teller, December 1877, all in Teller Manuscript Collection, Denver Public Library.

5.   Richard Irwin, January 11, 1878, John Hitching, December 26, 1877, N. A. Foss, December 13, 1877, William Bush, December 19, 1877, Hiram A. Johnson, December 24, 1877, Harper Orahood, November 6, 1878, John Thayer, March 5, 1878, Irving Stanton, January 2, 1878, John Routt, December 31, 1877, all to Teller, Teller Manuscript Collection, Denver Public Library. On women's suffrage see D. Kilhards? to William Jackson, March 15, 1877, William Jackson Papers, Colorado College.

6.   Joseph Sewall to Teller, November 18, December 27, 1877, January 9, 1878, E. Howard to Teller, December 10, 1877, Fred Stanton to Teller, January 21, 1878, all in Teller Manuscript Collection, Denver Public Library; William E. Davis, *Glory Colorado!* (Boulder: Pruett, 1965), 24–28; *Rocky Mountain News,* May 13, 1882.

7.   Moses Hallett, December 16, 1877, February 6, 1878, Richard Irwin, December 28, 1877, January 11, 1878, Henry Teller (uncle), January 19, 1878, C. A. Murray, January 15, 1878, O. Harper, March 10, 1878, Henry Leordz?, January 5, 1878, Philip Wilcox,

March 7, 1878, all to Teller, Teller Manuscript Collection, Denver Public Library. *Rocky Mountain News,* September 20, 1879, and Charles Henderson, *Mining in Colorado* (Washington, D.C.: Government Printing Office, 1926), 69–70, 77–78, trace Colorado's silver production.

8. Joseph Wolff, November 12, 24, 1877, January 3, 1878, James Belford, December 28, 1877, March 17, 1878, O. Harper, March 10, 1878, all to Teller, Teller Manuscript Collection, Denver Public Library.

9. Marshall Sprague, *Massacre: The Tragedy at White River* (Boston: Little, Brown, 1957), 57–58; George Manypenny, *Our Indian Wards* (New York: Da Capo, 1972 reprint), 413–417, 434; Mark Harvey, "Misguided Reformer: Nathan Meeker Among the Ute," *Colorado Heritage* 1 (1982), 39–40; *Rocky Mountain News,* April 22, 28, 1880, January 6, 1881. For the Ute issue, see Duane A. Smith, *Song of the Hammer and Drill* (Niwot: University Press of Colorado, 1999 reprint), and Duane Vandenbushe, *A Land Alone* (Gunnison: B&B Printers, 1980).

10. *Ouray Times, Rocky Mountain News,* and *Silver World,* 1877–1879; *Solid Muldoon, Denver Times,* and *Dolores News,* 1879; C. Clements, January 28, 1878, John Routt, December 20, 1877, Nathan Meeker, May 2, 1878, all to Teller, Teller Manuscript Collection, Denver Public Library.

11. Ben Ford, H. Mitchell, January 2, 1878, O. Mathews, November 25, 1877, H. Holladay, December 2, 1877, A. White, March 18, 1878, C. Clements, January 28, 1878, John Routt, December 17, 20, 31, 1877, March 12, April 19, 1878, all to Teller, Teller Manuscript Collection, Denver Public Library.

12. Uriah Curtis, December 24, 1877, and undated letter, Nathan Meeker, May 2, 27, 1878, all to Teller, Teller Manuscript Collection, Denver Public Library; Harvey, "Misguided," 42–44.

13. *Rocky Mountain News,* October 1879; *Solid Muldoon,* October 1879.

14. The best popular account of the Meeker troubles is Sprague, *Massacre,* chapters 18-24. Sprague was generally anti-Teller.

15. *Congressional Record,* December 7, 1877, 57, December 10, 1877, 81, January 24, 1878, 516, February 15, 1878, 1050, May 7, 1878, 3236, 3239, February 7, 1879, 1071, December 3, 1879, 21, December 8, 30, 1879, 69; January 26, 1880, 521; Teller to Routt, December 7, 1877, *Denver Times,* December 19, 1877, WEstern HIstory Collections, Denver Public Library; Dudley T. Cornish, "The First Five Years of Colorado's Statehood," *Colorado Magazine* (September 1948), 222–223.

16. Cornish, "First Five Years," 223–224, 226–231; Francis P. Prucha, *American Indian Policy in Crisis* (Norman: University of Oklahoma Press, 1976), 237, 240; *History of the City of Denver* (Chicago: O. L. Baskin, 1880), 169–170, 174–175; Sprague, *Massacre,* 228, 311; *Solid Muldoon,* August 12, 26, 1881.

17. Prucha, *Indian Policy,* 240; Cornish, "First Five Years," 232; Sprague, *Massacre,* 268, 276, 285, 305, 310–312; Jo Lee Behrens, " 'The Utes Must Go'—With Dignity," *Essays in Colorado History* 4 (1994), 42–44; *Georgetown Miner,* February 5, 1880.

18. Undated, unidentified newspaper article, "Teller Scrapbook," Chris Buys private collection; speech, *Congressional Record,* March 31, 1882, 2455–56.

19. *Georgetown Miner,* February 5, 1881; Alfonso Taft, May 15, 1878, John Ellet, December 24, 1877, Aaron Jones, January 3, February 6, 24, 1878, Willard Teller, January 1, May 18,

1878, Bella Buell, October 31, 1877, Hiram Johnson, May 1, 14, 1878, John Turner, March 2, 1878, Jerome Chaffee, December 26, 1877, Sidney Dillon, December 21, 1877, Gilbert Reed, December 13, 1877, Edward Berthoud, December 30, 1877, O. H. Henry, May 16, 1878, all to Teller, Teller Manuscript Collection, Denver Public Library.

20. Willard Teller, November 16, December 12, 1877, January 1, 29, February 13, 24, May 3, 4, 9, 10, 13, 14, 28, 30, June 1, 5, 6, 7, 1878, Harper Orahood, December 30, 1877, May 5, 1878, Welcha Teller, January 1, 1878, all to Teller, Teller Manuscript Collection, Denver Public Library.

21. William Bush, December 19, 1877, William Gorsline, February 5, 1878, A. N. Rogers, April 24, 1878, Charles Welch, March 5, 1878, Walter Cheesman, November 16, 1877, Joseph Andrew, February 21, March 13, May 15, 1878, all to Teller, Teller Manuscript Collection, Denver Public Library; *Rocky Mountain News,* August 9, 1881.

22. Jerome Chaffee, December 26, 1877, May 15, June 16, 1878, James Belford, December 28, 1877, January 2, March 17, April 4, 1878, O. Harker, March 10, 1878, Irving Stanton, June 7, 1878, Willard Teller, June 7, 1878, David Book, December 4, 1877, Richard Irwin, January 11, 1878, John Routt, March 12, 1878, Moses Hallett, December 16, 1877, Nathaniel Hill, October 10, 1879, January 2, 1878, all to Teller, William Bush to Nathanial Hill, December 19, 1877, all in Teller Manuscript Collection, Denver Public Library; R. G. Dill, *The Political Campaigns of Colorado* (Denver: Arapaho, 1895), 41; James Baker and LeRoy Hafen, *History of Colorado* (Denver: Linderman, 1927), vol. 3, 909; James E. Fell Jr., *Ores to Metals* (Lincoln: University of Nebraska Press, 1979), 52–53, *Rocky Mountain News,* January 5, 1879.

23. *Rocky Mountain News,* January 11, February 12, April 19, September 20, 1879, September 8, 1880, July 30, October 27, 1881; Robert L. Perkin, *The First Hundred Years* (Garden City: Doubleday, 1959), 323, 337–338.

24. *Colorado Miner,* October 30, 1880; *La Plata Miner,* October 2, 1880; *Evening Chronicle,* August 27, 1880; *Rocky Mountain News,* October 7, 1879, July 30, August 8, 27, 28, October 7, 12, 24, 26, 28, 1880; Dill, *The Political Campaigns of Colorado,* 56–58.

25. Willard Teller to Harper Orahood, December 3, 1878, Harper Orahood Papers, University of Colorado; unidentified, undated article, "Teller Scrapbook," Chris Buys private collection; Thomas Dawson, "Teller and Wolcott Manuscript," Colorado Historical Society, 4; *History of Clear Creek and Boulder Valleys, Colorado* (Chicago: O. L. Baskin, 1880), 489; Ben Eaton to Teller, February 24, 1878, Teller Manuscript Collection, Denver Public Library.

Secretary of the Interior

Teller's career took a new turn in 1882. His increasingly bitter split with fellow Colorado senator Hill was being fought both at home and in Washington. They contested each other's appointments and tried to remove federal appointees of the other faction. The bitterness spilled over into the state as they contested local and state elections, particularly as Teller's term neared its end in 1882. Both sides jockeyed for position to dominate the Republican caucus in the legislature.

Hill's newspapers, primarily the *Denver Republican,* viciously pounded Teller and his supporters. The *Denver Republican,* a rival paper claimed, "fairly reeked with foulness." Henry grew infuriated with his colleague, and his feelings would not change for years. In 1883 he wrote Thomas Dawson, newspaperman and his eventual longtime secretary, complaining that "while he [Hill] was my associate in the Senate he was not willing to take half of the appointees from among his friends; he wanted them all." Teller knew he faced an acrimonious fight from the local level right up to the statehouse to gain reelection to the Senate.[1]

The possibility existed once more that the Colorado Republican Party might split into two factions, potentially leading to another Democratic victory. Teller was not certain of victory in any event; Hill had built up a loyal, growing group of backers. The junior senator had boasted that Teller could not win reelection. His money and his newspapers gave Hill an advantage over his political rival.

The second development that affected Henry's career materialized with the tragic shooting in July 1881 and death in September of newly elected president James Garfield. That event placed Vice President Chester Arthur in the White House. The intelligent, cosmopolitan, fifty-one-year-old New Yorker had long been a Republican political boss who had proven an adroit campaigner in the 1880 campaign. To the reformers in the party, however, his close association with fellow New Yorker and pro-patronage senator Roscoe Conkling and the rambunctious, at times corrupt Stalwart wing of the Republican Party tainted Arthur. They also recalled his involvement with the political appointment scandal involving the New York Custom House when he served as collector in the 1870s. To the Reform wing of the party, this appeared to be strengthening the Stalwart and Conkling base. Arthur appointed competent men, but he also believed in rewarding party loyalty. Arthur was removed in 1877 because many believed he was too politically active.

The new president had much to prove to Washington and to the American public. As one observer noted, "Arthur's antecedents do not inspire confidence. He is now, however, entitled to support, unless he forfeits it." Arthur, much to the surprise of many, creditably measured up to the challenges and responsibilities of the presidency.

Determined to be his own president, Arthur set about to restructure the administration and the cabinet. Although he did try to retain some of Garfield's cabinet appointees, his overtures failed. Garfield's secretary of the interior, the elderly and ineffective Samuel J. Kirkwood, was no political friend of Arthur's and would go. Among others Arthur considered for the post was Colorado's Jerome Chaffee. All of the candidates carried political baggage, something Arthur had to consider as he steadfastly tried to separate himself from his past.[2]

Some Coloradans wanted a westerner to hold the prominent position of secretary of the interior, and they urged Arthur to appoint Chaffee. The position oversaw many issues vital to the West and was an important and attractive post because of its large budget, national scope, varied involvement in people's lives, and patronage positions.

Teller wholeheartedly supported his friend Chaffee and endeavored to secure his appointment. Then in late March the president's private secretary called Henry with an invitation to come to the White House that evening.

According to Teller's recollection in an 1890 interview, the discussion with the president took an unexpected turn. Teller had planned to present Chaffee's case. Arthur opened by commenting that he would not appoint Chaffee, but he had a man he hoped to secure. The president found too many public and party objections to Chaffee, especially because he was not a lawyer "fresh from a good practice." Henry disagreed: "I was rather nettled at this and I referred to the fact that a number of past secretaries had not been lawyers." Arthur proceeded to explain why he needed a lawyer and "to enumerate the quite remarkable qualifications" of the man he had in mind. Teller, "racking his brain to determine who the man could be," finally agreed that if the president could "find such a man for the place he ought to get him."

Colorado would not stand in the way "for a moment; the country needed him." The discussion continued:

> "Now, Senator Teller, I have decided that you come nearer to filling those requirements than any other man I know, and I want to offer you the place." I was thunderstruck. I jumped to my feet and excitedly exclaimed: "But I don't want it, Mr. President. I am in the Senate, and I can't leave it. I cannot afford it, and you must not offer me the place, for I cannot accept it."

Arthur asked Teller to think it over until Thursday, but Henry still had not changed his mind. The president then recommended Henry talk to his colleague, Pennsylvania senator and former secretary of war James Donald Cameron, who had also been mentioned as a possible candidate. He received enthusiastic encouragement from Cameron to accept. Somehow the news leaked, reaching Colorado. Telegrams promptly arrived pressuring Teller to accept this honor of being the first Coloradan offered a cabinet seat.

Cameron telegraphed Chaffee to come to Washington to confer with Teller. Realizing he had no hope for the cabinet appointment, Chaffee was "perfectly satisfied" with Teller's appointment. A later account reported his short and sweet advice: "Take it damn quick."

Henry still hesitated. Most Coloradans liked the idea of having one of their citizens in the cabinet; nevertheless, they could not push Teller into a hasty decision. With the pressure building, he carefully weighed the future before finally accepting on April 6: "My state urges acceptance and I can't decline."

President Arthur had wanted Teller because of his experience in the West and his ability as a lawyer. The president had also appealed to Henry on the grounds that the secretaryship would "give you a new broader field" in which to work. His appointment pleased both the Stalwart faction and some reformers. The famous editor E. L. Godkin, a reformer, highly admired Teller, calling him "a man of ability [who] brings to the discharge of his duties such an equipment as the experience of the Senate, of an active law practice in land and mining cases, and of Western life gives."[3]

Teller gave a few brief remarks at a Leadville reception in August 1882 that shed light on his thinking at the time. He had planned to be a candidate for reelection, and "from expression of public sentiment which I had received I had much confidence that I would be successful." Teller had been surprised when Arthur extended the offer of the secretaryship, but he considered it an honor for himself and Colorado: "I hesitated to accept. I was not sure that I ought to lay down the trust the people had confided to me. I knew the difficulties of the position offered me. I knew of the thousand intricate and perplexing questions that would arise. I know of the distinguished gentlemen who for many years held the position."

He elaborated further: "I knew that I differed with many—indeed with the majority of the people of some sections—upon the questions that would come before that department, questions that especially interested the great West." Henry knew westerners "are more interested than any others in the questions with which the Interior Department has to deal."

His concluding remarks illustrate much about the man and what he hoped to accomplish during his tenure.

> I am not vain enough to imagine that I shall make the best Secretary of the Interior that has ever served the country. I do not expect to do anything wonderful or astonishing. I do not claim to be a genius, or to be possessed by any exalted ability. But with my common sense—and I think I have a little of that—of my twenty-one years' familiarity with the matters with which I shall have to deal . . . I may so discharge the duty of my office that when I lay down the trust no citizen of Colorado will be ashamed.

He closed by commenting on something that was increasingly on his mind and capturing his political attention: "I have thought that the people of the Great West, and especially the people of this State, would like to have in the cabinet one man who believed that the great silver interests of the country were worthy of the attention of the administration."

A year later, when he arrived back at Central for a "few weeks enjoying the comforts of his old home," Teller received plaudits for his work. A "general good feeling prevails." The press was delighted that he looked "so good" and appeared in "better health than expected after his arduous labor at Washington." Coloradans were pleased, except for the diehard Hill faction.[4]

Teller's friends enthusiastically applauded the appointment. So did other Coloradans. Frank Hall wrote that "it was regarded as an honor conferred upon every citizen of Colorado without reference to political affiliations." Teller's old hometown Central could not contain its ardor; the town celebrated with firing of guns, a brass band, and speeches. Newspapers reported: "The kingdom of Gilpin was hardly large enough to hold the enthusiasms." With great pride the *Georgetown Courier* (April 13, 1882) said Teller "goes into the cabinet without a stain upon his character," and when he "leaves the cabinet his record will be as clean as now." His public and private lives "have been above suspicion," the paper contended. Among Colorado politicians in the 1880s, that was a rare compliment.

The *Colorado Miner* (Georgetown) proudly cheered how far Colorado had come since 1859. Local chauvinism carried the day. Colorado, "by her own energy and resources, in less than a quarter of a century has sprung from an Indian-scalping, buffalo-trodden wilderness to be[come] one of the most prosperous states in the union." Teller had come west when the state was a "trackless waste inhabited by wild beasts and wilder men. He put in his best licks with other pioneers, and the wild places yielded up gold and corn, the wealth of an empire."

Not everyone seemed so carried away or pleased. Hill's friends seethed. Teller's friends were unhappy when a rumor circulated accusing Hill of trying to prevent Henry's appointment, which would have "deprived Colorado of the honor of a place in the cabinet." Prominent Republican, former Maine senator, and ex-secretary of state James G. Blaine tried to bring the two men together by sponsoring an "old-fashioned tea party" for Teller, Hill, and their families. The split between the two proved too bitter and too deep, despite that pleasant gesture. Already planning for a presidential bid in 1884, Blaine wanted Colorado party loyalty to enhance his chances.[5]

The strongly Democratic *Rocky Mountain News* (June 2, 1882) chided Teller for ignoring his friends by not bestowing any offices on his "faithful henchmen." The *News* blasted: "His negligence in this matter cannot be attributed to any modesty on the part of his in signifying their desire to help in the great business of serving the country by drawing fat salaries."

Teller resigned his Senate seat in April 1882 and became secretary of the interior. The resignation set in motion a state scramble to appoint someone to serve the rest of his term and, more significantly, the upcoming full Senate term. The resulting campaign gained legendary status when it pitted two newly rich mining millionaires against each other. The San Juans' Thomas Bowen gained the victory over Leadville's Horace Tabor for the six-year seat. Tabor was to serve the last thirty days of Teller's term as a consolation prize. The race had been full of sensationalist rumors, including charges of bribery, political betrayal, and mining moguls buying a Senate seat. Something even more lurid followed—sensational accusations surfaced that Horace had married another woman while still married to his first wife.

When it came to news coverage, Tabor, a legend in his own day, completely eclipsed any previous Colorado senator, especially when he married Elizabeth McCourt in a glittering ceremony in Washington's famous Willard Hotel. "Baby Doe" trailed a less than glowing reputation from Central to Leadville to Denver. Shocked Colorado society turned its back on the pair. A reluctant Teller went to the ceremony along with President Arthur and a few other Washington politicians and officials. The churchgoing family man did not enjoy himself; Tabor had flaunted too many Victorian conventions. Teller recounted:

> Tabor has gone home, I thank God he was not elected for six years; thirty days nearly killed us, I humiliated myself to attend his wedding because he was a Senator from Colorado (but Mrs. Teller would not). I felt as if I could not afford to say that the State had sent a man to represent her in the Senate, that I would not recognize socially.

Teller's opinion of Tabor was not as bad as it may have seemed in those comments. Teller added: "Tabor is an honest man in money affairs, and I believe he is truthful, but he has made a great fool of himself with reference to that woman [Baby Doe], and he ought now to retire and attend to his private affairs." Tabor did so, but their paths merged again within a few years to lead the free silver fight in Colorado.

Meanwhile, brother Willard got caught up in the legal fallout over Tabor's affairs and managed to be cited for contempt and fined $500. The Teller brothers were not, as the nineteenth-century saying went, "two peas out of the same pod."[6]

Coloradans hailed Teller's appointment, not only because of state pride because Henry knew mining. As Frank Hall observed, Teller was "preeminently qualified to adjust the many complex questions relating to public lands in the West, more especially such as related to the mineral lands." The twin issues of public lands and mining dominated the attention of Coloradans at the time, and both fell under the Interior Department. After decades of frustration, Colorado had finally emerged as the number-one mining state in the United States and as a significant player in international financial and mining circles. Less newsworthy, although hardly less significant for the future, agriculture was making great strides throughout the state, especially on the eastern plains. Accessibility to homesteads and mining claims traced back to Washington and were within the secretary's domain.

Teller threw himself into his new office with his usual determination, preparation, and dedication. One eastern newspaper lauded the "delicate studious looking gentleman of unostentatious manner" for being at his desk by 8:30, taking no lunch, and "rarely leaving the office before 6 P.M." The reporter feared the secretary, who "has much the appearance of a college professor," might be undermining his health. The "wonder is his health does not fail under such arduous work." On his first day in office, Henry found out what it meant to be secretary of the largest federal bureaucracy at the time. Many callers, including congressmen, political friends, and office seekers, came to congratulate him and talk before he went to the White House to attend his first cabinet meeting at noon.

During the long territorial days and into statehood, Henry had become frustratingly familiar with what he believed were "some inconsiderate rules of the Interior Department and of the General Land Office." He vowed to try to revise and correct such problems and to hold prompt and proper hearings on contested matters. The western press hoped so; it had been a long and contentious problem.[7]

In his annual reports, a glimpse is seen of his response to such concerns and the multitude of other issues Henry had to contend with during his tenure. The Interior Department harbored a host of varied agencies the secretary watched over. The following commissioners and directors reported to Teller—Indian Affairs, General Land Office, Patent Office, Railroads, Education, Geological Survey, Pensions, Census, and Capitol Building and Grounds. Also, the Hot Springs (Arkansas) Reservation, Yellowstone National Park, Freedman's Hospital, and the Columbia Institution for the Deaf and Dumb fell under his jurisdiction.

Teller, in addition, oversaw the creation of the Civil Service Commission. The public's horror over Garfield's shooting—which may have occurred in part because the assassin had not received a political appointment—pushed the drive for civil service reform over the top, forcing Congress to act. Teller got the commission started and created a department made up of 213 clerks, copyists, and special examiners. Moreover, he put to rest one objection that the examinations "would be of such technical character as to exclude from public service all except those who have had the advantages of a liberal education." Teller felt "these fears were groundless, and that the examinations have been conducted on a sound and businesslike basis, calculated to secure efficient clerks for the various grades of public service."

Teller enthusiastically endorsed the idea of the Civil Service Department: "The law has in a great measure relieved the Department of the importunities of applicants and their friends for positions. I think the system a valuable one, and one that should have the hearty support of both executive and legislative departments of the Government."[8]

An interesting example of the department's responsibilities involved the nation's first national park, Yellowstone. As the Northern Pacific Railroad neared the park in 1882, Yellowstone emerged, in Teller's words, "a popular resort for recreation and health." Adequate visitor facilities—such as roads, hotels, liveries, and restrooms—desperately needed to be provided. The underfinanced small businessmen doing business in the park had neither the wherewithal nor the means to serve the hordes of tourists soon to venture west with the railroad. Concessionaires and a concessionaire policy were hit-and-miss propositions in the first decade of the park's existence.

Teller had to sort out what had been done against what needed to be accomplished. The concern that year (1882) focused on granting leases of land on which to "erect hotels for the accommodation of visitors." Teller decided that an "association of persons" would provide the best answer to offering "first-class accommodations." The department therefore granted the association a contract to build hotels and run stages to the "principle points in the park." They additionally had to construct a telegraph line from the park to lines outside it. A schedule of "charges for accommodations furnished and services rendered" was approved. The secretary asked Congress for further appropriations for roads, bridges, and other improvements.

The granting of a monopoly in Yellowstone seemed a pragmatic solution to a pressing problem. It would later be termed a "park steal." At the time, no thought that the Interior Department should build facilities and either operate or lease them gained official acceptance. The political climate stood foursquare against such "radicalism." The small-time operators did not provide the answer; expenses and risks remained too high. That left only a well-financed business monopoly as the logical answer. The monopoly lease policy thereby established lasted for nearly a century.

Locals did not agree with the policy, which produced an amusing story when President Arthur visited the park in 1883. A visitor protested when he was not allowed to hire the rig of his choice. The man complained to the president and leveled the accusation that his secretary of the interior worked in "collusion" with the Park Improvement Company. Arthur laughed, but he did revoke Teller's order giving two men control of the park tours. Henry also visited the park that year with an excursion organized by the Northern Pacific.

In his next two annual reports, Teller noted with pleasure that a hotel at Mammoth Hot Springs had opened and camps had been maintained "during the summer at other points of interest." The secretary emphasized, "Stringent regulations have been established for the prevention of injury of the game and national curiosities."

Sadly, that did not solve the problem because of "the inadequacy of the number of assistants to the superintendent for the proper supervision of so large an area." Part of the trouble came about because political "hacks" and relatives of well-placed individuals were hired as park employees during Teller's administration as well as others. Henry did make an effort to keep the force at the allotted ten, and most who served in the park proved at least adequate.

The secretary wanted Congress to give the superintendent more authority to enforce the rules and laws because, as Teller knew, "the nearest law officers of these Territories [Wyoming, Montana, and Idaho] are so remote." Wyoming solved that problem by providing justices of the peace and constables for park duty.

Yellowstone National Park grew more popular with the American public each year. The coming of railroads, the improved hotels and camps, and the maintenance of roads to the popular sites all made the park more accessible and enjoyable for visitors. It would take time, however, to educate the public and convince Congress of the special needs of this beautiful land.[9]

If Yellowstone looked to the future, the matter of pensions looked to the past. The Boys in Blue were growing older as the war marched farther into history. By the end of Teller's tenure, the surrender at Appomattox had occurred twenty years before. Illnesses, wounds, and old age were starting to take their toll. A grateful country, the victorious North, and the Union veterans' group—the Grand Army of the Republic—had not forgotten their heroes. Pensions rolled out of Washington for all who qualified, which meant nearly every veteran and widow.

Each year the number of pensioners increased, so did the amount spent. Teller reported in 1884 that 322,756 pensioners, veterans, and widows received $34,456,600.35, an average pension of $106.75. Included in these figures were more than 19,000 widows of men who had served in the War of 1812. The pension budget had become one of the largest in the total federal budget; nevertheless, that represented only a small amount of what had been spent or would be spent. Since 1861, nearly a million claims had been filed and over $678 million paid.

With that many claims, problems naturally occurred. Slowness in responding to applications worried Teller. He wanted to liberalize the process. The swamped bureau received 1.8 million letters and sent 1.3 million letters in 1884 alone. To try to improve the system, Teller had added 150 more special examiners that year, increasing the number to nearly 400. Critics seemed more worried about fraud than about slowness and wanted each case carefully examined. Teller, although not advocating illegal applications, wanted to enhance the system to benefit the veterans: "The Government has the means of detecting fraud if attempted, and injustice should not be done to the deserving and needy soldier for fear the Government may in some few instances be imposed upon."

Another source of anxiety involved fraudulent pension lawyers who "outrageously robbed claimants." During Teller's administration, "Many attorneys were suspended for practice before the pension [office]" and prosecuted for disregarding the "authority of the department." Henry instigated a policy in which fees were paid after disability claims were completed. One newspaper hailed the secretary for his "salutary influence" that produced a "marked change for the better," saying there was no one "better qualified for the position."

Teller only saw the tip of an oncoming financial iceberg. His successors would find the problems greater and the needs increasing. Teller helped the bureau in another respect during his administration; a new "brick and metal fire-proof" building was constructed "in a high and healthy part of the city [Washington, D.C.]."

He did not, however, succeed in reforming some of the pension acts, particularly that of March 3, 1879. The act stated that everyone who applied for a pension before July 1, 1880, would receive it from the time of his discharge or his widow from the time of the pensioner's death. Anyone who applied after July 1, 1880, would receive pensions starting only on that day. Teller protested, "No good reasons can be given why the claimants . . . ought not to receive their pension from the time of discharge if such disability then existed, or if not then existing, from the time such disability originated." Others, worried more about fraud and back payment expenses, did object; the debate continued.[10]

Other matters combined to make the secretary's days long. The number of patent applications steadily increased during the period 1882–1885. Teller repeatedly requested additional space and staff because "every succeeding year great labor and care are required in the consideration of applications, owing to the increase in the number of patents issued and the widening of the field of invention."

In the area of education, Teller's and the commissioner's recommendations echoed down through the next century. Improvement of reading skills, advancement of teachers' professional standards, national aid for elementary education, increased standards for collegiate instruction, and "increasing the efficiency of the school systems" were proposed along with federal aid to education. Teller never considered building a "national school system independent of state control, but [rather] to supplement the work already begun."

Henry clearly explained his views on education in a letter regrettably declining an invitation to speak at the National Education Assembly in August 1882. Heartily favoring an "enlarged State effort and only temporary national aid to education," he wanted "an efficient public school system extending to all the States and affording equal facilities for education to all classes of children free from rate bills." That goal "cannot be too highly prized." Provision for school facilities if a state "neglects or refuses" to do so rested clearly within the power of the federal government. All national appropriations for school purposes should be placed under the control of the state, "with only such guards as shall secure its faithful applications to the purpose for which it was appropriated."

Some sections of the country "cannot, I fear" or seemed unwilling to support public education without government aid. Teller concluded optimistically that if public education were maintained for the next ten to fifteen years, there would be no danger of abandonment because of public demand. The federal treasury would not have to be tapped beyond that time—or so he could "reasonably hope." The problem remained, how to get Congress to appropriate needed funds. The continual theme of "limited means" appeared yearly, and so did suggestions for the various reforms. Progress on a few fronts occurred, yet basically few advancements were made.

The physical condition of the nation's Capitol and grounds caught the attention of every visitor. Ongoing painting and repair helped; so did the introduction of the "apparatus for lighting by electricity [not entirely satisfactorily], improving the grounds, and modernization of the steam heating system."[11]

Westerners expected more from the one federal government agency they most likely came into contact with. Teller's constituents—thinking regionally, not nationally—were more interested in local matters. In his 1883 comments about the Geological Survey, Teller emphasized what westerners wanted to hear: "During the past year the work of the Survey has been vigorously prosecuted in the Western States and Territories, especially in the region producing the precious metals."

Westerners were happy to hear about what happened with the case of the Rico (Colorado) townsite versus Mill site claimants. The case went back to 1879, and Teller had reviewed it while in the Senate. Rico lost the first round; he appealed to the General Land Office in Washington, and there the matter rested when Teller became secretary. Henry reversed the decision in July 1882 and ordered that the patent be issued to the town intact. Naturally, the Ricoites were elated at the turn of events and commended him "in the manner [in] which he conducted the case."

Teller's image was also helped when he sent a letter to the Senate Appropriations Committee requesting federal funds for the 1882 National Mining and Industrial Exposition in Denver. The exposition would serve, local papers boasted, "as a means of exhibiting products and manufacturers [not only] of the West, but [of] the whole country."

Westerners also approved of his handling of mining matters. The Geological Survey, although cutting back fieldwork to attend to "the publication of the large amount of scientific matter on hand," still conducted an economic geology study of Summit County's Ten-Mile District just outside Leadville. In addition, it studied the Denver coal basin and Nevada's Eureka District. In 1882 the survey compiled lists of mines and mining statistics from the 1880 census for publication. Two years later the Geological Survey, again busy in the field, conducted topographical surveys in six western states and the southern Appalachian region and finished a map of Massachusetts.

In 1884 the survey created a division to study volcanic rocks in "relation to the occurrence of gold and silver ores." Overall, it kept crews in the field and continued special economic studies of mining districts in Nevada, California, and Colorado. Miners, mining men, and investors throughout the country appreciated what the survey was accomplishing. A pleased Teller noted in his annual report that in "the work of the Geological Survey there has been a material increase in comparison with preceding years. The work of this Bureau is greatly varied in character, but may be said to consist of two principal divisions, one of topography and one of geology."[12]

Teller drew accolades when he allowed the "cutting of timber for domestic use and mining use" on government land. A Colorado newspaper promptly praised the decision as showing "both . . . good sense and knowledge of the requirements of the mining industry." The *Rocky Mountain News* went even further and described what many westerners had thought of the department before Teller's arrival: "The promptness of action on the part of Secretary Teller in the premises and the clear common sense and sound legal construction of the statute, manifested in this decision, marks a new era in the old, slow and easy ways and stupid construction of statutes by the Interior Department."

To implement the plan, Teller had to overturn the decision of the land commissioner, who was trying to restrict such cutting despite the heated protests of westerners. The secretary was not finished with the issue of federal timber reserves in the West.

Henry also received plaudits for trying to resolve fraud occurring in the West involving the homestead, timber culture, and preemption laws, all of which could be manipulated by fraudulent practices that hurt the "ordinary American." Not everything went in the West's favor, though. Much to some westerners' displeasure, the Interior Department cracked down, through the Department of Justice, on illegal fencing of public lands by ranchers and some farmers. The difficulty in protecting public land, Teller explained in 1884, demanded that more "liberal appropriations should be made for the detection and punishment of fraud on the Government through the agency of said laws." Congress did not agree, and the problems continued.

The issue of land "frauds" agitated Coloradans when it became entwined with the issue of foreign land owners in Estes Park. A decade of complaints finally moved the Senate to request that the Interior Department look into the matter. After studying the problem, Teller sent the Senate a report complaining about the complexity and multiplicity of land laws. He did accuse one foreign company of fraud and compiled a list of foreigners' land holdings in the United States. Westerners wanted foreign investors and investment, not foreign ownership and monopolistic control.

In 1882 Teller oversaw the Utah commission appointed to investigate bigamy in that territory. The law "excluding polygamists from the exercise of suffrage" appeared to be working, or so Americans assumed. Utah's territorial legislature granted women the right to vote in 1870, second only to Wyoming. Maybe women would end the practice.

The "vexed question" of polygamy energized and infuriated many Victorians and pushed Mormon Utah beyond the pale of respectability. The commission did not resolve the concern, but it did recommend that Congress pass a law declaring that the "first or legal wife be declared a competent witness in all prosecutions for 'polygamy, bigamy, or unlawful cohabiting.'" The commissioners held out the hope that the enforcement of the law "will place polygamy in a condition of gradual extinction, and that the domination that is complained of by non-Mormons in Utah, and elsewhere, will, at no distant day, be much ameliorated." Teller had not seen the end of this issue either.[13]

Teller spent more time reviewing and discussing railroad matters than he did dealing with any issue except problems with Native Americans. Isolation and distance faced all westerners, and they knew the answer lay with the railroads. Americans had fallen in love with their steam locomotives and iron rails. The post–Civil War federal government spent much time, money, and effort trying to resolve westerners' problems through railroading, starting with the building of the transcontinental railroad by the Central Pacific and the Union Pacific. This led to graft and scandals as early as the 1870s when the infamous scandal involving the Credit Mobilier touched many congressmen. Teller sympathized with the problems of railroads in the unpopulated and geographically challenging West.

By Teller's day, much of the Interior Department's involvement proved routine. For instance, the Central Pacific and Union Pacific property and accounts of these companies each year had "been carefully and fully examined." The Northern Pacific, building westward from Minnesota and eastward from Portland, Oregon, received praise for "the rapidity with which construction has been progressing." Other railroads' reports were scrutinized and a summary was published, but that stopped after 1882.

Congress had encouraged such building by giving land grants to many railroads. Unexpectedly, this caused some problems in the West because if a railroad did not complete its road, it did not receive title to the land. This left a potential land buyer or farm purchaser in a quandary. Teller returned to the issue of lapsed land grants on several occasions, pointing out that problems existed for westerners—or anyone—trying to purchase land. He recommended that "some means of adjustment of these grants be provided" to allow the Interior Department to "reach a finality as to the titles and thus relieve an anxious and excited public feeling."

Another issue that vexed Henry and his department was the taxation of railroad lands. Land ownership, though, remained paramount to resolve a host of problems. In 1884, after two previous discussions, he angrily exploded: "I again call attention to the necessity for some legislation to compel the railed companies that have earned the land granted to them to take a patent therefore" so that states or territories "may have the benefits derived from taxing the lands within their boundaries." Of the estimated 34 million acres granted to the railroads, only 8 million had been patented. The matter perturbed Teller and a generation of western politicians and voters. He trusted that this matter would "receive the early attention of Congress." It did not.[14]

Teller knew firsthand the problems and temptations that came with building railroads through a newly opened and generally unsettled land. The West needed railroads as much as it had in Henry's decade of involvement. With this modern transportation method, the future appeared unlimited. Teller well understood, too, that eastern investors and eastern railroads were beginning to dominate the West.

Reformers had tried to curb the growing political, economic, and general influence of the railroads with little success.

Teller further appreciated, from personal experience and from his time in the Senate, that a deep love-hate attitude existed toward the federal government. Westerners wanted the government to organize territories, conduct surveys, provide military protection, give away or sell land cheaply, and generously give natural resources to local people to develop.

What they did not want were rules, regulations, and government officials to stand in their way of developing the West for the benefit, they believed, of the whole country. They wanted some things and rejected others. Teller understood this dichotomy and attempted to strike a balance, which softened but did not resolve the duality.

During his years as secretary of the interior, Teller worked hard for his region and with some successes; however, Congress ignored many of his recommendations. His concerns about Yellowstone National Park and fraudulent public lands transactions were well-taken. The secretary repeatedly called for the repeal of the timber culture and preemption laws and also urged that the homestead laws be revised to protect genuine settlers from speculators or land grabbers. His advice to homesteaders to cut fences cattlemen erected on public lands shocked some people and angered cattlemen in his state and throughout the West. When President Arthur pushed for preservation of forests on the public domain, Teller responded with a cautiously hostile western attitude toward such an idea. The Geological Survey, with his encouragement, continued its valuable field and publishing work.

Homesteaders and others cheered his willingness to overrule decisions by the land commissioner when he felt settlers had not received justice. Yet he tried to find parity between the needs of corporations and those of the public, as shown in his handling of railroad matters. He could say with pride that none of his rulings on railroad land grants had been set aside by the courts.[15]

The former teacher cherished the topic of education for the youth of America throughout his tenure as secretary. As will be seen, he carried his education ideas into the major problem facing him: western tribes and their future.

The public throughout the country applauded his crusade against swindler pension agents and lawyers. His efforts to improve the efficiency of the department and hasten response to public concerns and questions captured approval. His honesty, "versatile talent," and executive ability also received praise from the eastern and western press. After the turn of the twentieth century, Teller's secretary, Thomas Dawson, commented: "One still hears the remark among oldtimers in Washington that he was the best Secretary the country ever had." Henry did receive criticism, however. He was "sharply assailed" by "interested parties" for his decisions on public lands, railroad grants, policy involving Native Americans, and other issues.

Overall, though, westerners and many others approved of his actions as secretary. His old Central City colleague Frank Hall wrote a decade later, "Teller's record stands practically unquestioned as one of the most efficient that has been made in that office." The *Chicago Inter-Ocean* stressed while he was still secretary that Teller "is winning golden opinions, both for excellent appreciation of his duties and for his honest method of enforcing them." The *St. Louis Globe Democrat* praised his "unexpected grasp of the business of his complex and comprehensive department." The newspaper maintained Teller "has grown steadily in public esteem since he went into office" and his management "reflects not [a] little credit upon the administration."[16]

Both Washington and Colorado praised Teller when he stepped down in March 1885 to resume his seat in the Senate. The Washington rumor mill had buzzed about a Teller nomination for vice president in 1884, but that had not come to pass. Whether he was indeed "the best secretary of the interior the country ever had," as some Colorado constituents claimed, would be left to history to decide. Teller certainly had, as longtime political colleague James Belford insisted, never lost "sight of what is for the best interests of the country and the west."[17]

Teller realized that not everything he did would please some people or even a majority of folks east of the Mississippi River. Sometimes what appeared best for the West clashed with what was best for the country. Henry also stressed at Leadville that his well-known "opinions on the Indian question" would provoke "much opposition to me [in] some parts of the country." He still expressed his ideas and opinions on the issue.

Through his hard work, integrity, executive ability, experience, and common sense, Teller had brought credit to both himself and the Arthur administration. Henry instituted some original and new ideas for operating the department, but he could not be described as an innovator or a diehard reformer. He could view his term with satisfaction, though. He had lived up to what he had said in Leadville: "I hope I may so discharge the duty of my office that when I lay down the trust no citizen of Colorado will be ashamed." Neither they nor the vast majority of Americans were upset or ashamed.

NOTES

1. R. G. Dill, *The Political Campaigns of Colorado* (Denver: Arapaho, 1895), 64–66; *Denver News*, August 2, 1897; *Rocky Mountain News*, June 23, July 20, 30, October 27, 1881; Teller to Dawson, April 18, 1883, Teller Collection, Colorado Historical Society.

2   Thomas C. Reeves, *Gentleman Boss: The Life of Chester Alan Arthur* (New York: Alfred A. Knopf, 1975), 250–259; George F. Howe, *Chester A. Arthur* (New York: Frederick Ungar, 1957 ed.), 162–163.

3. Teller interview in the *New York Times*, September 1, 1890; James Teller, "How Teller Became Sec. of the Interior," Teller Collection, Colorado Historical Society; Godkin cited in Reeves, *Gentlemen Boss*, 259; Dill, *Political Campaigns*, 65–66; *Daily Republican*, undated article, "Teller Scrapbook," Chris Buys private collection; *Rocky Mountain Herald*, January 21, 1922; *Georgetown Courier*, March 30, 1882; *Rocky Mountain News*, October 27, 1881.

4. *Evening Chronicle* (Leadville), August 22, 1882; *Rocky Mountain News*, August 5, 1883.

5. Frank Hall, *History of the State of Colorado* (Chicago: Blakely, 1890), vol. 3, 30; *Colorado Miner,* undated article, *Republican,* undated article, "Teller Scrapbook," Chris Buys private collection; Dill, *Political Campaigns,* 65; *Georgetown Courier,* March 23, 30, April 13, 1882; *Dolores News* (Rico), March 23, April 15, July 1, August 19, 1882.

6. Teller to Dawson, March 8, 1883, Teller Collection, Colorado Historical Society. See also Duane A. Smith, *Horace Tabor: His Life and the Legend* (Niwot: University Press of Colorado, 1989), chapters 12–13; *Daily Herald* (Leadville), November 2, 1883. Amanda Ellis relates a strange story about Teller at the wedding that does not fit his character; see Amanda Ellis, *The Strange, Uncertain Years* (Hamden, Conn.: Shoe String, 1959), 198.

7. Hall, *History of Colorado,* vol. 3, 30–31; *National Veteran,* undated article, "Teller Scrapbook," Chris Buys private collection; *Weekly Tribune* (Denver), April 20, 1882.

8. Henry Teller, *Report of the Secretary of the Interior 1884* (Washington, D.C.: Government Printing Office, 1884), xxxix–xl. See also reports of 1882 and 1883 for an overall view of the department.

9. Richard A. Bartlett, *Yellowstone: A Wilderness Besieged* (Tucson: University of Arizona Press, 1985), 123–127, 237–239; Aubrey L. Haines, *The Yellowstone Story* (Yellowstone, Wyo.: Yellowstone Library and Museum Association, 1977), vol. 1, 279, 288. See Teller's reports as secretary of the interior for 1882, 1883, and 1884 for Yellowstone issues.

10. See Teller's reports as secretary for 1883 and 1884; unidentified, undated article, "Teller Scrapbook," Chris Buys private collection.

11. *New York Times,* August 21, 1882. See Teller's reports as secretary for 1882, 1883, and 1884; unidentified letter found in Thomas Dawson, "Scrapbooks," Colorado Historical Society, vol. 61.

12. *Rocky Mountain News,* June 16, 1882; *Dolores News,* July 1, August 19, 1882. See Teller's reports as secretary for 1882, 1883, and 1884.

13. *Rocky Mountain News,* June 2, 16, 1882; undated clipping, Thomas Dawson, "Scrapbooks," Colorado Historical Society, vol. 61; W. Turrentine Jackson, *The Enterprising Scot* (Edinburgh: Edinburgh University, 1968), 102; Teller's reports as secretary of the interior for 1882, 1883, and 1884.

14. See Teller's reports as secretary of the interior for 1882, 1883, and 1885.

15. Reeves, *Gentleman Boss,* 360–366; *Washington Post, National Veteran,* undated articles, "Teller Scrapbook," Chris Buys private collection; *Denver Post,* February 23, 1914.

16. Hall, *History of Colorado,* vol. 2, 31, vol. 3, 31; Thomas Dawson, "Teller and Wolcott in Colorado Politics," manuscript, Colorado Historical Society; Reeves, *Gentleman Boss,* 363–364; *Chicago Inter-Ocean, Globe Democrat,* undated articles, "Teller Scrapbook," Chris Buys private collection.

17. *The Messenger* (Montrose), June 15, 1882; *Silverton Democrat,* January 23, 1885; Belford cited in undated, unidentified article, "Teller Scrapbook," Chris Buys private collection.

"The Indian Question"

In a speech at the Carlisle Indian School in May 1883, the guest of
honor, Secretary of the Interior Henry Teller, observed that he always
wished "to deal with this Indian question dispassionately and upon the
plain, common sense principles of national and political economy." A reporter called the address the event of the day, and it "produced the deepest
impression upon his hearers." The reporter's only regret was that the speech
could "not be spread in full over the whole country."

Ever since the arrival of English settlers in Jamestown, Virginia, and
Plymouth, Massachusetts, more than 260 years before, the "Indian question" had vexed both cultures. The longest-running U.S. Civil War had
started in 1622 in Virginia between two American armies fighting on
American soil for their way of life, homeland, and future. Although wind-
ing down, the struggle continued in the courts and on the military field in
such widespread western regions as Montana, Arizona, Indian Territory,
and California.

That question had bedeviled the federal government since its creation and secretaries of the interior since the first one had been appointed. Now, in the 1880s, a more vocal group of Americans attempted
to sway Congress and the public to turn toward justice for the tribes,
particularly those in the West who still struggled to maintain their
homeland. Many westerners, on the other hand, simply wanted them
removed so their land could be opened for settlement. Colorado had

just been through that dilemma. Teller, recall, had been an active player in the Ute question.

When Henry Teller became secretary of the interior, he was well versed on the question. Teller held strong opinions about what had happened in the past, why, and how it could be changed. In his first annual report in 1882, called "one of the best of its kind in over two decades," Teller illuminated some of the problems and answers as he saw them.

> One great hindrance to the civilization of the Indian has been his passion for war and chase.
>
> In our dealings with the Indian we have fostered his passion for war and the chase. We have allowed him to procure arms and ammunition, and in many instances have assisted him so to do.
>
> When the Indian can be compelled or persuaded to give up his gun, he will be ready to devote his energies to earning a living, instead of wasting them in the chase or in raids on the frontier settlements.
>
> [The tribal system] is the best and only system adapted to the wants of the savage, or even partially civilized Indian, and its maintenance, for a time at least, is essential to success in attempting his civilization.
>
> Reservations ought to be sufficient for the support of the Indians who reside on them . . . but they should not be disproportionate to the wants of the Indians.
>
> The subject of Indian education has been one of interest to the people ever since the early settlement of the country.

For the next few years, Secretary Teller would work hard to carry out the ideas expressed in these statements, focusing on such key words as *civilizing, earning a living, assimilation,* and *education.*

Nevertheless, one idea stood out above all others in Teller's mind—the problem of education: "Within the past ten years much interest has been awakened among the people with reference to the cause of Indian education, and the national legislation on that subject has been in answer to the demand made by the people." Teller had no qualms: "The Indians being capable of and willing to receive an education, it cannot be doubted that is the duty of the government to provide the means."[1]

Henry Teller had always been interested in education. Henry agreed with the sage of his youth, Ralph Waldo Emerson, that "in yourself slumbers the whole of Reason; it is for you to know all; it is for you to dare all." It would be expected, then, that the education of Indian youth would be one of his main concerns as secretary of the interior.

In an August 1, 1881, letter, Teller discussed the difficulties with Indian education. Optimistically, he did not believe they were insurmountable, notwithstanding that the effects of the past 200 years were seemingly a failure. These young people could be made "useful citizens" if the government made "ample provision for putting the children in a properly conducted school." Teller wanted them to learn the "practical affairs of life" and also how to read. Education and labor (the "practical affairs") would place them "not far from civilization and usefulness [to] society."

Indian education in prior years had three primary goals: to teach the child the rudiments of reading, writing, and speaking English; to assist him and her to walk the Christian road; and to provide citizenship training. To help achieve these goals, in the 1870s the government had doled out reservation agencies to various church groups. Despite the best of intentions, the program had not worked well. Politics, church rivalries and jealousy, and personal ineptness interfered.

Despite his educational background, the impression swirled around Washington that Teller was not especially interested in education.[2] Washington did not know the man. He possessed liberal views on the subject and stood ready to act for himself.

After the Civil War, the question of what to do with the native peoples of the mountains, plains, and deserts increasingly confronted the American people and their government. Each year's delay in addressing the issue made the solution more difficult. Various ideas were tried, but by the time Teller became secretary, the idea of educational assimilation was at the forefront. Schools were being operated on reservations, but Indian parents' objections to white education, chronic absenteeism, and runaway students dimmed prospects for success. Reservation and off-reservation boarding schools offered advantages in stopping absenteeism and runaway students and consequently slipped into vogue.

Like his predecessor Carl Schurz, Teller hammered at the education theme. To a cost-conscious Congress and public, Henry rang a financial bell. He calculated that over a ten-year period the expense of waging war against the tribes and providing protection for western communities ran in excess of $22 million annually, a figure nearly four times what it cost to educate 30,000 children for a year. He successfully carried forward the program he inherited and expanded it. In his 1884 report Teller proudly pointed out, "There are now 81 boarding-schools, 76 day-schools, and 6 industrial or manual labor schools under Government control." Yet sadly, a short-sighted Congress remained stingy and negligent. The secretary went on to report that even at that, "14 boarding- and 4 day-schools are supplied with teachers and other employees, by some one of the various religious denominations, the Government paying a stipulated price for the care and education of the children therein." Why? Teller spoke bluntly: "This course has been necessitated by lack of sufficient appropriations to provide for all the children willing to receive an education."[3]

The subject of Indian education appeared in Teller's first report as secretary, along with the annual plea for additional financial support. Henry strongly argued "that he [Indian children] is capable has been fully demonstrated." He turned to the continually pressing issue: "The number of Indian children in school is limited to the provisions made for their support. Many more might be added if the appropriation was sufficiently liberal for their support."

In Teller's eyes and those of many of his contemporaries, the purpose of this expense for Indian education was simple: "to relieve the government ultimately of his support and dependency." That would never be accomplished, however, if they educated only a small fraction of a tribe's children. "If we educate a few Indian children out of the many in a tribe," Teller warned ardently, "the influence of the many uneducated will be more powerful than the influence of the few educated, and the educated will soon go back to the savage ways of the more numerous class."

The answers, Teller concluded, were "manual-labor schools, and more attention should be paid to teaching them to labor than [to] read. Neither should be neglected." His conclusion and that of other reformers was that "they can be made skillful farmers and mechanics much more readily than they can be made scholars." The idea of their assimilation into white society underlay these ideas, and Teller clearly expressed that fact when he wrote, "While in school they should be allowed to speak English only."[4]

Teller also advocated improving agency schools to educate children who "cannot be sent away." He saw military posts no longer needed and thought converting them into boarding schools would be cost-effective. He never ventured far afield from his theme of saving money.

During June 1882 Harriet and Henry visited the school at Carlisle, Pennsylvania, the crown jewel of the government's boarding school system, for a two-day inspection. Teller expressed clearly some of his opinions on Indian education, stressing to the assembled students how important education was to them and encouraging them to stay in school. Interestingly, he observed, he felt "education was what made the white man different from the Indian." That belief undergirded his educational philosophy.

In concluding his brief remarks, the secretary reverted to a favorite theme: manual labor. Education should not only teach reading and writing, the girls should learn sewing, cooking, and housekeeping; the boys farming and the trades. In this he echoed Emerson's observation, "there is virtue yet in the hoe and the spade, for learned as well as for unlearned hands. And labor is everywhere welcome."

Impressed by what he had seen at Carlisle, Teller pushed even harder to expand the off-reservation boarding school system. Among other ideas, Henry proposed a plan to create a permanent fund to finance Indian education by setting aside a portion of public land sales. Congress failed to act. His other idea, to give graduates of off-reservation schools a fully equipped farm to "prevent them from slipping back," also went no further.[5]

Congress authorized the appointment of an official inspector of Indian schools in the early 1880s, and during Teller's administration that individual became superintendent of Indian schools. The real issue, however, remained finances. In his 1883 report, Teller pleaded with Congress to honor its obligations. Many treaties, he pointed out, contained provisions for the "support of a school for every thirty children." Although implementing that plan may not be desirable, Teller argued, the provision was "inserted in consideration of the cession of land, and thus must be considered not as a gratuity but a payment to be made." The money could be used for educational purposes, such as building schoolhouses. The secretary urgently reminded his readers that "these obligations are as sacred as the public debt, and every argument that can be used in favor of strict probity in dealing with the creditors of the Government can be used with reference to these obligations."

Unfortunately, too few people considered these obligations a sacred trust. Education of Indian youth should have been of interest and concern to other taxpayers whose taxes maintained the tribes on reservations. Education would transfer these youth "from the list of non-producers to that of producers," and the public would be "relieved from the burden of their support." The public appeared not to be listening.[6]

Teller and those who supported Indian education and reform found time running out. Settlement and technology had caught up with the western tribes, and if the Indians and their culture were going to be saved, their supporters had to hurry. Opponents argued that the tribes retarded settlement and therefore national prosperity and needed to be pushed as far out of the way as possible. The reformers countered with a suggestion to quickly absorb them into the dominant society and culture where they could partake of the benefits of the "civilized world." Teller agreed more with the reformers than with their opponents, even if he was being pressured by his own state to end the "Ute problem."

Many Indian reform advocates, however, did not think the Indian culture was worth preserving. A "saved" Indian would become educated and civilized, would acquire an "acceptable" occupation, and would have "gotten right with God"—that is, the white man's God. That seemed more important than preserving the "inferior" Indian culture. Even the most sympathetic individuals realized that eventually certain aspects of native culture would be destroyed as assimilation and Americanization took place. Education and U.S. society would change them, just as it had the immigrants and the customs they brought with them when they flocked to American shores in the 1860s, 1870s, and 1880s.

Teller continued to focus on education for tribes, particularly manual education. The education problem persisted; Henry had neither the time nor the finances to make it work to best advantage. It would take at least a generation to see practical results, and Americans were not that patient or willing to spend the money needed.[7]

Long after he left the Interior Department, Henry would still be involved in the debate about how to answer this pressing question. He did see one of his cherished ideas develop. The off-reservation boarding school became a feature of Indian educational policy, along with assimilation, for the next twenty years. Two of the most notable schools operated in his home state. Near Grand Junction, the Teller Institute opened in 1886, and in the southwestern corner of Colorado, the Fort Lewis military post was converted into a boarding school in 1891–1892. Both schools nearly matched expectations. Some others did not. Homesickness and sickness plagued the schools (twenty-three in 1897), as did finding qualified teachers, developing a curriculum that worked, and finding students willing to leave their families and tribes to attend the schools.

During his term as secretary, Teller was pressured by noted Indian reformer Helen Hunt Jackson. Although they developed a congenial working relationship,

Henry failed to go far enough for her on some issues. The novelist and poet published her most famous book, *A Century of Dishonor,* the year before Teller assumed office. Living in Colorado Springs with her husband, William Jackson, who did not always share her views, as he said, of "these unworthy and troublesome children," Helen emerged as the popular champion of the plight of the American Indian. Her volume proved effective for arousing the public. Not since *Uncle Tom's Cabin* had a book so incited Americans to the cause of reform.

Jackson, at her own expense, had sent copies of her book to every congressman, and Teller knew she had called his predecessor Schurz "an adroit liar," among other things. Her present concern was the California Mission Indians, a cause that led to her fictional story "Ramona." Others wanted their land, and they were in the way.

Helen became convinced that the agent for the Mission Indians had done a poor job of defending their rights. She bombarded both Commissioner of Indian Affairs Hiram Price and Teller about the problems the Indians faced. She pleaded for government protection lest "they be driven off their lands." Do something "sharp and decisive for the protection of all these old Mission Indians," she pleaded in June 1882. Finally, Teller authorized her appointment as a special agent to visit the Mission Indians and try to locate suitable land for them. Teller told Price "she should furnish such minute descriptions of such lands if found as will enable this department to draft an executive order for setting them aside as Indian reservations."

The initial problem consisted of finding the money for Jackson. They used what Henry called the "civilization fund." Price, dedicated to Indian reform, outlined for Helen what he hoped would be accomplished: "The promptings of humanity, as well as a sense of justice, demand that these Indians should be placed in a position where the fruits of their labor will be for their own benefit, and where unprincipled white men cannot in the future, as in the past, deprive them of what is justly their own." Teller supported the Mission Indians, and other native people as well, by allowing no homesteading on their land. Such an intrusion, he argued, "though made under the pretension of preempting the land, was but a naked trespass."

Jackson experienced typical government delays in payment of her expenses (she received no salary), which resulted in much correspondence in 1882–1883. She continued her efforts regardless and in August 1883 touched former teacher Teller's heart. The salary of the teacher at Saboba had been reduced, she pointed out sadly. That teacher had been doing a fine job, Helen argued, and had achieved a close and affectionate relationship with her pupils. Not "one out of ten thousand could be hired for any sum to lead such a dreary, desolate life, and endure such deprivations." Teller promptly restored the salary.[8]

Her final report (July 13, 1883), fifty-six pages long, dealt mostly with Mission Indians in California's three southernmost counties. The recommendations included resurveying the reservation, removing whites from that land, moving the Indians or upholding their claims, establishing more schools that emphasized religious and industrial training, and implementing a "judicious distribution of farm equipment."

Teller submitted the draft of a bill to President Arthur, who sent it to Congress on January 14, 1884. The bill passed the Senate, then failed in the House. Jackson had been dead for six years and Teller was back in the Senate before a bill for the "relief of the Mission Indians in the State of California" finally passed Congress in January 1891 and was signed by President Benjamin Harrison.

Jackson was too late in defending the Mission Indians. White pressure and diseases had drastically reduced their land and numbers. Euro-American settlers' quest for land throughout the West proved too strong. Yet Jackson, with Teller's and Price's support, had awakened interest and an expanding desire to help among many people. "Her legacy," a biographer wrote, "was that, as a single woman, she undertook the tremendous task of alerting the public to the condition of the Mission Indians—a task she succeeded at eloquently."[9]

Teller praised Helen Hunt Jackson in his 1883 report: "Mrs. Jackson, having spent some time in California studying the history of these people, was well qualified for the work; besides, she has given much attention to the Indian question, and was known to have their interest much at heart."

The plight of the Mission Indians touched Henry's heart; still, there seemed little he could do in many areas, not just California. Americans' belief in manifest destiny, combined with their racial attitudes, greed for land, and lack of understanding and respect for the tribes and their culture, doomed many Indian reformers in the era. Teller never gave up; he launched several plans and advocated ideas that carried beyond his administration.

The secretary directed the commissioner of Indians Affairs, former Iowa congressman and businessman Hiram Price, to develop rules to abolish certain "rites and customs injurious to Indians." One result of this action was the development of a system of Indian courts. Teller explained in his 1884 report that the commissioner, "under my direction, in 1883, established a tribunal for the punishment of crimes among the Indians on their reservations, and entitled it a 'court of Indian offenses.' "

Teller enthusiastically supported the idea and thought it was successful. Joined by Indian police, the tribes could regulate themselves and take a step on the road to civilization, learning "to respect the rights and property of [their] fellows." Scholars have since taken a less enthusiastic view of the project, which reached its peak about 1900 with nearly two-thirds of the agencies having courts. With a vague legal basis, the courts functioned in selected areas—specifically having jurisdiction over dances, polygamous marriages, interference of medicine men, thefts, intoxication, the liquor trade, and misdemeanors.[10]

These matters were of particular concern to the secretary. He wrote in December 1882, "I desire to call your attention to what I regard as a great hindrance to the civilization of the Indians, viz., the continuance of the old heathenish dances, such as the sun-dance, scalp-dance, etc."

Polygamy among the tribes caught his attention, too, a practice he blamed on the government! He told Congress that the great "mass found themselves too poor to support more than one" wife, adding "since the government supports them this objection no longer exists and the more numerous the family the greater the number of rations allowed."

Medicine men, Teller and others concluded, "are always found with the antiprogressive party." Understanding the value of property, on the other hand, he considered "an agent of civilization." When an Indian acquires property "with a disposition to retain the same free from tribal or individual interference, he has made a step forward in the road of civilization." His conclusions and approach did not differ from many reformers of the era. The end project they all envisioned was to "civilize the Indians." To do this they "must be compelled to desist from the savage and barbarious practices that are calculated to continue them in savagery." Few bothered to try to understand how the beneficiaries of the government programs might feel about them.[11]

In another matter, Teller continued the policy of his predecessor—ending the government policy of giving agencies to various church denominations to administer. Teller appointed agents without regard to their religious affiliations, a policy for which he was widely criticized. When the secretary of the Methodist Board of Mission complained, Teller replied frankly, "I do not believe that the government has discharged its duty" when it turned the Indian matter over to churches. The Methodist Board did not like being told that as a result of this policy, "some of the grossest frauds have been perpetrated on the Indians and the government known in the history of Indian affairs."

Teller mustered out of service as many Methodists and like-minded brethren as he could. President Grant's heralded missionary peace policy thus came to an end.[12] Teller and Schurz had been correct; the policy had not worked well, and clearly in Teller's mind the denominational mission schools sadly had been little better than the ones they replaced. Concern had existed from the start over the separation of church and state. Now Teller's education policy would move forward without church hindrance.

Another dilemma that came to a head during his administration concerned cattlemen leasing Indian land, which had been done under arrangements made by the various tribes. That provoked Teller. He indicated that the amount "paid for such privileges is understood to be about 2 cents per acre." Double or triple that amount would be more fair, Teller believed.

The secretary recommended to Congress in 1884 that "some legislation should be had on the subject to enable the Government to demand and receive for the Indians the full value for the occupation of their lands, and to prevent conflicts between rival claimants holding such licenses or privileges." Interestingly, he expressed no objection to the tribes in Indian Territory leasing their lands but raised "serious objection" to those on reservations outside the territory leasing lands. Teller feared, often correctly, that such leasing proposals merely masked schemes to seize tribal land. Neither side was happy with his thoughts about the matter.

His attitude reflected another of Teller's long-held concerns: the belief that reservations were too large. If the reservation proved larger than required for tribal use so the tribes had surplus land to lease, the size should be reduced, "and all that is not needed for the use of the Indians should be opened to settlement." Teller, reflecting generations of western attitudes, maintained: "The time has passed when large and valuable tracts of land fit for agriculture can be held by Indians for either hunting or grazing lands to the exclusions of actual settlers."[13]

Reformers criticized both Teller and Arthur, whom they accused of bowing to western pressure for land. Their defenders called it a "wise and sane policy." When Teller convinced the president to open land in the Crow Creek Reservation in Montana Territory, reformers attacked the plan. Unquestionably, it all fit Teller's idea of self-sufficiency and assimilation of these people. The plan would, he argued, allow "sufficient land for each Indian to make them self supporting [and] self-dependent" and would open the rest for homesteaders.

Teller determinedly stayed the course. In his speech at Carlisle back in May 1883, he had ardently preached that the "time had come to teach the Indian to take care of himself." Without doubt, he had faith in Indians' "capabilities for improvement." If—and it remained a big if—the government would give him the money needed for industrial education and for his other ideas, the result, he asserted, would be the "final solution to the long-vexed Indian problem." At worst, it would "prove to the world the race is incapable of civilization." That was not his conclusion however.[14]

Paralleling these ideas was his view on severalty. In many people's minds, the hope for resolving the dilemma involving the tribes fixed on breaking up the reservations and granting individual tribal members an allotment. The rest of the land would then be opened to settlement. Indian rights reformers and various religious and women's groups supported this idea. Teller had opposed the plan even before he became secretary of the interior.

In a remarkable speech on January 20, 1881, and in the subsequent debate, Teller presented his views, foreshadowing what would go wrong when the government finally succumbed and tried the idea. In the debate he stood against the president, the current secretary of the interior, the commissioner of Indian affairs, and others: "I know the enormity of the crime of differing with such high and intelligent authority on this matter." With his wry sense of humor he joked, "I am running amuck against all the intelligence and all the virtue of the country, and therefore I must be wrong." In the long run he voted his conscience, believing he had "a heart that beats as warmly for the Indians as that of any other man living."

Teller argued that giving the Indians land would not civilize and Christianize them but that civilizing and Christianizing them would give them an understanding and appreciation of land holding. Severalty, in reality, would result in the Indians losing and selling their land: "If I stand alone in the Senate, I want to put upon the record my prophecy in this matter that when thirty or forty years shall have passed and these Indians shall have parted with their title, they will curse the hand that was raised professed in their defense to secure this kind of legislation." From experience, Teller understood that "Indians differ as much one from another as civilized and enlightened nations of the earth differ from the uncivilized and unenlightened nations of the earth."

Henry pleaded that if "those clamoring for [severalty] understood the Indian character, and Indian laws, and Indian morals and Indian religion, they would not be here clamoring for this at all." In that prediction he proved absolutely correct. The bill, he asserted, benefited "the interest of speculators; it is in the interest of the men who are clutching up this land, but not in the interest of the Indians at all."

In the debate that followed, Teller used history to bolster his argument. The question of severalty was not new; "a careful examination of history will prove that it has been an entire failure." Teller never wavered: "I say it in no unkind spirit, the bill ought to be entitled a bill to despoil the Indians of their lands and make them vagabonds on the earth, and a few years will demonstrate that what has been true heretofore with the Indians will be true hereafter."[15]

Teller did not think the encouraging reports of various agents year after year regarding their wards' progress were correct; he believed the truth lay in the opposite direction. His noble defense of tribal land ownership, now and later, did not sway his colleagues.

The aftermath of the Meeker troubles also haunted him, as did the question of the remaining Utes in southwestern Colorado. Josie Meeker lived and worked in Washington. In summer of 1882 Teller promoted her to his assistant private secretary, the last ray of sunshine for this unfortunate young woman. She contracted pneumonia just before Christmas and died on December 29. Teller attended her funeral along with her African American Sunday School class and a hundred other mourners.

The question of what to do with the Utes had not been settled in Coloradans' minds by the time Teller became secretary. Ouray had helped save the Southern Ute land before he died, but settlement grew in surrounding La Plata County and booming Durango. Again the old cry was heard: "The Ute must go." Montrose's *Messenger* (June 29, 1882) expressed the opinion of many Coloradans when it hoped the secretary would make the Utes "toe the mark."

Teller, who argued during the 1881 debate that Ute land was unfit for cultivation because the "arid and worthless land" suffered frosts every month and lacked water, had to confront the local assertion that the land actually appeared to be a "garden of Eden." Rumors persisted, too, that "remarkably" rich mining prospects existed on Ute land.[16] The questions would not go away.

Although Teller differed with Indian reformers on most issues, the newly formed Indian Rights Association applauded some of his efforts. The group especially appreciated his work to secure increased money for Indian education and in 1885 printed 2,000 copies of his speech containing his views. His conflicts with eastern reformers, however, reflected a decades-long difference between East and West regarding the Indian question. Theory and idealism ran headstrong into common sense and experience mixed with a dash of greed and cultural differences. Education had always been his main goal. Teller had not achieved his hopes, but at least he had made the public and Congress more aware of the issues and realities.

Teller moved cautiously on most Indian matters and tried to stay realistic, insisting that "men who have some knowledge of Indian affairs have a right to be heard." His insistence on practicality and thoroughness in working out proper solutions exasperated some reformers and others. The secretary realized far better than many that the Indian question would take time to resolve, but even he misjudged how much time.[17]

Henry Teller continued to be a leader in Indian education legislation. His impact is still felt in one area at least. In his last year in the Senate (1909), as the government was phasing out the off-reservation boarding schools, Teller added an amendment to an Indian appropriations bill. It stated that Fort Lewis, in the process of being transferred to Colorado, must be used for educational purposes. A clause was written into the transfer contract that "Indian pupils shall at all times be admitted to such school free of charge for tuition and on terms of equality with white pupils." They are still admitted today to what is now Fort Lewis College.

If Teller is evaluated against his generation and its objectives regarding native peoples, he must be considered a progressive. Assimilation by walking the white woman's and white man's road was the expected and rapidly anticipated goal. Americans, especially westerners, had little patience for idealism or cultural considerations. Teller understood both sides of the Indian question better than most. His emphasis on practical, industrial education was the principal answer available, as was retaining the tribal organization and the reservation until education had prepared the Indians for the world beyond their traditional life.

Teller's actions and efforts as secretary of the interior should put to rest the charge that he "hated" Indians. He did make his views better known and continued to fight after he left office. Perhaps the best tribute to his efforts was made by his longtime political ally James Belford. Trying to allay some people's fears in summer of 1882, Belford predicted Teller would be the "best secretary of the interior" the country ever had. He went on to affirm: "The People of Colorado may be assured that in Mr. Teller they have a secretary who will never lose sight of what is for the best interests of the country and the west." Although it can be debated whether Teller was the best secretary ever, it cannot be said that he did not try to do his best for the country as a whole while balancing decisions against the West's interests.

NOTES

1. Teller's May 1883 speech found in an unidentified, undated article, "Teller Scrapbook," Chris Buys private collection; Henry Teller, *Report of the Secretary of the Interior 1882* (Washington, D.C.: Government Printing Office, 1883), iii–xvii; *Dolores News,* May 3, 1882; Thomas C. Reeves, *Gentleman Boss: The Life of Chester Alan Arthur* (New York: Alfred A. Knopf, 1975), 262, 264.

2   Ralph Waldo Emerson, "The American Scholar," *American Poetry and Prose* (Cambridge: Riverside, 1957), 489; unidentified letter, August 1, 1881, Thomas Dawson,

"Scrapbooks," Colorado Historical Society, vol. 61; unidentified newspaper article, "Teller Scrapbook," Chris Buys private collection; David W. Adams, *Education for Extinction* (Lawrence: University of Kansas Press, 1995), 21–24.

3. Henry Teller, *Report of the Secretary of the Interior 1884* (Washington, D.C.: Government Printing Office, 1885), iii–iv; Adams, *Education for Extinction*, 18–20, 55–59.

4. Teller, *Report of the Secretary of the Interior 1882*, xii–xvi.

5. Three unidentified newspaper articles, unidentified article, June 18, 1882, Teller Scrapbook, Chris Buys private collection; Donald MacKendrick, "Cesspools, Alkali and White Lily Soap," *Journal of the Western Slope* (summer 1993), 3; Emerson, "The American Scholar," 485.

6. Henry Teller, *Report of the Secretary of the Interior 1883* (Washington, D.C.: Government Printing Office, 1884), viii–ix; Adams, *Education for Extinction*, 16–17, 29–30; Robert M. Kvasnicka and Herman Viola (eds.), *The Commissioners of Indian Affairs, 1824–1977* (Lincoln: University of Nebraska Press, 1979), 173–176.

7. For further discussion of this problem during Teller's administration, see Adams, *Education for Extinction*, 15–20; Francis Prucha, *American Indian Policy in Crisis* (Norman: University of Oklahoma Press, 1976), 270–272.

8. Sources for the section on Jackson and Teller are found in Helen Hunt Jackson Papers, Tutt Library, Colorado College; Valerie Sherer Mathes, "Helen Hunt Jackson: A Legacy of Indian Reform," *Essays and Monographs in Colorado History* 4 (1986), 49–55; Valerie Sherer Mathes, *Helen Hunt Jackson and Her Indian Reform Legacy* (Norman: University of Oklahoma Press, 1996 reprint), ix–x, chapter 4.

9. Mathes, *Jackson and Her Indian Reform Legacy*, 161–162.

10. Teller, *Report 1883*, ix–x; Prucha, *American Indian Policy*, 208–210.

11. Teller, *Report 1883*, x–xii. See also report of 1884.

12. Teller cited in Reeves, *Gentleman Boss*, 363–364; Prucha, *American Indian Policy*, 62–63; Mathes, *Jackson and Her Indian Reform Legacy*, 4–5.

13. Teller, *Report 1884*, x–xi; Loring Priest, *Uncle Sam's Stepchildren* (New York: Octagon, 1969), 160.

14. *National Veteran*, undated, unidentified article, "Teller Scrapbook," Chris Buys private collection; Peter Winne, "Sketches of the Indian Wars," *The Trail* (April 1912), 5–6; George F. Howe, *Chester A. Arthur* (New York: Frederick Unger, 1957 ed.), 212–213; Prucha, *American Indian Policy*, 130–131; Reeves, *Gentleman Boss*, 363–364.

15. Teller cited in Wilcomb E. Washburn (ed.), *The American Indian and the United States*, vol. 2 (New York: Random House, 1973), 1694, 1698, 1703–04, 1761, 1781–83, 1825; Prucha, *American Indian Policy*, 247; MacKendrick, "Cesspools," 3; Priest, *Uncle Sam's Stepchildren*, 224.

16. Washburn, *The American Indian*, vol. 2, 1699; *Inter-Ocean* (Denver), July 29, 1882; Marshall Sprague, *Massacre: The Tragedy at White River* (Boston: Little, Brown, 1957), 321; *Weekly Republican*, March 3, 1882; *Dolores News*, August 26, 1882; *Gothic Miner*, September 3, 1881; Reeves, *Gentleman Boss*, 364.

17. Priest, *Uncle Sam's Stepchildren*, 85; "Indian Rights Association Papers," microfilm, Center of Southwest Studies, Fort Lewis College, Durango, Colorado; Prucha, *American Indian Policy*, 135–136, 165; Teller cited in *The Messenger*, quoting the *Golden Transcript*, June 29, 1882; Dudley Cornish, "The First Five Years of Colorado Statehood," *Colorado Magazine* (September 1948), 231–232.

Photographic Essay: Henry Teller's Era

Colorado poet Thomas Hornsby Ferril has captured the time, spirit, and place of nineteenth-century Colorado as well as anyone in the twentieth century. His poem about Central City, "Magenta," has already been quoted. In another poem, "Two Rivers," he mused about the people who came to Denver and beyond those long years ago.

> Most of the time these people hardly seemed
> to realize they wanted to be remembered,
> Because the mountains told them not to die.

They did die, as did their era; only the mountains remain as they once were, and puny man changed even them in tiny ways. Most of these people would not be remembered, a fate that mattered little at the time because collectively Teller's generation left a heritage coming generations would expand on into the twenty-first century.

In the photographs that follow, ponder these Coloradans and their era. We will not see their like again.

Gilpin County placer mines started the excitement and were active throughout Teller's years there. Courtesy, Denver Public Library, Western History Department.

Hard rock mines and "stiffs" kept Gilpin County mining in Colorado's forefront for a generation; these miners worked at the Kansas Mine. Courtesy, Pettem/Raines Collection.

The Colorado Central Railroad Company took much of Teller's time; here, he has signed a stock certificate. Courtesy, Jay Hogan.

Henry Teller had both mining and legal ties to Caribou in neighboring Boulder County. Courtesy, Duane A. Smith.

Willard Teller followed Henry west from New York to Illinois to Colorado. Courtesy, Richard Tyler.

Colorado's premier early politician, and Teller's rival and later colleague, Jerome Chaffee. Courtesy, Duane A. Smith.

Nathaniel Hill saved Colorado mining with his smelter; later he was Teller's bitter rival. Courtesy, Colorado Historical Society.

Ambitious and ruthless, Edward Wolcott eventually made the wrong decision on the silver issue. Courtesy, Archives, University of Colorado.

Colorado's best-known nineteenth-century mining man, Horace Tabor. Courtesy, Henry E. Huntington Library.

Grand Rally!

A Feast for the Hungry

Senator Henry M.

Teller,

OF COLORADO,

WILL SPEAK AT

SOMERSET, KY.,

Monday, Sept. 21.

Senator Teller

Is a life-long Republican and was one of the founders of the Republican party. Come out and hear
this able advocate of the cause of Silver.

Hon. JO A. PARKER,

State Chairman of the Populist Committee, and

Hon. JAMES D. BLACK,

Democratic candidate for Congress in this District,
will also address the people.

Speaking from a Large
Stand on Public Square.

Reporter Print.

Teller campaigns in 1896. Courtesy, Chris Buys.

The Rocky Mountain News, *June 19, 1896, saluted Teller for his stand on silver. Courtesy, Duane A. Smith.*

Souvenir of the brief Teller presidential boomlet. Courtesy, Chris Buys.

One of the many Rocky Mountain News *editorial cartoons about Teller (April 13, 1899). Courtesy, Duane A. Smith.*

Teller for president pin. Courtesy, Duane A. Smith.

Two of Teller's longtime friends and backers, William Jennings Bryan and John Shafroth. Courtesy, Colorado Historical Society.

The Denver Republican *(May 15, 1902) did not like Teller's stand on the Philippine question. Courtesy, Chris Buys.*

Thomas Dawson, Teller's private secretary and friend. Courtesy, Colorado Historical Society.

Back to the Senate

Teller was never far removed from Colorado politics while he served in Arthur's cabinet. His split with Hill worsened as time passed, and it became even more paramount that Henry retain and buttress his state political foundation.

To complicate matters, Colorado politics boiled throughout these years as Leadville money and millionaires raced onto the scene, joining the mining men who already thirsted for political office. Teller's appointment as secretary of the interior set off the first scramble for his replacement as senator that throughout 1882 alternately fascinated and appalled Coloradans, as discussed earlier. Pueblo's George Chilcott, a longtime Republican from politically weak southern Colorado, gained the initial advantage when Governor Frederick Pitkin appointed him to fill the Senate vacancy until the legislature met in January 1883. Chilcott had too slight a base and too little money, so the advantage soon vanished. Almost everybody who was anybody decided he would make a fine U.S. senator—Thomas Bowen, Horace Tabor, John Routt, Frederick Pitkin, Henry Wolcott, William Hamill, and Jerome Chaffee. Republicans all, Democrats did not have a chance. The *Rocky Mountain News* guessed that there were over 150 candidates!

Denver's *Inter-Ocean* warned its readers that the Senate seat might become a plaything of the "Bonanza Kings": "Is Colorado to make these qualifications [ability and brains] a secondary consideration, and to make bonanzas the standard of fitness?" Later in the campaign the editor wondered if the politicians "would be able to trundle this state into their way of thinking." Would they "stifle the voice of the people?"

The Republican Party, meanwhile, openly broke into two factions. The Chaffee-Teller crowd, known as Windmills to their opponents because of their "tendency toward boastfulness," faced the Hill group, the Argonauts after the location of Hill's smelter at Argo near Denver. Hill wanted a friendly junior senator to serve with him and thus strengthen his reelection bid in 1885. Even more important, he also needed a pro-Hill governor and legislature. Challengers were already focused on his seat.

Two relative newcomers led the Hill charge—the Wolcott brothers, Henry and Edward. Ambitious, shrewd, and politically adept, they built a following in Clear Creek and Gilpin Counties, Teller's home bastion. Astute and opportunistic, Ed had hitched their fortunes to Hill back in 1878 after moving from Central to Georgetown. Now the Hill faction was advancing Henry for governor. Chaffee and Teller did not oppose Henry personally, but they were upset because he represented Hill. Neither side would forget a political defeat.

At stake, in order of prestige, were the Senate seat, the governor's chair, and the state legislature. Actually, the legislature was the most important because dominant party legislators decided who would be sent to Washington. In the background lurked what would happen with Hill's seat in 1885. The fight spread to every corner of the state and involved every newspaper. Money flowed freely.

With Teller in Washington and unable to do little more than advise, old pro Chaffee returned from New York—facing a carpetbag label—to lead his and Teller's forces against Hill. The old guard squared off against the young Turks, with the former enjoying richer coffers, longer involvement in local Republican politics, and an entrenched position.

The Windmills barely carried the state convention, thanks to Chaffee, money, and the event being held in the Tabor Grand Opera House, whose owner distributed passes to pack the gallery. The Argonauts were sent to the sidelines and stayed there for the duration of the campaign. Ed Wolcott convinced Hill to repudiate the ticket, which he did. That was a fatal error. The Democrats nominated one of their strongest candidates for governor, smelter man James Grant. Although Grant carried the day, the Republicans hung on to the legislature and the right to select the senator.

The party split, meanwhile, widened alarmingly with accusations of "scoundrelly and infamous" treachery and unbridled selfishness. It all came down to the fateful January 1883 meeting of the legislature.[1]

Henry initially announced that he would not be a candidate for senator and planned to finish his term as secretary. The *Rocky Mountain News* asked, "Is that a threat or a promise?" The paper wondered what would happen in two years when his friends would entreat him "to become Hill's opponent." Later, the *News* said Teller had suspended the policy "of disarming Indians" because he "is after hostile Argonauts at present." Pro-Teller and -Chaffee papers fought back, accusing Hill of bossism, "lying and a generally contemptible" prejudice. Hill's newspapers praised him:

"His work speaks for him in no uncertain terms." The *Inter-Ocean* (July 29, 1882) warned that if the Republican Party "goes to fooling too much at present with the prospective fight between Hill and Teller in 1884, there will be a risk of losing the state this fall."

With a few exceptions, Hill controlled the state machine, whereas Teller controlled federal patronage. At least to the press, it appeared a forgone conclusion that Henry would run in 1884.

Teller traveled west to Colorado in August and again in late October 1882. Not as partisan or as much an infighter as Chaffee, he was less inclined generally to mix in partisan quarrels. He had to retain his control in Gilpin County, however, which he did. He did hint in October that he would retire after his cabinet term expired to devote himself to his business affairs, which, Henry explained, had been "neglected to a considerable extent since he entered the Senate."

The political result of all this was an exciting legislative session that finally pitted Tabor versus Bowen. San Juan "bonanza king" and lawyer Thomas Bowen won the six-year term, and the Republicans unceremoniously dumped Chilcott and gave Tabor the remaining thirty days of Teller's term.

Teller had known Tabor for five years as Horace progressed from mining camp storekeeper to legendary millionaire. Tabor had asked Teller for assistance in the senatorial race. For Henry, the mere possession of wealth was not a justifiable criterion for election to the Senate, an opinion in which he was out of step with many of his Colorado contemporaries.

With his usual frankness, Teller advised the aspiring candidate: "You are mistaken in supposing that I could elect you. I could not do so if I wished and I would not if I could." He added that he felt this way "not because I do not like you and do not appreciate the use you have made of your money in the interest of the State, but because I know that you are not fitted by education, temperament, or general personal equipment for that office." Tabor's influence, particularly his finances, would continue to help shape Colorado Republican politics for a decade. Teller was not finished with Tabor, either.[2]

Candidates, meanwhile, had already started jockeying for Hill's Senate seat. Teller was in the cabinet, and if he bypassed the 1884–1885 election, the next seat would be Bowen's, which came up three years later. Henry had arrived at a crucial fork in his political career.

Teller's cabinet position rested on whether President Arthur would be nominated for a second term. Arthur had proven to be a better president than his career at the time he assumed the presidency might have suggested. He had won a place on the ticket to appease the Grant faction of the Republican Party, but the party reformers had never accepted him, and his one-time stalwart friends were upset by his handling of various matters. Ultimately, he was not renominated. The party turned to James G. Blaine in 1884, leaving the interior secretary's future in doubt.

Henry had considered retiring from politics if Arthur was not renominated. He had enjoyed in the past eight years honors and distinctions "rarely accorded" public men in so brief a period. No Coloradan since has matched his Senate and cabinet honors in such a short time. Further, he knew his political success would boost his legal career when he returned to private life. Teller carefully weighed the fact that his personal income and his practice had suffered over the past eight years of his public service. He needed to rebuild them for the future. His brother Willard and Harper Orahood, meanwhile, pressured him to return to their growing practice.

Pressure steadily built on Henry, however, to run for the Senate in 1884 against Nathaniel Hill. Many leading Republicans did not like the senior senator and wanted the best possible candidate to defeat him at the party convention. Teller thought former governor John Routt or Chaffee would be the best candidate. Teller's friends thought otherwise as Colorado Republicans jumped into another party fight.

Hill had done much for Colorado while in the Senate, but he proved, as one observer noted, "unsophisticated in the ways of politics." His faction's bolt in 1882 now came back to haunt him. Hill had the knack for making enemies, habitually held grudges, remembered slights, and did not forgive those who opposed him—all of which included a legion of Coloradans.

In a series of letters to newspaperman and friend Thomas Dawson, Teller described his feelings and political attitudes. Teller had met Dawson in summer of 1876 when he came to work for the *Denver Tribune,* and the friendship had grown.[3]

Talk of a bolt if one side or the other did not get its way aroused Henry's anger: "The men who bolt the ticket ought not to be rewarded." (Henry seemed to ignore the fact that he had done the same thing.) Was he a candidate? No, he confided to Dawson in November 1883, not at the moment: "I am not a candidate for anything. I may desire to be, however, and if I do shall so declare without hesitation."

Hurt and stung by attacks from Hill's leading newspaper, the *Denver Republican,* which during the campaign became the *Denver Tribune-Republican,* Teller commented privately on Hill as a senator and politician. Henry felt Hill claimed achievements not rightfully his; he could not be trusted, was sometimes untruthful, and appeared to be trying to destroy the state party for his own gain. Hill rather spitefully had threatened to investigate Teller's conduct as secretary of the interior, which led to these comments over a series of letters.

> He tells everybody even to the waiters and servants about the Capitol that he will investigate the Interior Department. . . .
> I only want him to put himself where I can meet him; if he will move the investigation he talks of I will show him up. . . .
> Now I do not want you to take any pains to defend me for I do not think I need it.
> But I want you to know that Sen. Hill's attacks on the Dept. will only make him [look] ridiculous and will do me no harm here. . . .
> He reports all sorts of stuff about the Department which he knows is untrue and if he calls for an investigation he will be compelled to admit he knew it was untrue. He will therefore make no charges directly.

Finally, in a February 1, 1884, letter, Teller pointed to the crux of the dispute: "I have been somewhat annoyed by Hill's talk, but it does not influence anyone here; still it is not pleasant to have a Senator from Colorado backbiting and slandering me all the time." To another friend he wrote, "At no time since the Interior Department was organized has it been in a better condition than it is now. It is clean and honest through and through and no one knows it better than Hill." The split widened to such a degree that it could not be reconciled.[4]

Hill energetically reciprocated, with his newspaper launching a continual anti-Teller and pro-Hill propaganda. For example, the *Tribune-Republican* trumpeted that there had never been a public man whose acts "were so entirely in harmony with the desire of his constituents." Hill blamed Teller's jealousy for this "disgraceful contest" marked by "such truculent scheming" and "silly malicious lies." Even though animated Ouray editor Dave Day was usually a Democrat, he supported Hill. Colorado's most outspoken editor, Day described Teller, whom he had known for "years," as follows: "I must confess, I have never entertained even a passable good opinion of him," adding that Teller is the "most cold blooded and unscrupulous [of] all the politicians who are seeking that exalted office [the Senate seat]."

The two factions skirmished from county to county, with the final battle fought out at the state convention. Thinking his two chief rivals would kill themselves politically by being locked in a deadlock, Horace Tabor jumped into the race again, trailing badly. Neither he nor anyone else stood a chance.

Teller had his newspaper as well. Central City's *Register-Call* leveled this blast at the county's smelter pioneer: "Socially Hill is a cold, heartless schemer; politically a blanket Apache who harbors no ambition beyond personal gain." He embodied, the article concluded, a man who found no principle "too sacred" to make him unwilling to "barter for political advantage."

The press not only blasted Henry. The Hill forces leveled their aim at the "interloper" Chaffee as well, calling him "a notorious and incompetent political fraud." Teller, they claimed, gave him "the only support he has."

Henry might have yearned to return to private life, but political reality and his personal feelings toward Hill drove him to run. As one account described the campaign, "Fur was made to fly in good earnest." An angry Teller was more than "annoyed by Hill; he probably disliked him more than any other person he had confronted in public life." Each man fought for his political life. A Teller faction spent the night in the Denver convention hall to gain control at the next day's convention by packing it with his supporters. Following the "disgraceful" Arapahoe County fight—a particularly nasty contest—one editor was moved to state: "It is a reflection upon the condition of morals and civilization in the Centennial State." Rumors of trickery, corruption, bribery, and betrayal whipped about like the wind.

The objections to Hill were interesting if one overlooked the personal vendetta between him and Teller. Hill had worked for the interests of Colorado and had listened to his constituents; few challenged that. Various newspapers commented that his personal "character was beyond question" and his standing in Washington was "of the highest." Hill the politician, not Hill the senator, was the issue. He "was surrounded by a class of men whose only interest in his success was the outgrowth of the purest selfishness." Nathaniel did not possess the political savvy, personality, or years of experience needed to control his followers or to understand the total implications of some of their actions. The bolt by his followers in 1882 had angered Republican leaders throughout Colorado, and he had failed to rebuild fences. Hill had simply alienated too many people.

At the state Republican convention in Colorado Springs in September 1884, legislative candidates would be chosen, and with a Republican victory in the state election, the senator would be selected in a caucus. Chaffee marshaled the anti-Hill faction very effectively, having previous experience at doing so. Both sides were willing to try almost anything to gain an advantage. It seemed that in many instances loyal workers "considered [the] success of their respective chiefs more important than the success of the party."

The *Gunnison Review-Press* called the Colorado Springs gathering "one of the most exciting state conventions ever held." The Democratic *Rocky Mountain News,* on the other hand, scolded that the convention "reeked with fraud and corruption from first to last. Honesty and justice had no weight with the clique of cunning and unscrupulous conspirators." Threats of a bolt and of possible rival tickets only added spice. Hill's ticket received what was nearly a mortal blow, losing to a ticket backed by Chaffee, Tabor, Teller, Routt (now Denver's mayor), Georgetown's consummate political pro William Hamill, and Samuel Elbert.[5]

A pleased Teller wrote Dawson, "I am pretty well satisfied he [Hill] cannot compel a compromise." He hoped his friends would stand by the ticket and that Hill "will be compelled to withdraw his ticket or to virtually withdraw from the Senatorial race." As the campaign moved toward a Republican victory, Hill lost ground. The opportunistic Edward Wolcott deserted his longtime ally to join Teller, although his brother Henry stayed loyal as one of Hill's managers for the upcoming January fight. Chameleon Ed did not seem adverse to changing horses in midstream. He, too, had aspirations for the Senate and no doubt realized which way the political power was moving.

Henry cornered the overmatched Hill faction in January, his victory constituting the "absorbing talk" in Denver. Chaffee arrived from New York to take up temporary residence in the capital city, and Teller came from Washington. The contest generated rumors throughout town from the "lobbies of the leading hotels" to legislative sessions. The *Rocky Mountain News* enjoyed attacking the Republicans. It accused both factions, with no doubt a large measure of truth, of trying to buy the election. Teller, the paper declared on January 11, 1885, had "always understood the art of running well on other people's money."

Amid accusations of falsehood and double dealing, the Republican legislators met January 19 in a boisterous and disorderly session in which the harassed chairman repeatedly had to gavel the caucus back to order. Both sides relentlessly tried to put through their rules, playing a "gag game," as each charged. "Indignation" reigned. Hill, Tabor, and Teller were nominated. The election finally focused on a debate over whether the vote for the final candidate would be by the customary ballot (which Hill preferred) or voice (Teller's preference). The Teller faction barely squeaked through; after a bitter two-hour debate, they won a narrow victory. Hill supporters stomped out, leaving the caucus to Teller. That prompted rumors that Hill planned to align himself with the Democrats and secure his reelection or, if that were impossible, the election of a Democrat. The *News* muttered, "There is no glory and plenty of shame for the Republican party of Colorado in the senatorial struggle."

Hill's people had fatally overestimated their support and underestimated Henry's. Before the official vote was taken in the legislature, Hill withdrew, taking his defeat "philosophically," a supporter claimed. Teller won the nomination on the first joint ballot by fifty votes, twelve more than needed. The time had arrived to close ranks, entreated the *Gunnison Review-Press* on January 24. Teller, the editor proclaimed, "is a careful prudent statesman." Dave Day leveled another blast at Teller's "gall" in asking Coloradans "to honor him with the highest and most important office within their gift." High in the San Juans, the *Animas Forks Pioneer* simply grumbled, it "is time for good men to leave" the Republican Party.

This election marked the beginning of the end of the bitter factional Republican fights that had gone on for twenty years. For the past six years, it had been Hill versus Teller. Henry, who had used his position as secretary of the interior and political sagacity to strengthen his threatened base and undermine Hill, triumphantly prepared to return to the Senate. Hill retired from public life the following March but remained a political factor through his ownership of the *Denver Republican* until his death in 1900. The two sides disbanded the "small armies" they had organized, and the factional bitterness and feud receded.

As stated, Teller had entered the race to defeat Hill. It had become obvious that no other Republican could do so. Although the era was one of scandal and mudslinging throughout U.S. politics and Teller's victory brought some stability to the Republican Party in Colorado, the editor of the *Animas Forks Pioneer* believed that "in history Senator Hill's star will shine brighter in defeat than the Honorable Secretary's will in victory."[6] The editor completely missed the mark.

In an interview in October 1884, Samuel Elbert expressed concern about the trend in Colorado politics. Many apprehensive Coloradans agreed with his assessment. He stated: "Corruption in our territory and State is of late date and chiefly in the manner of the election of U.S. Senator. They have got to using money in that direction to an extent that is utterly disgraceful and intolerable." At least Elbert judged there had been little "buying" of legislators for "this or that bill." As negative as this observation appeared, Colorado reflected the general political scene more than representing an individual aberration. The press had not nicknamed the U.S. Senate the "millionaires" club on a whim.

During the rest of the 1880s Teller faced few Colorado battles. A brief contest with Tabor in 1886 for the chairmanship of the Republican Party ended peacefully. William Hamill resolved the conflict by making Teller, "full of honors," temporary chairman and Tabor permanent chair. More important, the decision about Thomas Bowen's Senate seat, to be made in 1888, was stirring the political pot again.

Teller wanted a stronger man as his colleague than Bowen, whose main claim to fame was being the best poker player in the Senate! Bowen, in Henry's opinion "was markedly deficient in the qualities desirable for the high office of the Senate." As he had told Tabor and others, he firmly believed the Senate commanded "Colorado's representation by the State's best talent." He wanted "by his side a man of greater force, and finer dignity."

Ed Wolcott had his eye on a congressional seat and had been carefully laying plans for several years—undoubtedly the main reason he had opportunistically switched sides in 1884 and joined Teller. The two men found they agreed on a surprising number of issues, especially considering past events. Teller, to Wolcott's pleasure, offered him far greater support than Ed had "hoped for" or expected.

Initially, Ed was considering a seat in the House, but Henry advised him to go for the Senate seat, pointing out that incumbent George Symes was more firmly entrenched in the House than Bowen was in the Senate. Bowen lacked a strong following and came from the politically weak southern and San Juan regions of Colorado. Wolcott could prevail, Teller counseled, "if he would go to work from that time and make a systematic campaign." Wolcott did so with vigor and literally captured the party in 1886, becoming a "genuine dictator, and it was not long until he was absolute master of the situation." He eventually formed "alliances with the leaders of the Teller faction."

Wolcott could be as coldly ruthless as Hill, something Teller would ultimately learn. Tabor had learned it earlier when Wolcott dangled the governorship before him to head off a possible run by Tabor for the Senate. Tabor got neither post, as Wolcott orchestrated his own candidate and Tabor lost any realistic shot at the Senate. Bowen came home from Washington for a renomination bid, only to have the "splendid organization" of the Wolcott forces stop him in his tracks.

Teller got dragged into the campaign. George Raymond, the outspoken anti-Teller editor of the *Animas Forks Pioneer,* blasted him. Although Bowen was no favorite of the *Pioneer,* "in our opinion, he stands much better in the estimation of the people than Senator Teller." And, "If Colorado has disgraced herself, Teller is the disgrace."

Teller went on the campaign trail in 1888, appearing with Wolcott as he worked to build his legislative numbers. Wolcott was a powerful, persuasive speaker; that coupled with Teller's knowledge of government affairs proved a winning combination.

Wolcott won the seat in the January 1889 legislative session, and Teller had secured the man he sought. Henry had wanted an individual who could help with the silver fight and "effectively" assist him in battling for Colorado and the West generally in the Senate. A flap transpired, however, when Horace Tabor made a late bid for the Senate. The month before, the *New York Times* had reported that Teller had told friends he would not run for another term if the legislature chose Tabor. Henry claimed he had said nothing "whatever respecting his [Tabor's] personal habits or peculiarities." He admitting having commented "to a few friends . . . that if Mr. Tabor was chosen Senator I would not be a candidate for reelection two years hence." Why he bothered to express his views is a matter of conjuncture because, as the senior senator acknowledged, "there is so little prospect of his [Tabor's] election that any speculation upon the results of such an event would be a waste of time."[7]

RETURNING TO THE SENATE IN MARCH 1885, Henry found his years as secretary of the interior followed him. In his last days in office he had issued patents for over 680,000 acres of western land. That caused "much talk" in Washington and a few days of "hot attacks" for the Colorado senator. The crux of the matter centered on the differing attitudes of easterners and westerners regarding how land should be opened, settled, and developed.

The western lands and natural resources debate had heated since the 1870s. Easterners and some westerners were openly concerned about the waste of resources, particularly timber. Following his inauguration in March 1889, Benjamin Harrison's administration became particularly active in setting aside forest reserves—the forerunners of national forests—designating over 16 million acres. Westerners did not want their right to develop nearby natural resources as they saw fit altered. Teller ultimately became greatly involved in this dispute.

Teller was not simply a despoiler, however. He made a speech in July 1890 about complaints over land grabbing near designated reservoir sites. Westerners' protests over withdrawing the right to file such claims raced eastward. Henry sympathized with both sides and felt the government had been wrong from the start: "I do not want now, and never did want, the Government to do anything more than to indicate on its lands where these natural reservoirs were, what their capacity might be." He also disapproved of greedy westerners who hoped to benefit from such sites.[8]

The Committee on Privileges and Elections, on which Teller served, had to investigate the challenged victory of Ohio's Democratic senator Henry Payne. The charges against the seventy-six-year-old Payne involved Standard Oil men bribing state legislators to vote for Payne. Teller and two other Republicans voted with the Democrats in deciding no case existed on which to investigate the charges.

Payne's opponents immediately accused Henry and Illinois Republican John Logan of having used the same bribery tactics to gain their seats and thus of being unwilling to convict their colleague. Teller squirmed. His stated views on Tabor and Bowen must have come back to haunt him, at least in his own mind. He tried to take the high road, but considering all the facts, he did so somewhat unconvincingly. In July 1886 Senate remarks he had admitted realizing as well as anyone "the danger of filling this great body with men who only represent a bank account." Why, then, did he vote on the Payne case the way he did? He believed the Senate acted as a court in these cases:"If we proceed to condemn these things we must condemn them with the law; we must follow the usual procedure or else we shall be worse than they." The lawyer in him had triumphed.[9]

In 1887 Teller selected newspaperman Thomas Dawson as his private secretary, and Dawson became a close observer and chronicler of his mentor/friend's career. Dawson's writings offer our best view of the senator during his years in Washington. In an 1887 letter he provided some wonderful insights into Teller. During a "spirited debate" over a bill involving railroad and government lawsuits, "Teller made the most fiery speech I ever heard from him, and a good speech too. I tell you, I am beginning to feel proud of my Senator. He is certainly one of the most level-headed men and one of the great debaters in the entire body and is so recognized here in the Senate and out."

Granted, his ten-year friendship with Henry probably swayed Dawson's views; nevertheless, they do reflect the man:"Not only has he good judgment, but his information concerning the affair of the country is wonderfully varied and markedly accurate. All the senators consult him, and he is very popular with them—the biggest of them."

Dawson appreciated the fact that Henry treated everyone equally:"He is never 'stuck up'—always the same. He does not treat me as other senators do their secretaries." Teller trusted Dawson and gave him a great deal of free reign. Dawson recalled oversleeping one morning and not arriving at the Capitol until ten: "I apologized. He said, 'That's all right; sleep all you can.'" Henry's well-known "difficult to decipher" penmanship revealed his humorous side. When Dawson wrote letters for him, Teller said, "'Tom, you are going to spoil my reputation for penmanship.' 'No, Mr. Teller,' I always replied, 'I am simply doing my level best to make your constituents think they are getting autograph letters.'" Teller, according to Dawson, "appreciated that his writing was not the plainest in the world, but he gave his clerks so much opportunity to read it that they became adept in doing so."

Even after senators were provided with stenographers, Teller rarely dictated. He wrote letters he felt he "must give personal attention to, turning them to be copied on the typewriter." He did not like to dictate and did not like to have a "clerk dangling at his heels wherever he went." Dawson believed Henry was "so considerate" that he followed this course to save double work "for the clerk, if for no other reason."[10]

His senatorial years in the 1880s seemed in many ways like those of a decade before with one physical exception. Neither Edward Wolcott nor Representative Hosea Townsend, from Teller's Colorado district, had a committee room or much of an office, so they both made their "headquarters" in the senior senator's official apartment. As Dawson said, "It was of ample size for the entire delegation."

Teller was involved with national and international issues that touched Coloradans. For instance, Leadville miners and others wanted a limit placed on lead imported from Mexico. The "ruinous competition" of sixty cents a day paid to Mexican miners threatened declining Leadville almost as much as the collapsing price of silver. Teller eventually succeeded in having a high tariff placed on lead and in getting a fish hatchery located in Lake County, although Leadville never got its desired federal building. He thoughtfully watched over the Ute issue in southern Colorado because his constituents there still wanted to have the remaining tribal members removed.

Obligatory matters always needed to be taken care of as well. Interested potential settlers wrote him about locating in Colorado; through Dawson, Teller replied. Henry met Lt. Gen. Philip Sheridan when he visited Denver in October 1886 on a "rest and recreation" tour. Teller did the "honors with his usual grace and geniality," noted a *News* reporter. When the first train arrived in Aspen on November 1, 1887, Henry rode aboard it. Much to the pleasure of Aspenites, their senator "enthusiastically exclaimed that it beat any railroad celebration he had ever seen."

He went to the national Republican convention in 1888 as a member of Colorado's delegation. Henry supported his old cabinet friend Walter Q. Gresham in his failed bid for the presidential nomination. The entire delegation followed Teller's lead and then joined him in supporting the eventual winner, Benjamin Harrison.

Soon after his election, Harrison made a friendly overture to Henry. Teller had written the president-elect congratulating him on his victory and boasting of Colorado's fine effort. Harrison responded, "I am very much obliged to you for your friendly congratulations and to the Republicans of Colorado for the magnificent result achieved by them. You are right in saying that it will be hard for any rival State to establish its claims to precedence."

On the national scene, Henry was asked to support the candidacy of a man who wanted to serve as U.S. marshal in Louisiana. When Secretary of State James Blaine wrote him about increasing the salary of the American consul in Paso del Norte, Henry advised him that it was unlikely unless all consuls in Mexico received an increase. Congress considered the sum recommended too large "for the place." Teller watched with interest the 1887 passage of the Dawes Severalty Act relating to native peoples. He had long opposed granting individual allotments and citizenship to members of tribes because he believed they were not ready for either. He tried to amend, but failed. Henry was right; the Dawes Act provided no panacea, for reasons previously discussed.

His support for what he considered the answer, education, however, never wavered. Reflecting his policy as secretary of the interior, Teller worked steadfastly to increase federal appropriations for government schools. Many Americans wanted to abolish the remaining church schools on the reservations, but Henry would not close the denominational schools that still existed. Teller would "never vote to run the Indian children out of a denomination school until the Government had opened an opportunity for them to go into another school."

He spoke on one of his favorite subjects, women's suffrage. He had attacked the anti-Mormon Edmunds-Tucker Act and its section removing Utah's women's suffrage. The territory had granted that right, and Congress threatened to take it away for nonpolitical reasons. The question came up again in April 1886 in a debate over

Washington Territory, which favored granting women the right to vote. Kentucky Democratic senator James Beck, among other southerners, attacked the idea because of the precedent for women in general mainly because, as Henry suggested, they "worried about colored women."

Westerners Teller and Oregon senator Joseph Dolph replied vigorously. Referring to neighboring Utah, which granted women the right to vote in 1870, Teller praised what had happened: "It has been my opportunity to live by the side of a community which granted to women equal rights at the polls with men. Order, good government, decency has been the result." He did not appreciate the innuendos and denunciations about suffrage that flew around the male Senate: "I say from observation that the evils from so doing which have been emphasized and suggested will not come."

Senator Teller could be partisan. His 1888 speech attacking President Cleveland and the Democratic Party for their "free trade" views hit hard and were well supported. The Republican Party printed 50,000 copies of the speech for campaign purposes.

In the detailed speech, Teller used history to prove that the tariff benefited farmers and industrial workers alike. "American laborers," Henry intoned, "get better pay, better compensation for their labor" than anyone else in the world. Why would immigrants come, Teller asked, if not for the better conditions in America? Democrats had not been a free trade party until recently, a mere "party looking for patronage." He hammered home a host of issues. Grover Cleveland and the Democrats planned to destroy this protective system that had so greatly benefited America and Americans. Free trade would allow the lower-paid Mexican, Japanese, Chinese, and English laborers to compete unfairly with American workers, thereby lowering their wages and standard of living. The protective tariff produced glorious results and had "brought to the people of this country a prosperity, a richness, a contentedness, and a glory that no other system has brought to any other people in the world."[11]

Teller would regret some of those words within a decade. For the moment, however, he considered the Republicans the party of the people; the Democrats wandered somewhere in the political wilderness.

HENRY KNEW WHAT IT WAS LIKE TO BE IN THAT WILDERNESS. When Americans generally criticized and demeaned the Mormons and their Church of Jesus Christ of the Latter-Day Saints, Teller defended them on constitutional grounds. While secretary of the interior, he had involved himself with the problems of Colorado's western neighbor. Jeopardizing his career, he championed in a losing cause the constitutional freedom of all persons "regardless of religious creeds." Henry "Mormon" Teller threatened the sanctity of home life and the purity of domestic relations and sanctioned immoral conditions, screamed various Colorado newspapers. Hill's *Tribune-Republican* (January 5, 1886), called him little more than "a Mormon attorney." At issue was the Mormon doctrine of polygamy.

Congress had passed laws trying to punish polygamists and prevent polygamy, without discernible success. Henry had received letters during his previous term from constituents who wanted to have those laws enforced. Utah's "unbridled sin continued unabated," however. In early 1886 the Senate debated what became known as the Edmunds-Tucker Act. A few of the provisions of this vindictive legislation included forcing wives to testify against their husbands, ending polygamous marriages regardless of consequences to the families involved, prohibiting Mormon women from voting in any territorial election, and bringing witnesses to court without subpoenas. Further, the corporate structure of the church would be abolished, the territorial school system would be controlled by a group of federal commissioners and heavily Mormon Utah election districts were to be reapportioned.

In Teller's mind, polygamy was wrong, but the issues transcended that. Freedom of religion, civil rights, and civil and criminal law stood on the docket. Congress was trying to deny the constitutionally guaranteed rights implicit in the Fourteenth Amendment, which promised "equal protection of the law." He knew the personal and political cost of his position, but he spoke his conscience: "I believe that my ear has always listened to the cry of the oppressed and distressed. I believe that I may have a weakness: when people complain of oppression, no matter from whence it comes, I ought to have a desire to look into it."

On January 6, 1886, Teller attacked the entire bill, which he believed contained far-reaching implications. Why make martyrs of men and women who had married more than a generation ago and "bastardize their children?" The Mormons had been persecuted in the past; Teller recalled, "I myself left a courtroom in that Territory so outraged" that he could not stay for fear "I should be compelled to rebuke the presiding judge." Matters would only be worse with the new bill: "This bill, in my judgment, bristles everywhere with vengeance and blood." He continued:

> They are an honest, painstaking, hard-working, industrious people. I went to their capital city when there were 15,000 people there and to their credit be it said not a place in it where whisky could be sold . . . not a house of prostitution, not a gaming place in the whole territory with 80,000 people.
>
> I know that no man stands upon this floor and defends that people without being slandered and traduced through this land. I know that the bigotry and hatred that grows out of religious enthusiasm and zeal can never see beyond the very question that is presented, that polygamy is a crime.
>
> I am not to be deterred because somebody says "you must be a Jack Mormon," I will not vote contrary to my conscience and judgment for anything although it may accomplish, even if I believed it would accomplish, the purpose for which it was intended if it is contrary to law. I hold my allegiance to the law.[12]

That speech took as much courage as anything Teller did in his political career, and it speaks much about the man.

Aroused proponents viciously attacked Teller and his views. Former Illinois governor and longtime Republican senator Shelby Cullom, a bitter foe of Mormonism, accused Henry of being "an especial advocate of the Mormon people." After all, in the Illinois senator's inconsistent and illogical view, "there has been no persecution of them." Teller fired back that Cullom was thinking, like most men, "from his prejudices."

His own view on polygamy remained abundantly clear: "It is a crime against civilization as we view it, and yet more than three-fourths of the world today are in favor of and practice this institution of polygamy." He might support the Mormons as people, but he was not a proponent of Mormonism: "I know these people as well as anybody here does, and I regard their chief prophet as an arrant knave."

Teller captured the better of the debate on constitutional and logical grounds, whereas Cullom seemed more intent on damaging Teller's reputation. Henry's position was one he had repeated often, one based on the law and the constitution—the defense of which "I believe to be a constitutional right that these people have, not the right to practice polygamy but the right to be treated as we treat every other citizen of this great country until they infringe [upon] the law." Teller would never sanction ignoring the constitution or laws to reach the result: the destruction of polygamy. He deemed nothing more sacred than the rule of law and the constitution.

Teller could not stem the tide, however. Powerful Vermont senator George Edmunds and his backers held the votes. The final total was 38 to 7, after which the bill was sent to the House where it was eventually amended. It went back to a conference committee and was finally approved on February 18, 1887. Standing by his principles, Teller again voted no. President Cleveland refused to sign the act, but he did not veto it either, and on March 3 it automatically became law. The official church newspaper (*Desert Evening News*) praised Teller for putting the real situation in a "true and forceful light." Much to its credit, the *Rocky Mountain News* (January 11, 1886) had already come to Teller's defense. He had been cowardly attacked "because he dared to express the belief that gentler legislation would prove more efficacious than Senator Edmunds's drastic [plan] in the extinction of polygamy."

> Senator Teller makes no defense of polygamy. He is sincerely anxious for its
> overthrow, as any man that lives, and said so in his speech.
> Senator Teller, very proper we think, questioned the wisdom of the means
> provided by the Edmunds Bill. He held the government had not done its
> duty in the past in dealing with the problem and he expresses grave doubts of
> the wisdom and justice of harshly punishing the Mormons for the mistakes of
> the government as well as their own evil behavior. But if Senator Teller never
> does anything worse than that he will not forfeit the confidence of honest
> and intelligent men.

The *News* went on to speculate that if such things could be done to the Mormons, could they not equally be done to the Methodists or Catholics?[13]

If the hearings on Senator Payne had been one of Teller's low points, his attack on the Edmunds bill represented one of his finest moments during this term. The dark side of the American character had overwhelmed Teller's correct concerns. Self-righteousness, misunderstanding, and bigotry surface occasionally in American life.

Considering the hue and cry at the time, one might think Teller's stand regarding the Mormons would affect his reelection chances. After the senatorial fight in 1884–1885, political harmony prevailed in the Republican Party for the first time in two decades. Some rumbling surfaced about the old Hill faction trying to defeat Teller, but its newspaper, the *Republican,* came out in favor of Teller's reelection. Hill might not like Teller, but as one wag said, he "liked Wolcott less."

Few, if any, Republican leaders wanted Teller to be defeated. The Republicans in the legislature sent him a dispatch before the vote to dispel any uncertainty he may have had about the outcome: "Your splendid service to the country and to Colorado are recognized and appreciated by every good citizen . . . and we shall but voice the wish of every loyal Republican in Colorado when we cast our votes for you." They expressed their "cordial and hearty friendship and . . . our personal regard and esteem as well as our high respect for your distinguished public service."

On January 21, 1891, the joint session of the legislature reelected Teller. One supporter telegrammed him that there "is a feeling of general relief" in his victory. It had not been that easy in reality. Teller, who had feared Colorado might go Democratic in 1890, wrote Dawson revealing some of his inner feelings. If the state did so, "we will have until March 4th to pick up our things and get out, and I am confident I will be happier out than in, so I am not disturbed over the prospect."

Looking ahead, Teller saw an old problem on the horizon. In a letter Henry returned again to his long-expressed concern: "I do not like the idea of inducing certain persons who have money to enter the race for the Senate simply because they have the money to control the Legislature or the Conventions that nominate members of the legislature."[14]

Entering his third six-year term, Senator Teller found that one issue dominated his time: the silver issue. The metal's international price had fallen steadily since the 1870s, whereas mining costs in older and deeper mines had risen. Colorado and world production had increased, which added to the miners' troubles. Colorado silver mining needed assistance. The decline in mining could affect the entire state economy.

Teller dealt with other matters ranging from state pride to international issues. He supported federal funding to help the Colorado School of Mines: "We are very proud of our School of Mines. We think it is one of the best in the world." With the funding, Teller believed, the United States could help education in general. The state retained control, and the whole country benefited from the training of mining engineers. Teller was not wrong. The Colorado School of Mines exemplified the best America offered, and it pleased Henry to see professionally trained mining engineers making an impact on the industry. He remembered all too well his early territorial days when self-proclaimed experts made some grievous mistakes involving Colorado mining.

On a more local level, Teller looked into a pension concern for Mrs. Edward Wynkoop, whose husband had opposed the Sand Creek attack. One constituent advised him that this was not a good time for New Mexico statehood. The writer worried that there "is no hope of making the state Republican." Supporting the wishes of Colorado's laboring men, he favored a bill requiring registration of Chinese workers in the United States. True to his earlier position, he declared, "I have always insisted that the right of the Government to exclude this class of people should be exercised. I am in favor of exercising it now."

Henry visited Pittsburgh's Bethlehem Iron Works, along with other congressmen, to witness its operations and examine how government military contracts were being spent. As fellow senator and former Civil War general John Hawley wrote, "It [the company] takes pleasure in showing that those [government contracts] it has have been wisely awarded" and also takes "just pride in its mechanical triumphs." He also received advice on a South Carolina judicial appointment.[15]

These issues paled in significance before the all-consuming question of silver, the common man, and the financial future of the United States. Trouble was brewing from farms to mountain valleys, and Henry's beloved Colorado landed in the midst of a brewing revolt Teller had worried about when he feared a state Democratic victory in 1890. Colorado had reached a watershed era in its history, and few understood where the state might be going.

NOTES

1. See *Rocky Mountain News, Inter-Ocean, Denver Tribune, Denver Republican, Leadville Daily Herald,* and *Solid Muldoon* (Ouray) April–October 1882; R. G. Dill, *The Political Campaigns of Colorado* (Denver: Arapaho, 1895), 63–68; Duane A. Smith, *Horace Tabor: His Life and the Legend* (Niwot: University Press of Colorado, 1989), chapter 12.

2   Thomas Dawson, "The Personal Side of Senator Teller," Colorado Historical Society, 4; Teller to Dawson, March 8, 1883, Teller Papers, Colorado Historical Society; Charles Thomas, "Reminiscences," Special Collections, Colorado College, 84–85; *Denver Republican,* December 31, 1906; *Inter-Ocean,* July 29, September 9, 1882; *Georgetown Courier,* March 23, 1882; *Rocky Mountain News,* April 3, June 16, August 31, September 16, October 21, 22, 1882; *Weekly Republican,* April 13, 20, 1882; *Evening Chronicle* (Leadville), October 10, 1882.

3. Teller to R. A. Cameron, December 10, 1883, Teller Papers, Colorado Historical Society; Dill, *Political Campaigns,* 87, 98–100; Thomas Dawson, "Teller and Wolcott," Colorado Historical Society, 3; Dawson, "Personal Side of Senator Teller," 2–3; Thomas Dawson, "Scrapbooks," Colorado Historical Society, vol. 61.

4. Teller to Dawson, March 8, November 1, December 10, 11, 24, 1883, February 1, June 3, 1884, Teller to R. A. Cameron, December 10, 1883, all in Teller Papers, Colorado Historical Society.

5. *Gunnison Review-Press,* August–September 1884; *Solid Muldoon,* August–September 1884, January 23, 1885; *Rocky Mountain News,* August–September 1884; *Weekly Denver Tribune-Republican,* August–September 1884; *Opinion* (Denver), May 10, 1884; undated clipping, *Register-Call.*

6. Teller to Dawson, September 20, 1884, Teller Papers, Colorado Historical Society; *Animas Forks Pioneer,* December 20, 1884, January 31, 1885; Dill, *Political Campaigns,* 85–

86, 92–94, 100–101; Frank Hall, *History of the State of Colorado* (Chicago: Blakely, 1890), vol. 3, 43–44; Dawson, "Teller and Wolcott," 5–7; *Rocky Mountain News,* November 1, January 11–18, 1885; *Gunnison Review-Press,* January 17, 24, 1885; *Solid Muldoon,* January 16, 23, 1885; *New York Times,* January 21–22, 1885.

7. Samuel Elbert interview, October 21, 1884, Bancroft Collection, Special Collections, Colorado College; *Denver Republican,* September 6, 1888; Thomas Wiswall, "Tabor," Bancroft Library, Berkeley, California; Dill, *Political Campaigns,* 103; Charles Thomas, "Old Timer," Colorado Historical Society, 11; *Rocky Mountain News,* August 2, 1897; *Animas Forks Pioneer,* February 20, March 27, 1886; *Evening Chronicle* (Leadville), October 28, 1888; Dawson, "Teller and Wolcott," 8–9; *New York Times,* December 12, 13, 15, 1888.

8. Benjamin Harrison to Teller, November 14, 1888, Teller Papers, Colorado Historical Society; Allan Nevins, *Grover Cleveland* (New York: Dodd, Mead, 1964), 225–226; Teller speech, *Congressional Record,* July 18, 1890, 2053.

9. Albert H. Walker, *The Payne Bribery Case and the United States Senate* (Hartford, Conn.: Clark and Smith, 1886), 4–3, 25–29, 32–33; Chester W. Destler, *American Radicalism 1865–1901* (New York: Octagon, 1963 reprint), 153; Teller's comments, *Congressional Record,* July 1886, 7269–70, 7311–12.

10. Dawson, "Personal Side of Senator Teller," 2–4.

11. Thomas Dawson, *Edward Oliver Wolcott* (New York: Knickerbocker, 1911), vol. 2, 8; John Ingalls to Teller, April 6, 1889, Teller Papers, Colorado Historical Society; *Rocky Mountain News,* October 4, 1886; Benjamin Harrison to Teller, November 14, 1888, Teller Papers, Colorado Historical Society; *Leadville Herald-Democrat,* November 2, 1887; Irving Howbert, *Memories of a Lifetime in the Pike's Peak Region* (New York: G. P. Putnam's Sons, 1925), 267–268; *Congressional Record,* January 6, 1886, 461, April 1, 1886, 3316–17; Henry Teller, *Prosperity Under the Protective Tariff* (Washington, D.C.: Government Printing Office, 1888), 1–30; Edward McPherson to Teller, August 3, 1888, Teller Papers, Colorado Historical Society.

12. Speech in *Congressional Record,* January 5–7, 1886, 406, 461–462, 514.

13. *Congressional Record,* January 6–7, 1886, 460–461, 506–508, 512–515, February 18, 1887, 1904; *La Plata Miner,* January 23, 1886; *Animas Forks Pioneer,* January 16, 1886; *Denver Tribune-Republican,* January 10, 1886; *Desert Evening News,* January 16, 20, 1886; M. Paul Holsinger, "Henry M. Teller and the Edmunds-Tucker Act," *Colorado Magazine* (winter 1971): 1–14.

14. Dill, *Political Campaigns,* 135–136, 144–146, 157; Teller to R. W. Steele, December 29, 1891, E. Ammons to Dawson, January 21, 1891, Teller to Dawson, November 1, 1890, all in Teller Papers, Colorado Historical Society; *New York Times,* September 1, 1890, January 8, 1891.

15. *Congressional Record,* September 3, 1898, 1077, September 5, 1893, 1114, October 28, 1893, 3184; S. B. Elkins to Teller, December 14, 1892, Elihu Root to Teller, October 14, 1893, Teller to Dawson, November 13, 1892, J. R. Hawley to Teller, February 4, 1892, all in Teller Papers, Colorado Historical Society.

The Silver Issue

What you are about to read is the death of an American dream. You may approach it with logic, although few people did during its 1880s and 1890s heyday, or with more emotion than logic, as they did then. In reality, this is a crusade, a revivalistic, passionate crusade to save "their" America. To understand what is about to transpire, one has to try to return to a time and place as foreign to today as the Salem witch trials seemed to the generation of the late nineteenth century.

This is the saga of the determined stand of a vanishing America against the onrushing future. The promised land of a better life for oneself and one's children had always been tied to owning land. Now westerners and farmers elsewhere doubted that premise, less sure that the dream would emerge as real life. The hopes and expectations of two centuries collapsed against the restless drive of tomorrow's reality and that of the day after.

The tragedy inherent within this is that those long-held hopes and expectations created their own demise. Who could have killed them? Plots swirled. Many of these plots, believed religiously at the time, make no logical sense except in the darkness and desperation of the times. Despair brewed will-o'-the-wisp elixirs, held out and drunk as the gospel of salvation. Innocence, gullibility, hardheaded reality, naïveté, hypocrisy, bamboozling, and ambition were mixed together in a helter-skelter fashion.

Intermingled with all this breathed the dreams of other Americans who worked equally hard to reach their promised land. They too included both natives and recent immigrants. The big difference was that they lived in the bustling cities, worked in factories and businesses, and lived the urban life. Their outlook on life and the future differed from that of their rural cousins.

The two groups, urban and rural, had not intended to contest one another. They, after all, had pulled the country back together during the catastrophe of the Civil War. Nevertheless, they could not rationally prevent a clash. The city dwellers could not understand the radicalism that seemed to be exploding in the hinterland of their homeland, and the rural folk could not grasp their city cousins' lack of compassion and understanding. In the end, the situation had to be sorted out before the turn of the century. For some, the dream died; their promised land faded like last night's dream.

Sundry trends in American history came together in these years—they included rural America, industrialization, urbanization, old America versus new America, foreigners and foreign investment, and the role of money in American finance and life. It had all started several generations before.

Fundamental changes were occurring in the United States before the Civil War, although few understood their long-range implications. Industrialization was taking root in the northern states. From 1810 to 1860 the value of manufacturing rose roughly tenfold to just under $2 billion. The United States stood second only to Great Britain and within a generation became the industrial leader of the world. With industrialization came factories, steam power, corporate organization, and a decline in the worth of the laborer.

Along with this came urbanization in and around the industrial centers. Although by 1860 only 16.1 percent of Americans lived in towns or cities of more than 8,000 people, that number was fivefold what it had been in 1800. New York City and its boroughs already topped a million people, and its commercial and banking importance outstripped its claim as the country's largest city. In the mining West, urbanization grew as it never had before in the settlement of what Americans called the frontier.

Agriculture still dominated the U.S. economy at the start of the Civil War. Nonetheless, industrialization increased greatly, and with it came a transportation revolution. The railroad changed the United States, rural and urban. Americans had fallen in love with the steam engine and the iron horse and dreamed of a transcontinental line. Each little hamlet yearned for a railroad station and rail connections; without them the future looked bleak.

The West had long been a debtor region; investment was needed to open, settle, and develop the land beyond the Appalachian Mountains. In the 1850s, as settlement moved beyond the Missouri and spread all the way to Oregon, California, and Pike's Peak country, that need became even more paramount.

Meanwhile, the U.S. monetary system was strained. Because of problems with paper money during the colonial and confederation periods, the federal government attempted to establish a bimetallic monetary system. The principle of free and unlimited coinage of silver and gold had been adopted in 1792. That meant anyone could take gold or silver to the mint and have it coined, with a silver dollar containing a dollar's worth of silver. Establishing a price ratio between gold and silver proved a mistake that came back to haunt Henry Teller. The price of gold was stable on the international market; silver's price floated. Finally, during President Andrew Jackson's administration, the U.S. ratio was established at 16 to 1—16 ounces of silver equaled 1 ounce of gold. In international monetary terms, that ratio undervalued silver

Within two years the California gold rush changed everything. The forty-niners unintentionally helped set the stage for the rest of the nineteenth century. They mined so much gold that it became less valuable in relation to silver, thus compounding the earlier troubles.

By the 1850s the international price of silver was higher than the U.S. price, making a silver dollar worth $1.04 in gold. Silver coins almost disappeared; they were melted down for their silver. In 1853 Congress abandoned the free coinage of all silver coins except the dollar, placing the country on a de facto gold basis. Few Americans noticed or cared.[1]

The Civil War changed the situation further. To help finance the war, the federal government issued paper money, or greenbacks. Inflation followed, and the value of greenbacks decreased compared with that of gold and silver. Had Washington been able to position the country to use all paper currency, many later problems would have been avoided. It could not do so.

At the end of the war, businessmen, eastern bankers, and eastern investors wanted to return to a gold basis as soon as possible and retire paper money. Their position was bolstered by the orthodox fiscal philosophy of the day that supported gold because it had an intrinsic value. They wanted to avoid the inflation that resulted when the country did not have "sound money." They did not want inflated currency paying for their products or repaying the money they lent, which would "dishonorably" shift some of the debtors' burden to the creditors.

Westerners and southerners, who were often debtors, did not want a resumption of gold. Inflated currency seemed fine to them. Inflation promised to raise crop prices, stimulate the local economy, and thereby make it easier to pay off debts. They had put their finger on the real problem: the U.S. currency, backed by an insufficient gold supply, lacked the flexibility to grow with the population and the economy.

Despite this, in 1874 the Republican-controlled Congress passed an act providing for a return to gold payments on January 1, 1879, at which time paper money would be backed by gold. The government maintained official parity of all other forms of money with gold. Washington had firmly committed the country to gold.

All this came about as the industrial-transportation-urbanization revolution moved into high gear after 1865. It was a fascinating time to be living in the United States, although many changes came on the heels of this revolution that gave birth to concerns and stress. Where was America going?

With silver coins having disappeared, replaced for all practical purposes by paper money in five to fifty cent denominations, Congress in 1873 decided to drop the silver dollar. This meant the mint would no longer coin silver at the old 16 to 1 ratio. Few cared then because the market price of silver ($35) was higher than the government price of $20, and little silver consequently came to the mint for sale.

The dropping of the silver dollar caused a furor that lasted a quarter of a century. Several countries adopted the gold standard and stopped buying silver. The industrial needs for silver continued to be negligible, and silverplate and jewelry could not take up the slack. Meanwhile, Nevada's famous Comstock basked in the "big bonanza," pouring out silver ore, joined by its only rival, Leadville, and lesser western silver-producing districts. Within three years silver had glutted a deteriorating market, and the international price of silver dropped. As Americans celebrated their national centennial in 1876, silver miners had little to cheer; the price of the metal had slipped to $1.16. The treasury had once offered $1.20, so the miners attempted to sell their silver to the government. To their amazement and horror, they discovered the government no longer purchased silver. All hell broke loose. The miners wanted to know what had happened. Uncle Sam had always come through before to help the West. Why not again? Politicians bailed out. President Grant, for instance, claimed he did not know what he had signed back in 1873.

What had once seemed an innocuous act became the "Crime of '73." That "crime" gave birth to the silver issue. Henry Teller watched all this from Central, then when he arrived in Washington in the centennial year he was swept up in the "cause."

Initially, the silver issue entailed the slumping price and the government's stopping silver purchases. This aroused an early effort in two related directions to restore silver coinage and secure a government-guaranteed price for silver. Teller sat in Congress when it passed the Bland-Allison Act and repassed it over President Rutherford Hayes's veto. Henry did not take an active role in the debate.

The bill authorized the secretary of the treasury to buy not less than $2 million or more than $4 million worth of silver each month for coinage into silver dollars. No guaranteed price for silver was set, however. The secretaries of the treasury in the following years purchased the lower amount.

The Bland-Allison Act might have seemed primarily to benefit miners, but farmers supported the idea, too, because debt and the country's inelastic currency caused agricultural hardship. Too little money circulated in the United States, especially in the agricultural regions. This hurt farmers when they marketed crops because money was unavailable when they needed it most. This slowed business transactions and lowered the prices they received. Further, with virgin farming areas opening and new equipment, methods, and seeds allowing more production per acre, an agricultural surplus developed. Crops prices joined silver in a downward cycle.

Most farmers may have been unfamiliar with the intricacies of monetary theory, but they knew they were receiving less when they sold their animals and crops. The gold dollar purchased more corn, for example, than it had twenty years before. Using

1873 as the benchmark for $1.00 worth of goods, by 1893 that same dollar purchased $1.40 and three years later $1.64 in goods.

Silver coinage promised to provide an answer to their worries. Miners, for their part, just wanted a better price to allow them to mine. The two groups eventually joined to back silver.

As had been discussed in previous chapters, the silver issue climbed steadily to the forefront of Coloradans' concerns. Teller received letter after letter about silver even in his first term; newspapers wrote editorials about the issue throughout the 1870s and 1880s.

A miner writing to the *Rocky Mountain News* in 1876 asked who "is responsible for the demonetization of silver." He saw a plot led by the "money kings" to make gold "the only medium of exchange in the world." Philip Wilcox, U.S. marshall for Colorado, wrote Teller two years later, heartily in favor of the Bland-Allison Act and government help. Another writer the same year cheered him on, saying he was "glad to see you square on the silver question," as all Colorado politicians should be.

In September 1879 the Republican state convention passed a resolution wanting legislation "to restore silver as money metal to its equal with gold, and to this end we *demand that Congress enact a law providing for the unlimited coinage of the silver dollar.*" The next year in Leadville, Republican delegates were greeted with banners demanding "equality of the gold, silver and paper dollar, each convertible into the other." That October Georgetown's *Colorado Miner* published an editorial that praised silver's contributions to the state, benefiting everybody and every town: "Every citizen of Colorado ought to feel a lively interest in maintaining this prosperity and in encouraging the production of silver."

"The single gold standard is a curse to the country," bemoaned the *Georgetown Courier.* A blow "at silver is a blow" to every interest in the far West. The *Silverton Democrat* (February 12, 1885) felt the creditor class demanded the suspension of silver coinage.[2]

People could clearly see the fundamental arguments of the cause. Colorado speakers repeatedly reminded listeners about the bimetal standard of gold and silver, government help in restoring silver's price, the prosperity silver brought, and loyalty to silver over all else. The cry for silver echoed down the mountains and over the prairies.

A few months before he became secretary of the interior, Teller had discussed the silver issue in the Senate. Henry admitted that "heretofore" he had not "been very radical on the silver question." He laid out many ideas he would emphasize over the next fifteen years. Speaking for the "people of the great West, more than half the people of the United States [he included the South]," he said they wanted free coinage of silver: "Only a few people want gold." Pointing to the depression of the 1870s and the positive impact of the Bland-Allison Act on those hard times, Teller concluded, "I think that proof can be easily made that in a great degree the revival of business in this country was due to that act."

At the same time, he defended Colorado against attacks by the progold forces. They claimed Colorado silver production had declined and that "many" mining camps had played out. Pointedly, they asked about the Colorado railroads that had not paid dividends as expected. Investors' money disappeared downtrack to mining camps that promised much and produced little. Teller lashed back: "There is not a single mining camp in the State of Colorado that does not today enjoy a degree of prosperity that it never enjoyed before. No railroads have been built to mining camps that were of doubtful value, not a mile, because such camps cannot be found."

In March 1882 he authored a resolution that said in part "that the experience of mankind has demonstrated the necessity of the use of both gold and silver as circulating mediums; that the destruction of the money faculty of silver is in the interest of a few only and not calculated to benefit the great mass of mankind." He wanted the government to coin "annual domestic production of gold and silver." The resolution, like so many others, was tabled. Teller predicted that the people of the United States would "demand and will have a law" to put silver on "equal footing with gold."

As soon as he reentered the Senate, Teller reemerged as a vocal champion of silver. Appearing in winter-locked Silverton in February 1886, Henry gave a "very able and exhaustive" speech on the silver question. Although admitting that free coinage aroused more interest in Colorado than in "any other state in the union," he believed the real question was whether world commerce would be conducted in both metals or only one: "Let the judgment of mankind be taken on silver's value as money." Money scarcity meant dull times, low wages, and money changers. He spoke for all who toiled "in mills and fields," now joined in defense of their rights. He made the same appeal in hundreds of places over the next decade.[3]

Teller was not above criticism. Leadville's *Carbonate Chronicle* (January 24, 1885) gently castigated him for staying in Arthur's cabinet. The editor charged the president with opposing silver and Teller with "practically" endorsing that stand by "remaining in the cabinet."

When Edward Wolcott assumed his seat, Teller gained a vigorous, dynamic ally. The two became a strong team. Wolcott—the orator and debater who did not "ordinarily enjoy detail"—and the organized, thorough senior senator raised the silver banner.

In Wolcott, Henry found the firebrand for the cause. Fellow politician and later governor Charles Thomas said Wolcott easily ranked as "the most brilliant and forceful man in our state." Impatient with detail, he also disliked committee work. His mercurial temperament swung from "companial to disagreeable." Henry had gained a useful junior senator if he could keep him focused and motivated.

Teller and other silver spokesmen, meanwhile, had been agitating relentlessly for greater government purchases of silver at a guaranteed price of 16 to 1. The price of the metal continued to slip, reaching 94 cents an ounce by 1890. They lobbied the secretary of the treasury and other government officials, all to no avail.

The gold folks answered with their own emotional appeal. They feared silver would drive gold out of circulation, harm business, and make the United States a pariah in world finances. Free coinage was a leap in the dark: "No one can tell where, if it be made, the country will land." They were blunt regarding the silverites: "There is not much use in combating pleas of this sort. They come from minds that can hardly be said to have reasoned themselves into their present position, and cannot easily be reasoned out of it."

Mining engineer and Geological Survey veteran Samuel Emmons also disagreed with the silver backers. Silver, he argued, compared with gold, was "too bulky" to use as a medium of exchange for large sums. Further, on the international market it "is practically valued on a gold standard in all matters" of exchange. It would not matter, Emmons asserted, what value an individual nation might give it by legislative agreement. The "law of the survival of the fittest" would prevail. He did hold out hope for silver. Emmons predicted that eventually the price would rise and "prosperity" for the industry would return.[4]

Throughout these years in Colorado's mining districts, disgust and desperation increased alarmingly. In the older districts like Georgetown, Caribou, and Leadville, deeper mining meant higher costs and lower-grade ore. The miners found themselves trapped in a crushing economic vise.

The opportunity to do something finally came in 1890 when eastern senators wanted a higher tariff. As Wolcott explained in a speech, the mountain states "are less benefited than any other portion of the Union by a high protective tariff." Further, Colorado does not have a single stream or lake benefiting from the "great annual appropriations" for the improvement of rivers, harbors, and coast defenses. He drove home his point. When Colorado wanted Washington's help for free silver, "we are called speculators and told our ideas are those of a dissatisfied and visionary people." Ed was upset when senators opposed to silver accused its supporters "directly and by imputation with holding sordid and unworthy and unpatriotic opinions."

This was Wolcott's maiden speech, but, Dawson wrote, as Ed was "wont to do, he went after his antagonists." Nevada senator and longtime silverite John P. Jones, among others, jumped to defend silver. With great emotion he declared to his colleagues that silver represented the most momentous "question of public policy within the memory of this generation. It embodies the hopes and aspirations of our race." There would be no compromising.[5]

Teller had hoped President Benjamin Harrison would favor the remonetization of silver. With the support of newly admitted western states (Wyoming, Montana, Washington, and both Dakotas), this seemed like the ideal time to push for that goal. The western senators, who made up more than 20 percent of the Senate, held a causal view toward party obligations and often acted independently. They wanted to do something for their distressed farmers and silver miners. Although their states might not be able to influence a national election, they could wreck a party's legislative program.

The first setback for Teller occurred when he met with the president in January 1890. Harrison stated plainly that he harbored no sentiments for free silver. After that, Harrison and Teller parted ways. Thomas Dawson recounted a story that after Henry visited Harrison he told his Senate colleagues: "At last the President and I have discovered a subject upon which we could agree. The President said it was a fine day. I assented that it was, so that after these many years we got together."

Try as he might for free coinage, Henry gained no headway in the Senate. The tactic now became to hold the eastern-supported tariff measure hostage to force a resolution of the silver issue. Party discipline fell apart, and tempers rose. Finally, a party caucus worked out a solution agreeable to everyone. The treasury would purchase 4½ million ounces per month, paying the miners and smeltermen in legal-tender certificates. This figure had been arrived at as equaling the amount of silver mined per year (54 million ounces) in the United States.

Gone was the secretary of the treasury's flexibility to purchase lower amounts of silver. More silver would now be purchased. The silver people could achieve nothing more right now. For a brief time, the Sherman Silver Purchase Act did raise the price of silver to $1.05 before it started down again.

A time bomb lurked in the Sherman Silver Purchase Act. The silver certificates now circulating because of the act could be redeemed in either gold or silver. This carefully phrased measure preserved the gold standard by allowing the secretary of the treasury to redeem silver certificates in gold, a practice universally followed. That appeased easterners.

The fragile party unity in the 1890 session did not last through the year. The split between the factions proved too deep, too fundamental. Tensions flared particularly in January 1891 when Teller and other silverites interrupted longtime Ohio senator John Sherman, a leading gold proponent, during a speech on the Sherman Silver Purchase Act. Sherman, who was especially upset with Henry, stormed: "Now, the whole tone of this debate on the part of the Senator from Colorado has been irritable to the last degree, like a schoolmaster bossing his boys. We are not children here. Certainly I have passed the age of infancy."

John P. Jones joined with Teller. For the Nevadan, the war had escalated. The silver question "is a contest between European bondholders and the laborers of the world." He declared, "The people of the United States cannot submit to dictation from either New York or Europe." "Civil liberty," Jones ringingly concluded, "cannot survive financial slavery."

Sherman had made the mistake of saying silver could be mined at a little more than fifty-one cents an ounce. An amazed Teller challenged: "I hope the Senator will succeed in convincing the people of the United State that silver can be produced in Colorado at the figure he names, because we shall then have all the spare capital of the United States going into Colorado next year." Asked by Teller and Nevada's other senator, William Stewart, where these fifty-one cent mines were located, Sherman embarrassingly had to confess he did not know.

Sherman rebutted: "The Senator from Colorado, with his disinterested view of the silver question, looks down on them [bankers, businessman, and others] with contempt, and upon me, because he says I have some influence with these ignorant and deluded people." Sherman denounced Teller for advocating a single standard of silver. Henry hotly denied having done so. The debate ended in a shouting match.[6]

Silver senators stood together while the cause gained support elsewhere. Omaha newspaperman and silverite William Jennings Bryan shared Teller's view. Bryan supported Teller's silver fight and sent Henry editorials he wrote for the *Omaha World*. Their correspondence grew in the years that followed, with Bryan requesting copies of Teller's speeches to distribute in Nebraska. Henry, meantime, continued a lively correspondence with the secretary of the treasury, "advising" him on financial matters and silver.

The political landscape was about to be rocked as it had not been since the turbulent 1850s. Farmers, joined by others angry with the two older parties that seemed unresponsive to the needs of the people, organized the People's Party, or Populists. It grew less as a party than as a campground, a religious revival—emotional, fiery, and marching to a silver zion. The year was 1892. At their national convention Populists bitterly denounced the U.S. economic system and the Democrats and Republicans. In Populists' eyes, they had been interested in "a sham battle over the tariff, so that capitalists, corporations, national banks, rings, trusts, watered stock, the demonetization of silver, and the oppression of the usurers may all be lost sight of." They shouted, "All power to the people."

Populists wanted the Australian secret ballot, adoption of initiatives and referendums, direct election of senators, a one-term presidency, a graduated income tax, and the free and unlimited coinage of silver. They blamed railroads, middlemen, bankers, foreigners, and big corporations for their troubles. Coloradans became enchanted. Neither of the older parties seemed responsive to Colorado's crisis but appeared more concerned about not offending their monied eastern friends and supporters.

Henry was troubled. The new party represented much of what he stood for; however, he questioned its ability to carry the national political scene. Teller knew Coloradans' support came mostly from the silver issue and might prove fleeting. He decided to stay in the Republican Party.

Teller went to the national convention in 1892 hoping to have the party recognize silver in the platform. Henry further wanted to defeat Harrison, a "most unrelenting enemy of free coinage." As he had written Horace Tabor in February 1892: "If we are to support Mr. Harrison in convention as our first choice it is a declaration that we care but little about the free coinage of silver." Tabor, one of the early and leading Colorado silver spokesmen, desperately needed an increased silver price to help right his sinking business empire.

Both goals proved unattainable, but Henry was not discouraged. Wolcott declared Henry's "ringing speech" at the state convention the best he had ever heard him make. Teller "showed the folly of silver men leaving the Republican Party."

Optimistically, Henry and Ed set out on the campaign trail. "I think we can do both [carry the state and national tickets]," Teller encouragingly wrote Dawson. They got little help from the national party; in fact, it actually hurt them. Teller's old nemesis John Sherman made a speech in Cincinnati on gold that Teller felt "hurt us badly, but I don't think he cares."

At home, he, Wolcott, and others found themselves "greeted with hisses, cat-calls, and hooting" as they tried to support the Republican Party's candidates and platform. Speakers "were fairly howled from platforms." Teller had not faced such hostility for twenty years. One shocked observer reported, "In the mountain towns especially, a reign of terror was inaugurated." Businessmen who supported Republicans were "plainly told" they would be "compelled to go out of business" by a Populist boycott.

State silver Democrats gained control of their party, leaving the Republicans trying desperately to straddle the gap between their national stand and Colorado's needs. The *Denver Times* correctly observed that "the average Colorado Populist is simply a Republican or Democrat with a grievance." That was true, but that grievance concerned silver, the most potent campaign issue that year.

The campaign ended with the worst defeat Republicans had suffered in state history. Colorado's electoral votes went to the Populist candidate, James Weaver, and voters elected two Populists to the House of Representatives, placed Populist Davis Waite in the governor's chair, and with the aid of the silver Democrats controlled the state Senate. The Republicans scraped through with a one-vote majority in the House. Coloradans cast a vote for silver and "people power" and against corporate power and the entrenched power of the financial community in the two old parties.[7]

For the first time since the Civil War, the Democrats captured the presidency and both houses of Congress. It proved a pyrrhic victory, as President Cleveland and his party quickly learned.

As soon as Congress reconvened, the silver fight broke out. Opponents wanted to repeal the Sherman Act, whereas Teller and others energetically supported it. The senior senator, too, now saw a plot. The advocates of repeal, he argued, belong to that class of financiers "who suppose that whatever is done across the water by the English is exactly the thing. They are English in their finances." Henry ventured that there "must be expansion and growth of currency with the growth of the people." Silver remained the answer.

A progold publication, *Sound Currency,* chided Teller and other silver advocates. Gold monometalism "is the unavoidable destiny of this country," the editor proclaimed. Silver producers "are wholly secondary in comparison to the immense advantage the country" would gain with gold. The United States was part of the "civilized" world, which did not accept the "snare" of bimetallism. All the silver agitation had only hampered industry and deranged business "by [creating] financial unrest and commercial apprehension." Coloradans, of course, cheered on the "magnificent fight" Teller and Wolcott were conducting on "behalf of silver."

The political turmoil of 1892 overshadowed a growing economic crisis. Times were not good. Teller alluded to this crisis in a letter to a constituent in which he discussed paying silver rather than gold for greenbacks and treasury notes. If silver were adopted there might be "some financial disturbance," he cautioned, but that was far better "than to continue to pay in gold and keep all the industries of the country in their present distressed condition and continue the disturbed financial condition of the past 15 months."[8]

Agricultural distress had worsened since the late 1880s, and in consequence business earnings dependent on farm markets or goods also suffered. U.S. industry had expanded too rapidly, creating debt, which combined with urban growth nearly drained the nation's investment resources. Industrialization and growth led to poverty for many immigrants and workers. Foreign markets also shuddered. Panic struck in April 1893.

The panic was created by psychological fear. Americans confidently assumed that when the treasury held a reserve of at least $100 million in gold, all was right with the country. At the time of the silver and tariff debate in 1890, however, the reserve had been double that amount. Inept Republican tariffs, combined with lavish pensions for aging veterans, cut down revenue, and cautious financiers started hoarding gold. It took extreme borrowing from New York bankers for the Harrison administration to keep the reserve above the $100 million safety line until it limped out of Washington.

Cleveland and the Democrats arrived in 1893 and found the gold reserve barely above the safety line. By the third week of April, it had dipped below the line. Fear, alarm, then panic raced across the country, smashing almost overnight the hopes and dreams of a generation of Americans.

Over the next six months 8,000 businesses failed, 400 banks closed, and 156 railroads followed each other into receivership. Industrialists cut payrolls, merchants ended purchases, brokers dumped stocks, and people demanded relief. Only debts failed to decline during summer of 1893.

With miners and farmers already reeling, it did not take much to push Colorado over the brink. A report by the Colorado Bureau of Labor Statistics on September 1 showed graphically what had happened during the past two months. More than 45,000 people had been thrown out of work, 435 mines had closed, and 377 businesses had failed. The report summarized the condition of various towns.

> Blue: Crested Butte, Castle Rock
> Depressing: Denver, Idaho Springs, Ouray
> Bad: Alamosa, Fort Collins. Grand Junction
> Very Bad: Silver Cliff, Glenwood Springs
> Gloomy: Brighton, Breckenridge, Durango
> Dull: Delta, Erie, Florence
> Dark: Cheyenne Wells, Canfield, Cortez
> Disheartening: Holyoke
>
> Deplorable: Las Animas
> Desperate: Longmont, Loveland
> Hopeless: Rico
> Dead: La Veta

The report included comments from various unidentified sources about that summer, clearly illustrating mining's significance to Colorado. From Custer County came this summation: "The people are almost destitute, owing to failure of crops and the decreasing price of silver." Washington County contributed this observation: "The situation in our vicinity is indeed gloomy. The death of silver is the death of farming in this state." In Garfield County: "The situation is very bad; all credit business is stopped, and [people] are in need of the common necessaries of life. Crime and poverty is rapidly increasing." Finally, Bent County's plight was described: "Low prices of farm products and scarcity of money have made the condition of our people a deplorable one."[9]

A friend lamented to Henry in November, "Money is not plentiful and the poor creditors are crying for blood." He especially targeted eastern creditors who "are grasping everything in sight." Edmond VanDiest concurred, writing from Colorado Springs that all "you can make here at present is a bare living."

Why was Colorado struggling? In 1892 Colorado silver production hit an all-time record of $20.88 million (half the country's production) as new districts opened and old ones tried to produce more to compensate for the falling price. The whole state, as mentioned earlier, came to depend on mining. Yet mining, even without the silver price crisis, had nearly reached the point of diminishing returns. Higher labor costs, mining expenses, smelter fees, and transportation charges cut deeply into profits in the older districts. Increasing lower-grade silver deposits only made matters worse. Silver priced below 80 cents an ounce meant catastrophe, and it dipped below that amount in early 1893. Investors demanded dividends, and mine owners expected a return. Neither was forthcoming. Even before the crash, Coloradans watched angrily and worriedly as matters raced out of control.

Despite national cries for government help and public works, Cleveland followed the conventional wisdom of the day. The problem was a business matter outside the realm of politics, and businessmen would have to solve it. Meanwhile, he would keep the government solvent and preserve the gold standard.

The president did call a special session of Congress to repeal the Sherman Silver Purchase Act. The conservative Cleveland, supported by all "sound" money men, pointed the finger at silver. With its purchase and redemption in gold, they rather simplistically believed, the villain had been unmasked. The road to recovery was at hand.

That special session preceded the tensest, most active months of Teller's Senate career. From August to October the *Congressional Record* dramatically documents his involvement.

Henry debated, spoke (one speech stretched over three days), presented petitions, and worked continually on the floor and off. He attacked his old nemesis Senator Sherman for trying to convince the country that the panic "arises out of a distrust by the American people of the currency of the country." He introduced relief bills for some of his hard-pressed constituents, including Horace Tabor. He presented petitions and memorials supporting free silver and opposing repeal, including ones from the Pioneer Ladies Aid Society of Colorado, Montezuma County citizens, railway conductors of Colorado, citizens of Leadville, and the Franklin Club of Cleveland, Ohio.[10]

His finest moment came in a speech that started Saturday, September 9, 1893, and ended the next Tuesday. It was typical Teller—detailed, thoroughly researched, well fortified with facts and historical precedents, carefully organized, and forthright. As his secretary Dawson warned, "Woe betide the man who questioned his array of facts and precedents in debate."

More passion and emotion than usual were evident in Teller's presentation. For example, he opened with his view about the times—"[This is an] extraordinary session and there is an extraordinary condition of things in this country"; "I intend to debate this [the silver] question until I am thoroughly satisfied that I have discharged my duty to my constituents, that I have discharged it to the people of the United States, and that I have discharged it to the unborn millions, who are to suffer, in my judgment, from this pernicious proposed legislation."

He felt obliged to respond to an allegation: "I have no more interest in silver mining individually than any other member of this body. I repeat, I have never mined an ounce of silver in my life. I have no properties in silver." It does seem inconceivable that not one of his Gilpin County mines had failed to produce an "ounce" of silver. He defended his conduct in the Senate during the session: "And above all, I have endeavored to conduct myself so that I would have the approval of my conscience."

Like many politicians before and since, Henry was upset with the press, which was pressuring for a quick vote: "Is the American Senate to be lectured to by the newspaper press and ordered as if they had masters to proceed without deliberation?"

After praising and defending Colorado, Teller launched into the main body of the speech. Starting with the writing of the Constitution, Henry traced the money question through the "Crime of '73" to the Sherman Act. The act had not caused the depression; it "actually brought prosperity." The blame for the crash lay at the "feet of people manipulating stocks, Europe, bankers, and mistrust of the government."

During his address he paused to answer queries from listening senators. Although he was not a Populist, he defended them, believing they had justifiable grievances. They might have put in their platform "some things that would better have been left out," not including the free coinage of silver.

He concluded with statements that summarized his views past, present, and future.

I am a bimetallist. I wish to say that I consider it no kind of reproach to say that a man is a bimetallist. I am proud of the term. I am proud to be called a bimetallist, with all that that term implies. I can be called a lunatic, a crank, a fanatic, and it does not affect me a bit. I am in the company of the most reputable people who ever lived. I am in a company with more intelligence than any man who assails it. . . .

Bimetallism is founded upon a principle, and it is defensible in any court in the world. It is the only system by which the finances of the world can be held, as ought to be, in equilibrium. . . .

I should consider myself craven to such a degree that I would not be worthy of a seat in this Chamber or among men if I should allow this great crime, as I consider it, to be carried out without a protest here.

Wolcott joined his colleague in a desperate fight against repeal. With even more emotion he stated that when silver "is destroyed" and a great section of the economy laid to waste, "we are to be led into the valley of the shadow of death with no rod and no staff to comfort us. The step when taken will be irrevocable." Their pleas fell on unhearing ears in Washington and on the Senate floor. The free coinage amendment went down to defeat: twenty-eight senators for, thirty-eight against. They could no longer muster the strength to filibuster or defeat the bill.[11]

Defeated, the silver men gave their valedictories. In a chamber "silent as death," on October 27, 1893, Teller addressed his colleagues and the large audience beyond in the most "terrible moment of my legislative life. We are neither downcast nor dejected. We shall not abandon the faith that is in us." The silverites would not give up. Wolcott, more excitable, eulogized in part: "These are indeed grave and sad days for us. Your action drives our miners from their homes in the mountains, and compels the abandonment of hamlets and of towns that but yesterday were prosperous and populous." He lamented:

> The wrong, however, which you are inflicting upon us is cruel and unworthy, and the memory of it will return to vex you. Out of the misery of it all, our representatives in this Senate will be always glad to remember that they did their duty as God gave them the vision to see it.
>
> It is for us, standing together on this question, to save our common country from greater suffering and impoverishment than even the horrors of war could inflict.

Unmoved, the Senate promptly repealed the Sherman Silver Purchase Act. In what was described as an "impressive silence," the vote stood at forty-eight yeas, thirty-seven nays.

Writing to William Jackson Palmer on October 29, Wolcott shed some light on these events: "You can have but little idea of the pressure that had been brought to be on us from every conceivable channel. Most of us have lost whatever standing or influence we had established in the east." The silver people could have compromised, extending purchases another year, but they felt "that would have done us far more injury than unconditional repeal." They feared every owner with ore in sight would gut his mine. That "abnormal productivity" would give opponents of silver additional arguments against the metal. They also feared small merchants and others would try to sell their property within the year, causing great problems for real estate and property values.

According to Ed, the "vicious character" of the Sherman Act, which made silver a commodity, made it "impossible to tinker it into anything sound or satisfactory." He concluded, "Until silver shall be treated as a standard, I can see little hope for its permanent recognition."

Palmer greatly appreciated what the two had done: "The devotion of our Senators to the interests of Colorado, of the western half of the United States and to the cause of Silver is signal and unquestioned. They have striven with marvelous courage and energy to guard our mining interests and to secure the more extended use of silver as money."[12]

The repeal of the act solved little except ending the purchase of silver and satisfied few, if any, Americans in attempting to ease the country's woes. The continued redemption of greenbacks with gold kept the bullion reserve below the safety line. Enraged westerners lusted for revenge. The Democrats, they believed, had sold out to bankers, whereas the Republicans continued to be hopelessly reactionary. That left the Populists, the party of the common man.

Despite the defeat, Coloradans cheered Teller and Wolcott. Henry warned his constituents that until Congress heard from them "at the ballot box and . . . in a way that will compel attention to their desire," no favorable silver legislation would appear. Letters arrived from admirers throughout the country for "so brave and splendid [a] fight for silver." Invitations came for him to speak. The fight had made Henry Teller a national figure. In an interview in Chicago Teller cautioned again that the repeal of the act would not produce better times, as its opponents claimed: "There is not a single indication of revival of business and there will be none."

When Henry returned to Denver, the feelings expressed by the people, one observer proudly wrote to Dawson, compared only to "the feeling that the whole country had for Lincoln. It would have made your heart throb with pride and joy and pleasure and everything else, to have witnessed the reception given Mr. Teller at the Brown Palace."

The silver forces gained strength throughout 1894. Eager Populists excitedly looked forward to the next presidential election year two years hence. The Republican Party, for all intents and purposes, had married itself to the gold standard. Where did that leave the silver bloc? Teller received a cordial letter from one presidential candidate, Ohio governor William McKinley. The genial McKinley, a party regular, had supported the silver cause while a congressman in the 1870s and 1880s. A possibility existed for silver there.

On the Senate floor, however, Teller threatened to vote with the Democrats on another tariff bill. The Republicans were trying to filibuster, and Teller almost gleefully reminded them that they had joined with Democrats to repeal the Sherman Act. He would take "great pleasure in giving them a dose of the same medicine they so cheerfully prescribed for them [silver senators] during that memorable contest." Bitterness ran deep. Wolcott, meanwhile, sailed to England to attend an unofficial international bimetallic conference. Nothing resulted from the conference, as both men feared.[13]

Facing reelection that year, Wolcott discovered he was not especially popular despite his silver heroics. His dictatorial control of the party angered some; other Coloradans did not like his confrontational, sometimes "superior eastern" personality. Teller had worked to build Ed's image for reelection by, among others things, allowing the junior senator to sponsor nearly every local bill for Colorado. Still, Wolcott faced another fight, especially if the Populists continued their momentum.

As Teller had foreseen, though, the Populist tide started to recede. He felt they had gone too far, as he said in a Washington interview: "It is not a question of the defeat of any one individual but of the entire party."

Governor Waite, whose antics hurt the party and embarrassed many Coloradans, lost his reelection bid—blaming, among others, women who had just received the vote. Besides his infamous "bloody bridles" comment, he had proven very quotable, much to the delight of the nation's press. He was a staunch free silverite, and the manner in which he supported the cause shocked people: "Except [for] a few damned fools, the people [of] Colorado, without distinction of party, are in favor of free coinage of silver at 16 to 1." Teller, embarrassed, sharply criticized Waite's "rabid frothings" as "erroneous and unrepresentative of the sober opinion of the state."

The Republicans recaptured the governor's chair and regained a slim majority in the legislature, thus assuring Wolcott of a second term. Usually politically astute, he committed a blunder near the end of the campaign. He promised that if free coinage could be implemented through another party than the Republicans, "I will leave that party."

During the great debate of 1893, with Henry busy in Washington, Coloradans voted to give women the right to vote, the first state to do so by an election. Because of the silver crisis, Teller did not have time to get as involved as he had earlier. His work in the past was appreciated, however. Susan B. Anthony invited Harriet and Henry to the annual convention of the Women's Suffrage movement to celebrate the victory. She wanted him to say a few words, to "express your belief in the entrance of women into the body politic of Colorado. I hope you will say yes." Back in Colorado, men wondered what impact suffrage would have. One confided to Dawson that he had no doubt that it would change "things rather materially . . . but no one can tell just exactly what will be the outcome."

IN THE MIDST OF THE SPECIAL SESSION, Teller lobbied for the federal government to donate money from mineral land sales to Colorado to help keep the School of Mines open to all. He had proposed this idea earlier without success. With a great deal of pride Henry affirmed there "was none superior on this continent" to Mines, perhaps none in the world. He continued: "Mining is an industry that must occur in this country as applied to iron, coal, silver, gold, and copper. It certainly is proper that we should have a place in this country where American youth can go without great expense being entailed upon them."

In a January 1895 speech, Teller discussed the proposed federal income tax. Although he thought "the income tax is an objectionable tax," he could not "recall any tax which is not an objectionable tax." Teller made a prediction: "In my judgment the time will never come again when the American people will be without an income tax, although I know the present tax is limited to five years. It has become the system of revenue in nearly every civilized country in the world since 1842." Henry did feel incomes derived "from high professional labors or which are derived from property should bear a proper and just burden of the support of the Government." The income tax traveled a twisting path before a constitutional amendment adopting it was ratified in 1913. Nor has it gone away, as Teller predicted.[14]

During 1894–1895, cheered on by Coloradans and silverites everywhere, Teller and Wolcott doggedly fought for free coinage against nearly impossible odds within the national Republican Party and in Congress. There were speeches to give, meetings to attend, letters to write, congressional debates to participate in, and a host of other activities.

The economic anguish did not ease in Colorado. Teller wrote gloomily in 1895: "I know a large number of mining men who thought three years ago that their fortunes were secured, who today feel that they had no fortune at all." The price of silver must improve or "it is only a question of time when silver mining must cease in this state."

Nationally, the economic situation seemed little better. Dismay and distress caused an army of the unemployed, led by Jacob Coxey, to march on Washington from points throughout the country. They wanted, among other things, government aid with building roads, issuing legal-tender notes, and paying $1.50 a day to all who needed employment. Coxey and 500 followers arrived determined to lay their demands before Congress, now a worried body. Conservatives and many other Americans looked on in horror, shocked at what they deemed to be the threshold of revolution.

Teller did not think so. In a May 10, 1894, address, Henry gave a clear explanation of his political philosophy while taking about the Coxey situation and the depression. Although, Henry denied that Coxey represented a "great mass of people," he reminded his colleagues that their sentiments and distress were real. He chided his fellow senators: "The average American legislator does not keep himself in sympathy and accord with the sentiment of the people and has not full knowledge of their distress." The people had the right of petition, he argued, not the right to invade the Senate or necessarily to "present the petition on the steps of the Capitol." Some senators thought of them as ignorant people who knew little about finance and that therefore they "do not need and are unworthy of our sympathy." That was not true, asserted Henry.

He spoke for those forgotten, ordinary Americans whom the Senate seemed hell-bent to ignore: "I sympathize with these people. I suppose it is unstatesmanlike." He continued:

> I do not think there is any waste of time, even in the American Senate, in the discussion of questions involving the liberties and rights of the citizen. I am

old-fashioned enough to believe that there is a great deal in this country which is more valuable than money—that life, liberty, and the pursuit of happiness . . . are of infinitely more value to us than the mere question of [whether] . . . the tariff [shall be] for revenue or for protection.

I know it is not fashionable for a man to stand here and speak for the lowly and the distressed. I know a man loses caste in the financial circles of the country when he does so. I know that because I have stood in the Senate for years insisting the laboring people were after all God's elect I have lost caste in certain circles, and I am set down as a crank. But I am not disturbed about it. My heart goes out to the man who labors.

Teller had spoken for the people for forty years. He updated this speech with references to the silver and tariff debate, but Henry had defended the "forgotten American" since the exciting 1850s.[15]

Coxey and his followers got nowhere. The police arrested the leaders of the demonstration for trespassing on the Capitol lawn. His dismayed followers eventually disbanded, as did other marchers coming to Washington. The movement might die, but the ideas lived on.

Teller's main political problem had become the fact that although he was out of step with the national party, he paraded in step in Colorado. Silver and free coinage aroused every corner of the state. Wolcott, on the other hand, tried to straddle party and state. His effort proved impossible, although he kept his eyes on the East and his own career.

The two men got along well during these months. In an 1890 speech Wolcott praised his "good fortune" to be associated with a colleague who "has stood as the exponent of the views of an intelligent constituency upon this real subject [silver], and who has left nothing pertinent unsaid."

All the issues had at last merged. Debtor stood against creditor, western ruralite squared off against eastern urbanite, silverite opposed goldbug, older America conflicted with new America—Teller probably understood all this as well as any of his Senate colleagues. Behind the rhetoric flared a battle over America's future.

Heated rhetoric fired from both sides, with logic and reason going "out the window." On the silver side, *Coin's Financial School* (1894)—simplistically and with drawings—explained what had gone wrong, who was guilty, and how the country could be cured. The author, William Harvey, had professor Coin bewildering goldbugs with unanswerable logic. The *Banker's Magazine* (May 1895) took care of "Coin" and his unanswerable logic, at least in the editor's eyes. The review described the book as a "series of ridiculous" pictures accompanied by a text "containing many absolute misstatements together with the gross suppression of fact." It was, he intoned, aimed mainly "toward uneducated voters." William Jennings Bryan, on the other hand, thought it a "most potential[ly] educational influence on behalf of bimetallism."[16]

The probusiness *Banker's Magazine* despised *Corporation Rats in Our National Corn-Crib* written by twenty-seven-year-old lawyer Albinus Worsley. The emotionally charged title page blasted all the villains. The general thrust of the attack can be gathered from this excerpt:

> These Corporation Rats have burrows under ground from Wall Street to Washington. And from Washington to Europe, and you may put in new planks, put on a new roof or get a new lock—they have the key and will continue to steal the corn and leave the people bare cobs to gnaw until we place in power a new party with a new platform, which means a new corn-crib built in modern style up off from the ground so that the rats cannot get in.

The banks "have an absolute control of our financial legislation. They are the power that must be overthrown or liberty is gone forever." The cunning, villainous Republican and Democratic administrations not only sold out to England; far worse, they became "inefficient, corrupt, and traitors" to the American people. The answer was to vote for silver and the People's Party.

Coloradans read and believed. They fought to uphold their way of life based on mining and, to a lesser degree, agriculture against the oncoming new United States. To them it seemed the old moral values, the traditional America (rural, small-town America) was being sacrificed on the altar of greed, or "a cross of gold" as Bryan preached. As Senator Jones had vowed, this "is war."

Henry fervently believed in the cause. In a series of letters written in 1895 to constituents and friends, Teller reiterated his positions. If greenbacks were redeemed with silver there would be little economic disturbance, "but we cannot hope for improvement if we pursue the course marked out for us by the Treasury Department or eastern sentiment."

Henry strongly emphasized what he had only touched upon before. The Sherman Act, in reality, had been a "goldbug scheme and not a silver scheme." Although he was still loyal to the Republican Party, the conduct of "Eastern Republicans at the Special Session in 1893 has greatly aggravated our people and done great harm to the party." Teller judged that party ties and obligations "set very lightly on the people of the West at this time." President Cleveland, he charged, had betrayed the United States to England on the silver question.

Making matters more despicable in western eyes, the president had worked with J. P. Morgan and other eastern financiers to float bond issues to keep the gold reserves above $100 million. The investors received a very favorable rate of return, albeit not without damnation for Cleveland for working "hand-in-glove with the plutocrats." This split the Democratic Party.[17]

Printed and reprinted, Teller's speeches circulated throughout the country. Those from 1893 and those discussing the fight over the Sherman Act were the most popular; his prosilver efforts throughout these years also appeared in print. He attacked gold-backing Great Britain in a May 1894 speech more bluntly than he had ever done before. The thesis of his argument was that "we cannot afford to let Great Britain steal our markets, and at the same time destroy the monetary conditions of the world, and bring the laboring people not only of this country but of every country under the sun to a state of degradation and want." He repeatedly chastened Republicans for having lost the faith and confidence of the people.

At the same time, he championed Coloradans at every turn against the allegations hurled at them. They were, Henry proudly declared, "well informed on political and economical questions. They are not the dolts some of our Eastern friends think." Populated with "active, energetic, intelligent, educated men and women," Colorado need not fret. He turned it back on the detested easterners, the best of whom, Teller felt, had migrated west: "We think we have the 'pink and pick' of the Eastern people, and the number of college men here engaged in business and in the learned professions supports that conclusion."[18]

Coloradans believed. They had the faith, and so did others. That provided the key to understanding what was happening and what would happen. Everything pointed toward 1896, the presidential election of the century, many people thought. In their opinion, the fate of the American republic hung in the balance.

NOTES

1. Material for this overview was found in Gilbert C. Fite et al., *An Economic History of the United States* (Boston: Houghton Mifflin, 1965); Ross M. Robertson et al., *History of the American Economy* (New York: Harcourt Brace Jovanovich, 1979); John W. Reps, *Cities of the American West* (Princeton: Princeton University Press, 1979); Arthur Schlesinger Jr. (ed.), *History of U.S. Political Parties,* vol. 2 (New York: Chelsea House, 1973).

2. *Rocky Mountain News* (weekly), September 20, 1876; *Colorado Transcript,* September 30, 1876; Philip Wilcox to Teller, March 7, 1878, C. Clements to Teller, January 28, 1878, both in Teller Collection, Denver Public Library; *Rocky Mountain News,* September 20, 1879, August 27, 1880; *Colorado Miner,* October 30, 1880; *Georgetown Courier,* March 16, April 27, 1882; *Silverton Democrat,* February 12, 1885; Schlesinger, *History of U.S. Political Parties,* vol. 2, 1704–06; Gene Clanton, *Populism* (Boston: Twayne, 1991), 121–122; Paolo E. Coletta, *William Jennings Bryan* (Lincoln: University of Nebraska Press, 1964), 206.

3. *Congressional Record,* January 27, 1882, 447–449, March 21, 1882, 2100; *Silverton Democrat,* February 13, 1886.

4. Charles Thomas, "Reminiscences," Special Collections, Colorado College, iii; *New York Times,* January 8, 1891; Thomas Dawson, "Teller and Wolcott," Colorado Historical Society, 11; Samuel Emmons, *Progress of the Precious Metal Industry in the United States* (Washington, D.C.: Government Printing Office, 1893), 92–94.

5. Edward O. Wolcott, *Free Coinage* (Washington, D.C.: Government Printing Office, 1890), 3–8; Thomas Dawson, *Edward Oliver Wolcott* (New York: Knickerbocker, 1911), vol. 2, 7–8, 20–21, 571–572, 576; John P. Jones, *Speech* (Washington, D.C.: Government Printing Office, 1890), 112; Wm. Windom to Teller, November 6, 1889, Teller Papers, Colorado Historical Society.

6. Dawson, "Teller and Wolcott," 14–15. Dawson speculated that the story might have been apocryphal. John Sherman, *Speech* (Washington, D.C.: Government Printing Office, 1891), 13–18, 31–38; John Jones, *Speech* (Washington, D.C.: Government Printing Office, 1890), 3, 4, 25; George H. Mayer, *The Republican Party* (New York: Oxford University Press, 1967), 224–226.

7.   Bryan to Teller, June 31, 1891?, March 21, 1892, note, 1892?, Secretary of the Treasury to Teller, September 3, 24, 1891, S. McCullon to Teller, September 15, 1891, Teller to R. W. Steele, December 29, 1891, Teller to Dawson, July 24, September 12, 18, October 10, 16, November 13, 1892, all in Teller Papers, Colorado Historical Society; Teller to Tabor, February 15, 1892, Tabor Papers, Colorado Historical Society; R. G. Dill, *The Political Campaigns of Colorado* (Denver: Arapaho, 1895), 165, 193–194; *Great Southwest* (Durango), September 22, 1892; *Rocky Mountain News,* July 14, 1892; Wolcott cited in Thomas Dawson, "Scrapbooks," Colorado Historical Society, vol. 61; James Wright, *The Politics of Populism: Dissent in Colorado* (New Haven: Yale University Press, 1974), 81–83, 138, 158; Schlesinger, *History of U.S. Political Parties,* vol. 2, 1701–04, 1763–65; Clanton, *Populism,* 122–124; Jeffery A. Frieden, "Monetary Populism in Nineteenth-Century America," *Journal of Economic History* (June 1997): 367–369; Thomas Cronin and Robert Loevy, *Colorado Politics and Government* (Lincoln: University of Nebraska Press, 1993), 61.

8.   *Sound Currency,* March 1, 1893; *Great Southwest,* February 7, 1893; Leon Fuller, "Governor Waite and His Silver Panacea," *Colorado Magazine* (March 1933): 43; Stephen Kneeshaw and John M. Linngren, "The Republican Comeback, 1902," *Colorado Magazine* (winter 1971): 15; Teller to Everett Winship, February 2, 1892, Teller speech, February 5, 1893, both in Teller Papers, Special Collections, Colorado College.

9.   *Effects of Demonetization of Silver on the Industries of Colorado, July 1 to August 31, 1890* (Denver: Smith-Brooks, 1893), 1–33; Edmond VanDiest to H. J. Menten, August 2, 1893, VanDiest Letters, Special Collections, Colorado College.

10.   Robert Steele to Teller, November 24, 1893, Teller Papers, Colorado Historical Society; VanDiest to M. H. Gillot, October 10, 1893, VanDiest to Menten, August 2, 1893, VanDiest to James Bloner, September 20, 1893, all in VanDiest Letters, Special Collections, Colorado College. See the *Congressional Record,* for example, on the following dates in 1893: August 9, 35–36; August 15, 72; August 17, 191; August 19, 247; August 30, 857; September 3, 1068; October 10, 236; October 26, 309; October 27, 3140.

11.   Henry Teller, *The Panic and Its Causes* (Washington, D.C.: Government Printing Office, 1893), 1–52; Dawson, "Teller and Wolcott," 11; Edward Wolcott, *The Silver Discussion* (Washington, D.C.: Government Printing Office, 1893), 16.

12.   Edward Wolcott, *Causes of the Panic* (Washington, D.C.: Government Printing Office, 1893), 3–6; Allan Nevins, *Grover Cleveland* (New York: Dodd, Mead, 1964), 542–547; Dawson, *Wolcott,* vol. 2, 593, 596–597, 639; *Congressional Record,* January 12, 1895, 894–901; Teller, *The Panic,* 1–25; Wolcott to Palmer, October 29, 1892, William J. Palmer, note, October 18, 1893, both in William Jackson Palmer Papers, Special Collections, Colorado College.

13.   *Durango Herald,* October 31, 1893; John Reagan to Teller, November 21, 1893, R. W. Steele to Dawson, November 24, 1893, R. J. to Dawson, November 22, 1893, Edward Wolcott to Thomas Reed, March 15, 1894, Wm. McKinley to Teller, March 17, 1894, Wolcott to Teller, May 24, August 8, 1894, all in Teller Papers, Colorado Historical Society; *Denver Republican,* May 17, 1894; unidentified clipping, "Teller Scrapbook," Chris Buys private collection; Coletta, *William Jennings Bryan,* 118.

14.   *Evening Star* (Washington), August 20, 1894; Steele to Dawson, November 24, 1893, Anthony to Teller, December 2, 1893, both in Teller Papers, Colorado Historical

Society; *Leadville Daily Herald,* July 7, 1893; *Denver Republican,* July 18, 1893; *Congressional Record,* October 28, 1893, 3138, January 12, 1895, 892; Fuller, "Governor Waite," 41–42; Charles Hartzell, *History of Colorado . . . Davis the First* (Denver: C. J. Kelly, 1894), 6; Henry Teller, *The Financial Problem and Its Solution* (Washington, D.C.: Government Printing Office, 1895), 2–3.

15. Teller to Wharton Barker, Teller Collection, University of Colorado; *Argus* (Fort Collins), March 2, 1895; Henry Teller, "The Coxey Movement," copy of speech, Special Collections, Colorado College, 3–11.

16. William Harvey, *Coin's Financial School* (Cambridge: Harvard University Press, 1963 reprint); *Banker's Magazine,* May 1895, 756, 758, 761–775, July 1895, 33; Wolcott, "June 17, 1890, Speech," Special Collections, Colorado College; *Salida Mail,* July 5, 1895; *Chaffee County News,* March 12, 1895; *Pagosa News,* April 19, 26, May 10, 1895; William J. Bryan, *The First Battle* (Chicago: W. B. Conkey, 1896), 153–154.

17. Albinus Worsley, *Corporation Rats in Our National Corn-Crib* (Chicago: Chicago Sentinel, 1895), 5–6, 13–14, 111, 116, 120–128, 135–139, 145 (quote on pp. 5–6); Teller to Everett Winship, February 2, 1895, Teller to Wharton Barker, August 21, 1895, Teller to Robert Cameron, December 23, 1895, all in Teller Papers, Colorado Historical Society; Schlesinger, *History of U.S. Political Parties,* vol. 2, 1720–21.

18. For Teller's speeches see *The Financial Problem and Its Solution* (Washington, D.C.: Government Printing Office, 1895); copy of speech, "International Agreement on Silver," Teller Collection, University of Colorado; *Miscellaneous Speeches* (Washington, D.C.: Government Printing Office, 1893); *Shall the Bonded Debt Be Increased?* (Washington, D.C.: Government Printing Office, 1893); *Silver Coinage* (Washington, D.C.: Government Printing Office, 1892). See also Teller to Wharton Barker, August 21, 1895, Teller Papers, Colorado Historical Society.

Year of the Jubilee

The year of the jubilee was a year of rejoicing, a year of deliverance from tribulation, according to American folksong and story. Many Americans prayed and dreamed that 1896 would be the dawn of future happiness.

The year was the most momentous in sixty-five-year-old Teller's life. He had speeches to give and Senate business to take care of. In the Senate, civility was cast aside, a casualty of the passion of the times. Teller lashed out at Vermont's venerable senator Justin Morrill: "I am a Republican in the truest and best sense. I helped create the Republican Party. I was in it before the Senator from Vermont." Teller warned prophetically, "He must allow me to go out of it in the way I came in." He reminded long-time antagonist John Sherman that westerners "get no more sympathy and no more support than if we have been aliens in an alien land." Finally, he bitterly took to task gold Republicans and the Democratic Cleveland administration: "If there ever was a nation in the world that seems to be governed by imbeciles and men without thought or men without reason it is fair to say we are now in the hands of that class of people."[1]

Henry had other matters to contemplate. His long-ago political ally James Belford wrote to him in March. He anticipated no relief for silver from either the St. Louis or Chicago (Democratic) conventions. Nevertheless, Belford warned, "no Republican can carry this state on a gold platform or on a straddle platform—on this you can rely." Teller agreed.

Teller looked toward St. Louis and the Republican presidential convention. First, the state delegation had to be selected. It would wholeheartedly support silver. The only question for the May 14 state meeting in Pueblo to resolve was whether Wolcott or Teller would lead the delegates.

Wolcott seemed to be gaining momentum until it was revealed that widespread corruption had led to his delegate victory in Arapaho County. Ed's eastern leanings and sympathies and his down-the-line support of the national Republican Party finally took their toll. Teller won, and Ed barely escaped censure.

Teller wrote to Irving Stanton, state chairman, telling him that "I do not intend to support a candidate on a gold-standard platform or on a platform of doubtful construction." Neither did the delegates who championed Teller and his opposition to fixing the country on the gold standard. A supporter wrote Henry that he was happy to see that "we have demonstrated emphatically that the Republican Party of Colorado was first for the interest of the State and was not out for party spoils." He wondered what impact this might have on the Democratic national convention. He thought it ought "to be very great."[2]

Even before St. Louis, the goldbugs had apparently seized control of the Republican Party and were set to nominate their man, William McKinley. Teller and the other western silverites, determined nevertheless to take a stand, went to the convention anyway. Talk had surfaced that Teller and the silver Republicans might join with the Populists and, it was hoped, the Democrats to select their own candidate. The name most frequently mentioned was Henry M. Teller. Speculation centered on whether the Democrats would agree to such a deal. If not, some surmised that Teller might run anyway and hope to prevent any candidate from winning a majority. That would force Congress to decide the winner.[3]

In June Teller went to St. Louis. That same month Colorado began showing signs of recovering from the depression. Silver mining might be doing poorly, but gold mining was doing well. Gold bonanza Cripple Creek boomed, as did the rejuvenated San Juans. The Gunnison "gold belt" showed promise. Even silver Aspen and Creede mined steadily, desperately trying to make up for the decreased silver price with volume. Signs of business recovery surfaced in many towns. Miners, however, struck in Leadville and in some coal districts over wages, working conditions, and union recognition.

Despite the defeat in St. Louis, Colorado stood proud. Governor Albert McIntire telegrammed Teller that a twenty-one-gun salute was being fired at the state capitol in his and the delegation's honor for their "brave and patriotic stand. We are proud of you and the delegation and delight to show it." Teller received a reported 700 telegrams of congratulations the day he bolted, and hundreds more came every day after that. Henry, meanwhile, went to visit his mother in Morrison, as she "is expecting him." He needed some rest and did not anticipate arriving home until July.

Even while "resting," though, he kept active politically, encouraging Idaho senator Fred Dubois that the "friends of silver made no mistake in St. Louis." Henry did not think the gold Democrats could control their party's convention; he hoped for a silver nominee. If so, he counseled, silverites must overlook "all minor differences" to put the country on a sound financial system. A "little more patriotism and a little less partisanship is what our country needs at this time." Teller repeatedly returned to that theme.

When Teller returned he was hailed as Colorado's greatest hero. Railroads offered special rates to bring people to Denver for his arrival, and the organizing committee "was determined to make it a memorable evening." Over 300 folks came out, and two bands were there from Central and Gilpin alone. Colorado did itself proud. Those who could not come sent telegrams. Banker Alfred Camp, merchant Thomas Graden, and "hundreds of others" sent telegrams from Durango congratulating him for his "noble stand" and that of the Colorado delegation and other silver men "of whom you are the acknowledged leader." They would be with the crowd "in spirit."

After spending part of the day (July 1) in Greeley, Henry reached a "gayly decorated" Denver. A parade "fully 5 miles long" escorted him from the depot to the reviewing stand. Bands, banners, fireworks, and cheers greeted the "Patriot, Statesman, Pioneer." Crowds lined the streets, an estimated 100,000 people; Coloradans had never seen anything like it. "One continual roar" echoed throughout the area of Broadway and Seventeenth as the parade took three-quarters of an hour to pass the reviewing stand. Finally, speakers prepared to laud Colorado's foremost citizen. Cheers and shouts for Teller almost drowned out others who tried to speak.

Henry spoke only briefly, thanking the people for this "magnificent demonstration" that fully "compensated" him for his political labor. For nearly twenty years he had represented Coloradans, endeavoring to do so "honestly and conscientiously and advocating the sentiments that they entertained." He turned to silver, encouraging his listeners—amid continuing applause—to stand united. They would then secure "a true, honest American system of finance."

With that he returned to his carriage and, with police assistance, went to Willard's home. There Henry would rest a few days, visit Central, and prepare for the campaign.[4]

The Teller presidential boomlet that started in St. Louis gathered momentum among the silverites. Wishfully, the *Ouray Herald* (June 11, 1896) hoped Teller would be the man the Democrats chose. The *Fort Collins Argus* (June 27, 1896) headlined "Teller Is Boomed." Other newspapers sounded the call. Accolades poured down on the "Moses and deliverer" of the common people.

> All hail that grand and courageous man, Colorado's able senator and pure and unsullied statesman, Henry M. Teller. (*Boulder Camera*)
>
> Colorado is with him wherever he may lead. (*Cripple Creek Times*)
>
> Teller for President. (*Aspen Tribune*)
>
> By a series of brilliant maneuvers, he compelled its [Republican Party] leaders to completely unmask themselves, [which] is in our opinion a service for the common people. (*Chaffee County Record*)

Senator Teller is the grandest, noblest patriot in the United States today. (*Ouray Herald*)

Many Coloradans hoped the Democratic Party, meeting in Chicago July 7–10, would select silver and Teller. Congressman John Shafroth wrote Teller, "There is an absolute unanimity of opinion that you would make a most excellent president."

Teller might have wanted rest, but he would not get any. Telegrams inundated him with encouragement, suggestions, and praise. Behind them loomed the Democratic national convention.

It might seem unbelievable that Democrats would seriously consider Republican Teller as a potential nominee. For decades Henry had challenged, criticized, and contested the party. His stand on silver, his concerns about railroads, and his views on income tax made him appealing, however, to the silver/reform wing of the party.

His comrade Fred Dubois advised him that this was not the time "for hasty expressions," as did the chairman of the new National Silver Republican Party. On July 2 a cheerful Dubois predicted Teller would be the Democratic nominee; if not, they must join with the Populists. Either way, a silver party would emerge. Nevada Democratic congressman Francis Newlands insisted that Henry represented the only hope of the silver Democrats: "Your honor and career will be crowned with success in this coming contest." An unidentified silverite described what silverites thought of their hero: "I regard Teller as one of the broadest and purest statesman of a century. He is as plain as the plain people, his statesmanship and humanity are as broad as were Lincoln's, and I predict that before this campaign is over the people will discover in him the closest prototype of that great man in every quality."

Teller privately told a friend he hoped he would not be nominated. Harriet implored emphatically: "No, no; we pray that that will not happen." Chicago would be the Rubicon for silver and Teller.[5]

Teller's friend William Jennings Bryan and other silver Democrats had been working for years to capture and change their party. To them, the conservative Cleveland-gold wing of the party appeared little different from the orthodox Republicans. They feared losing the West and perhaps the South to the Populists on issues people genuinely cared about. The answer seemed simple, albeit bold: accept the silver banner and other reforms and absorb the Populists.

In hot and humid Chicago the silver delegates gained control from the start, putting the gold wing on the defensive. Their platform came out for silver against a minority report for gold, thus repudiating their party's current president.

Bryan spoke last in the debate over the platform. He spoke for silver and the majority report. When his turn came to speak, he sprang from his seat, bounding for the platform. Raising his hand and asking for quiet, Bryan began what has become known as the "Cross of Gold Speech."

With a powerful, trained voice, Bryan reached listeners in the farthest corners of the hall. Defending every reform in the platform, he hurled verbal shots at the gold standard and gold delegates. He heralded war following a silver banner: "Our war is not a war of conquest; we are fighting in the defense of our homes, our families, and posterity." He spoke for the people, "the struggling masses against the idle holders of idle capital." He continued:

> The sympathies of the Democratic Party, as shown by the platform, are on the side of the struggling masses who have ever been the foundation of the Democratic Party. There are two ideas of government. There are those who believe that, if you will only legislate to make the well-to-do prosperous, their prosperity will leak through on those below. The Democratic idea, however, has been that if you legislate to make the masses prosperous, their prosperity will find its way up through every class which rests upon them.

The audience, Bryan later wrote, "seemed to rise and sit down as one man. At the close of a sentence it would rise and shout, and when I began upon another sentence, the room was [as] still as church." Delighted silverites heard their thoughts and ideas cascading forth.

By the time the dramatic climax came, the audience was nearly mesmerized. Bryan used every oratorical skill in his abundant arsenal:

> Having behind us the producing masses of this nation and the world, supported by the commercial interests, the laboring interests, and the toilers everywhere, we will answer their demand for a gold standard by saying to them: you shall not press down upon the brow of labor this crown of thorns, you shall not crucify mankind upon a cross of gold.

Stretching his arms out from his sides as if on a cross, Bryan stood silent for a moment, then dropped his arms and stepped back.

Stunned silence greeted him. Then, as he descended back to his seat on the floor, a demonstration began that lingered in his listeners' memories for the rest of their lives. The walls of the hall shook. Delegates carried Bryan around the hall. Cries for his nomination crescendoed.[6]

Bryan instantly became the front runner, and his speech gained immortality. He was nominated on the fifth ballot. Teller, never officially nominated, gained a handful of votes, but the Democrats were not going to vote for a lifelong Republican when one of their own so powerfully carried the day. Even some Colorado delegates, although they liked him, did not favor Teller's candidacy. "He has not been a Democrat," said one. Teller's friend and Democratic delegate Charles Thomas wrote to him about Bryan's performance: "After he finished it, he stood alone as the one man to whom the convention looked for its leader." Thomas concluded that destiny had "surely reached down," and it was "foolish to think of your [Teller's] nomination."

With the Democratic nomination out of the way, supporters encouraged Teller to try for the Populist nomination. Their convention met in St. Louis on July 22.

Neither Teller nor Dubois liked the idea. Dubois telegrammed Teller on July 10: "I cannot see why we should not accept him [Bryan] at once." Others told him to finish the course and go for the nomination. In a long letter written on July 13, Henry explained his position to a Populist. Although he was uncertain what silverites' political affiliations would be, he reiterated, "I know for myself it will not be with the Republican Party." He urged support of Bryan, although not necessary declaring "our adherence to the Democratic Party or its principles."

Populists, Henry urged, should maintain their platform, with its all-important principles, "yet make Bryan [their] nominee. I believe the cause of the people and of good government will be promoted by his election." Sounding a great deal like Thomas Paine, Henry concluded: "This is the time when partisanship should give way to patriotism and when sacrifice of party affiliation and personal preference must be made in the interest of the people."

Teller gave the final word on his hopes and views early in the campaign. In an interview he replied to a reporter, "I didn't want the nomination." The old-pro politician understood the realities: "I knew the Democrats would not commit such a blunder as to nominate me, for it would have been charged that I left the Republican Party to get the nomination. No, I did not want it and was glad when Bryan was nominated." He continued:

> I have made my sacrifice, and I will now support Bryan, not because he is a Democrat but because I believe him to be a statesman and a patriot, and because I believe his election will inaugurate a new era in American politics that will give to the plain people of the country what they have not had for some time—a voice in the affairs of the government.[7]

The Populists did nominate Bryan, then stubbornly selected a different running mate for him than the one the Democrats had chosen. The skirmishing had finished; the final battle now began. Teller took to the national campaign trail as never before. He had to carefully watch the home front as well because the senior senator stood for reelection during the battle of the standards.

IN THE THICK OF THE GREAT FIGHT FOR SILVER, Teller and Wolcott found themselves on almost opposite sides of the question. Once they had worked closely as a team for silver; now fundamental differences turned them down different paths. Never as popular as his colleague, Wolcott faced a personal dilemma in 1895–1896. Calculatingly ambitious, he desired to remain in the Republican Party, which he believed offered him the best opportunity for advancement. Also, like Teller, he had little faith that the Populists would endure. Although he favored bimetallism, Wolcott looked to an international agreement as the lone answer, and that, he strongly advocated, could only come through Republican leadership. The Republicans had promised to attempt to promote international action on the issue. He believed them. Wolcott did not join the silver Republicans.

Although his constituents left the party in droves and Teller dramatically joined them at the St. Louis convention, Wolcott stood firm. Ed's words came back to haunt him. He had promised earlier that he would leave the Republicans if some other party took up the silver cause and the GOP had not. Both the Populists and the Democrats now backed the cause; the Republicans did not.

Wolcott's supporters had been trying to undermine Teller's position in the party since the start of the year to increase Ed's chances of leading a regular party delegation to St. Louis. Their efforts failed, and Ed withdrew his name. Before the convention Wolcott had discussed with Teller his position and his intention to publicly support the nominee and the party's platform. Henry urged him not to do so. Determined, Ed proceeded, backed by the depleted regular Colorado Republican organization. With that move, Wolcott signed his political death warrant in Colorado. He signed it again by supporting McKinley and the party during the campaign.

All hell broke lose. The press attacked "our English friend from Colorado." The *Ouray Herald* sarcastically dismissed his contention that free coinage would come through the GOP: "Either Eddie has the faith that should move mountains, or else he is greater than Ananias at the art which the latter once excelled [dishonesty and lying]." Wolcott promoted his "own personal and political ambitions" at the expense of bimetallism, charged the *Denver Republican*. La Junta's *Democrat* expressed the view of the plains' people: "Senator Wolcott's loyalty to Colorado and to Silver has a string attached to it." Red Cliff's *Eagle County Times* leveled this blast: "Colorado silver is generally all right, and it is rare indeed that such rank counterfeit specimens as Silver Ed are traced home to this state."

Those attending a meeting in Creede declared, "Compared with E. O. Wolcott, Benedict Arnold was a patriot and Judas Iscariot a saint." Puebloans branded him a traitor to Colorado "who will sacrifice" his state's interests "and those of the masses rather than party." He received hundreds of letters demanding that he resign, many containing personal threats, and Ed was burned in effigy. When Wolcott tried to speak, the crowds hooted and jeered, forcing him to limit his appearances.

Tensions between the two senators grew equally impassioned. The disagreement splashed into the open at the election of the convention delegates, ending eight years of harmonious relations. They barely spoke to each other the rest of the year and favored almost diametrically opposed solutions to the silver question. Although they remained personally cordial in the years that followed, they never reforged the close political bonds of the early years.[8]

With Teller, bimetallism appeared to be almost a religion, paramount to all other issues. He went where silver went. If that meant leaving the party, so be it. Wolcott's party ties remained stronger, as did his personal ambition. Fiercely calculating, Wolcott remained unwilling to sacrifice his national reputation and future for the sake of his state or silver. He bet on the Republicans to achieve a silver policy through an international agreement. If Wolcott could get bimetallism through the party, fine; if not, he would abandon it. To him, Bryan was right about silver and wrong about everything else. When Ed made a speech on September 15 in support of McKinley, criticism rained down on him. He spoke at his oratorical best, urging Coloradans to stand

against "Bryanism, Populism, Coxeyism, and Socialism." It did no good. His popularity, already negligible, sank to a new low.

Wolcott more accurately judged national currents; Teller better understood Colorado. Wolcott committed political suicide at home, and the national Republican Party
never rewarded his loyalty either personally or by offering something in support of
silver to appease his Colorado constituents. Teller, meanwhile, continued to be the
political power in Colorado.

Colorado Republicans knew they had no chance. Their new chairman, Irving
Howbert, commented later that he quickly became "convinced that it was utterly
useless" to keep Republican voters in line for McKinley and gold. He moved his
energies toward achieving success at the state level. Nationally, a different story
unfolded. McKinley's campaign manager and friend, industrialist Mark Hanna, proved
a political genius. His organization, fund-raising, and political acumen foreshadowed what would come in the next century. Newspapers attacked Bryan, silver, and
anything else they could. McKinley clubs appeared everywhere with buttons, banners, booklets, and loaded "banks" (campaign treasuries). With more money behind
him than any candidate had ever raised, Hanna hired speakers and writers, published campaign material, organized rallies, and wisely kept his candidate home
in Canton, Ohio, for a front-porch campaign. McKinley fell far short of Bryan's
charisma and oratorical ability. Hanna refused, however, to write off the West.
At this juncture, Wolcott and the disheartened regular Republicans fit into his
strategy.

If an endangered species list had been compiled, Colorado Republicans would
have ranked at the top. When the *Montrose Press* editorially supported McKinley and
gold, the neighboring *Ouray Herald* exploded. Montrose and its newspaper depended "upon us" for their income and "for their food." Although the newspaper
had the right to advocate for the gold standard, for those "of us of the silver camps
it is aggravating" to have to see such "traitorous action." Finally, in the July 30 issue,
the *Herald* editor announced with pleasure that Montrose's "patriotic people" had
forced a change; the "offensive" name McKinley no longer graced the *Press*.[9]

The campaign sprinted ahead. The "magnetic young boy orator of the Platte"
(Bryan) instantly became a "hit" in Colorado. Teller again felt obligated to refute the
charge that he owned silver mines. He was upset because the sheriff back in Whiteside
County, Illinois, declared that Teller had mortgaged his Illinois lands to buy silver
mines. In a revealing insight, he wrote an old Morrison friend about his gold mines;
they were "not at this time paying, but [they are] all paid for."

Although he had earnestly come to Bryan's support, others hesitated. Teller advised Bryan in late July not to "crowd some of our friends who have not just yet
forget" being Republicans. He also worried about Bryan running in two parties with
different vice presidential candidates. This upset some Coloradans. The *Ouray Herald*
(July 30), for example, called the Populists "knaves" and said a vote for them was a
vote for McKinley.

With the dominant Republican Party split between the majority silver group and the minority regulars, many Coloradans feared the Populists might gain control of the state. State chairman Howbert wrote Teller with two worries. Should they fuse with the Democrats "upon the state offices? If we endorse their electoral ticket, they might be willing to join us in state affairs." Second, he hoped to convince Wolcott to come out for Bryan to regain the people's goodwill: "I have been sorry to see him abused by the papers as he has been; we must try to keep down this spirit of intolerance that certainly manifests itself." He failed utterly with Wolcott but made some progress with the Democrats.[10]

In August Teller made his only Colorado tour during the campaign. He knew the combination of the silver Republicans and the Democrats were going to carry the state. Henry needed to campaign outside Colorado in crucial areas essential to Bryan in November to gain victory for the Democratic candidate.

Teller continued to receive letters from his constituents about their problems, none more moving than one from Horace Tabor. Tabor's once-flourishing "empire" lay shattered; he desperately needed help. Horace complained to Henry, "On account of my being such a strong advocate of Free Coinage it is at this time . . . impossible for me to make a loan. I feel that the judges of this silver state should protect [us] until after the election for then there will be no trouble to make a loan." Horace placed all his hopes on Bryan and silver.

Henry also busily wrote letters to friends and answered his mail. He admitted to his Central City friend Dunham Wright (an Oregon resident now) that he received such a "great number" of letters that he found it "quite impossible" to answer them all. Henry expressed his view of Bryan and his expectations for the 1896 campaign.

> I am in hopes we have found our Lincoln in Bryan. I am giving him my hearty support and I hope Oregon will be in the column of states that supports him.
> I think the chances of his election [are] good. I never expected to be the nominee of Chicago. It was the proper thing to nominate a Democrat and the nomination was as good as could be made. Bryan is a first class man and if elected will be a President of all the people and not of a few only.

He sent encouraging letters to silverites, telling them not to be discouraged even with "the odds against us." Teller was sure the people would see the truth: "I am a firm believer in the good sense and honesty of the American people, and that gives me hope." He told them not to fear the rumors of panic if Bryan wins, adding that even if he loses, "the cause is not [lost], and we must if defeated now reorganize our forces and continue the fight."[11]

Not all letters Henry received came from admirers. George Dorr of Pittsburgh, who had been at the Republican convention, started his letter with "what a miserable man you are" and ended by questioning Teller's motives and "honesty of purpose." Unfortunately for George, Willard—at his curmudgeonly best—answered the letter: "I do not know who or what you are, never having heard of you except by this letter.

From this letter I think I am safe in saying that you are an impertinent hophead who thinks he has a mission." He closed sarcastically, "Now please don't waste any more of your valuable time by taxing your great brain in expressing opinions that nobody on Earth except you can affirm, and if you must do it don't send it this way for you are too small game, I judge, to warrant anybody replying to you."

MOST OF HENRY'S TIME WAS SPENT CAMPAIGNING. He received so many offers to speak that he had to decline most of them. He would have liked to have gone to his old home state but regretfully turned the invitation down: "I fear New York is 'joined to its idols' and will support the gold standard." He guessed correctly. Teller did not have time to go to New England, saying he had better "confine my efforts to those sections that we hope to carry. I don't believe we can carry a New England state." Correct again. Henry sadly declined Bryan's offer to speak in Lincoln, Nebraska, because he was already scheduled to go to Illinois.

The *Silverton Standard* (August 29, 1896) boasted that a Bryan "tidal wave is sweeping over every quarter of the land." Mining engineer James Hague, investigating Telluride's Tomboy Mine, wrote his wife: "In Colorado Bryan is regarded as a Moses, a divinely appointed leader of the people, or, at least, a Lincoln, raised up to save and redeem his people." The *Mancos Times* (September 11) put it in perspective: "Our Religion! Silver First."

Sixteen-year-old Vachel Lindsay never forgot that summer or the campaign. In his poem "Bryan, Bryan, Bryan, Bryan," he remembered those exciting, enchanting times. Lindsay wrote:

> I brag and chant of Bryan, Bryan, Bryan,
> Candidate for president who sketched a silver Zion,
> The one American Poet who could sing outdoors,
> He brought in tides of wonder, of unprecedented splendor.
>
> July, August, suspense.
> Wall Street lost to sense.
> August, September, October,
> More suspense, and the whole East down like a wind-smashed fence.

With his "best girl," Lindsay heard Bryan speak in Springfield, Illinois: "He lifted his hand and cast a new spell."

Henry started his national campaigning in neighboring Cheyenne in late July with "cheer after cheer renting the air." He spent most of his campaign time, though, traveling through the Midwest and upper South. Harriet went with him. Teller appeared in parades and at rallies and gave speeches day after day, always the center of attention. Henry spoke in Morrison on the courthouse grounds where so long ago he had started his career. Then he traveled to Cleveland, Lansing, Ft. Wayne, Kalamazoo, Detroit, and places in between in Kentucky, Indiana, Michigan, Illinois, and Ohio. His familiar message reached out to his listeners—points included Bryan being of the people and for the people, the paramount silver issue and bimetallism, the hardships of the gold standard, Republican betrayal of the people, and his belief that America's future rested on this decisive election. Teller concluded with an emotional flare: "I cannot support the gold standard, nor can I give aid to a party that advocates it. I believe the gold standard in a few years will change the very character of our institutions and destroy the liberty of the people, and I cannot support a party that advocates it."

Henry was well received. In Ashland, Kentucky, a newspaper reported that at the conclusion of his speech, deafening yells filled the air along with flying hats and waving banners, canes, and umbrellas: "No such demonstration has been accorded any speaker in this city for years." Detroit's *News-Tribune* (October 4) called his appearance the "most impressive and profitable public gathering" since the Civil War days. This was remarkable because the "careful, patient [Teller] did not once descend to the ordinary catchy trick of the stump speaker. He spoke under the solemn consciousness of addressing a jury upon a momentous question that involved the life of a beloved client."[12]

November finally arrived, and Colorado voters found nine parties from which to choose. The ballot contained the regular two through variously named silver parties to socialist, labor, and prohibition parties. Teller advocated voting a straight Bryan ticket, and Coloradans did. Bryan gathered 85 percent of the vote, McKinley 13 percent, and scattered parties the rest. There had never been such a landslide, nor would there be again. The *Rocky Mountain News* headlined the November 4 edition "BRYAN BELIEVED TO HAVE WON."

Nationally, a different story emerged. A downcast Lindsay never forgot that day.

> Election night at midnight:
> Boy Bryan's defeat.
> Defeat of western silver.
> Defeat of the wheat.
> Victory of letterfiles
> And plutocrats in miles
> With dollar signs upon their coats,
> Diamond watch chains on their vests
> And spats on their feet.

Not until November 6 did the *News* concede. The Glenwood Springs *Avalanche* expressed the feelings of many: "It was a great struggle." Both papers and others proclaimed the struggle was not over.

Teller stayed equally optimistic. In an interview in his Denver law office, he had much to say: "There is no reason why we should be discouraged. Our candidate was all that we could desire and performed his part to perfection. We must not look backward but forward." Education would open the door to victory: "Silver will win in 1900." Unlimited money, subsidized newspapers, lies, and terror tactics had worked, Teller charged. Further, Henry expected to see the Republican Party abandon all pretense to secure international bimetallism. The reporter observed, however, that Teller revealed "a visible tinge of sorrow and regret and how could it be otherwise."

One of the Republican allegations during the campaign involved the amount of money Colorado silver miners had donated to Bryan. New York's *World* claimed they contributed over $300,000, a highly unlikely amount. Teller wrote during the campaign, "We could have raised $100,000 four years ago easier than we can raise ten now." Silver men like Tabor no longer had the funds. How much Teller did raise will never be known, but it was probably far less than $100,000.

In one of the paradoxes of the campaign, new Cripple Creek gold millionaire Winfield Scott Stratton offered to bet $100,000 on Bryan against $300,000 on McKinley. Fortunately, no one took him up on it. Without question, Cripple Creek gold production harmed silver's long-range cause by restoring a measure of prosperity to Colorado. Stratton, though, wanted to protect the working people against "exploitation by the rich."[13]

Teller had helped Bryan win in the agrarian/mining South and West and helped him amass the highest total a Democratic presidential candidate had ever received. Some powerful western allies helped raise money in a losing cause. The Midwest, where he had campaigned so long and ardently, went for McKinley. Bryan thanked Teller for doing "yeoman service upon the stump for the Democratic ticket." Henry was one of the three champions of bimetallism to whom Bryan dedicated his book *The First Battle,* which discusses the 1896 campaign.

Teller now needed to be nominated for another term. Charges of "Treachery to Teller" had been leveled during the campaign to try to stop his reelection. Fascinatingly, James Hague wrote that "everyone is mad at Sen. Wolcott because they believe he secretly supported the Populists." Why? Wolcott hoped to elect a Populist legislature, thus "defeating Teller's reelection to the Senate." The *Pagosa Springs News* in January 1896 also hinted at the combination of Colorado goldbugs and Populists. Regardless, Henry gained overwhelming support throughout the state. As the *Rocky Mountain News* declared on November 5, "Voting for him will not be a mere perfunctory act, but one of love and deep conviction."

The final legislative vote was 92 to 6—nearly 16 to 1, noted state senator Charles Newman in congratulating Teller. Newman concluded: "That it [the landslide] was merited, and just, no Coloradan will for a minute doubt." A group of supporters ordered a floral offering to be placed on his Senate desk the moment the vote was announced, "being desirous of testifying their appreciation of Senator Teller as a man, a citizen, a patriot and a statesman."[14]

Teller won, Bryan lost. Silver also lost. Why? Maybe the answer will never be known, but a few insights help explain it. Bryan made few inroads into the metropolitan centers east of the Mississippi River. The Republican campaign slogan of a "full dinner pail" meant more to urban workers than Bryan's "Free Silver." Further,

Cleveland and gold Democrats did not appreciate Bryan blaming the depression on the administration's policies, a view they felt was myopic. Concentrated in the East, they boosted McKinley's total in key states.

In the midwestern farm belt, a rising price of wheat before the election reflected a crop failure abroad. Bryan had assiduously cultivated the intimate connection between the rise of silver's price and that of farm prices. That belief burst when wheat went up and silver stayed down. Many farmers thought a general upturn of prices was coming and returned to their traditional Republican allegiance. Teller's appeals, therefore, fell on increasingly deaf ears. Scholars have felt Bryan's campaign emphasized silver almost to the exclusion of everything else and was too narrow in scope.

Hanna had defeated the Democrats in every detail of campaign management, especially educating the voters. He portrayed the Republicans as the party of prosperity and respectability. Kansas newspaperman William Allen White thought Bryan's campaign inspired wrath and fear among nonwestern voters. Bryan seemed to be pitting class against class. White's famous editorial, "What's the Matter with Kansas," did not win friends there, even if it carefully laid out many Americans' concerns. Additionally, Bryan was not helped by some radical Populist orators and their statements over the past years. Frightened easterners united against this threat to their interpretation of national life and prosperity. Civil War veteran McKinley, on the other hand, appeared to uphold traditional values, particularly that hallowed belief in individual responsibility for success or failure.

The goldbugs and Republicans had been right on several issues. At least 80 percent of international trade was transacted with gold standard countries. Silver would have isolated America. With the country finally pulling out of the depression, why jeopardize recovery? They hammered at the question of specifically how free silver would benefit the farmer and laborer. The Democrats offered few specific answers. The U.S. situation in 1896 differed from that in the 1870s when the silver agitation started. Times had changed even for the mining industry. Colorado, for instance, had become a gold state, thanks largely to the astonishing production of Cripple Creek and renewed effort by the San Juan mines. Where once prospectors had wandered and miners tramped, corporations now reigned supreme.

Complaints of political shenanigans and outright blackmail also arose. Businessmen reportedly threatened to cancel orders if Bryan won and to double them if McKinley won. Eastern insurance companies offered borrowers five-year extensions on loans at low interest rates if McKinley won. Rumors flew of workers being told not to return to work if that heretic Bryan captured the White House. People accused more than one bank of refusing to extend credit or renew loans for Bryan supporters. How much truth or impact any of these accusations may have had will never be known.[15]

Would free silver have saved the day for Colorado and its national backers? Even with faith, it seems doubtful. The country's financial and banking systems and attitudes were not ready for that type of inflationary policy. It would take the changes ahead with the Woodrow Wilson administration, the 1929 crash and Great Depression, and Franklin Roosevelt's New Deal for the ideas and reforms of 1896 to take hold.

The sharply sectional election of 1896 marked the end of an era. The financial crisis of 1893–1896 reached its swan song as a political issue. The U.S. middle class recovered from the jitters. Bryan and his passionately devoted followers saw their America end. Bryan was one of the last nineteenth-century leaders to give voice and shape to the Jeffersonian and Jacksonian agrarian political ideologies.

Now Americans found new problems, new issues, foreign affairs, and growing prosperity. The anti–regular party theme the Populists had championed became a growing tradition in the elections ahead and dominated much of the twentieth century. Straight party voting slowly became a relic of past politics.

The election ended an era for both major parties. The Republicans would no longer run against Jefferson Davis and the Confederacy. Business and prosperity became their themes. They won a decisive victory that laid the groundwork for presidential victories in six of the next eight elections. The Democrats became more of a reform party and separated themselves more from conservative Republican ideals. Unfortunately and political damagingly, however, Bryan and many party leaders remained unaware of new urban problems and needs of city dwellers or at best were unable to articulate and respond to them. For a while, they were unable to propose pragmatic solutions.

The Populist Party, for all practical purposes, died in 1896; however, its platform lived on, except for free silver. The Populists had not died in vain. The party flourished at a time of momentous political upheaval and left the political landscape permanently altered. Populist oratory and idealism moved a generation toward reform and paved the way for the Progressive reform movement in the twentieth century. Initiative, referendum, direct election of senators, and a host of other ideas now seemed acceptable. Finally, the idea that government could play a positive role in people's lives would live on, flowering in the twentieth century under Democratic presidents Woodrow Wilson and Franklin Roosevelt.

Actually and unintentionally, as mentioned earlier, Colorado helped undermine the silver issue. Ironically, it ultimately realized the dreams of the fifty-niners who thought they were going to find gold near Pike's Peak. Located on the west side of Pike's Peak, Cripple Creek—Colorado's greatest gold district—erupted on the scene in the 1890s. After producing only $1,000 in gold in 1890, the district's production soared to $18 million in 1900. Combined with the Alaska/Yukon strikes and an international increase in gold production, gold helped ease the monetary crunch.

America and Americans moved toward the twentieth century with renewed confidence. Many might not have realized it, but they had passed a watershed in their country's history and weathered a political-economic crisis. Those who yearned for the "vanished" America of the nineteenth century did so at their peril. It would soon be apparent how and where Henry Teller would fit into this new world.

The year of the jubilee had not ended the way Teller, Bryan, the silverites, and their supporters had wanted, but they kept the faith. Voting Americans throughout the land had simply failed to catch the vision. They had stirred the country and made inroads they did not realize at the time. Perhaps Kansas newspaperman William Allen White portrayed it best: "It was a revolt of the man with one talent or with five talents against the man with ten, who was hoarding his gains in unfair privileges."[16]

NOTES

1. Henry Teller, *Revenue Not the Remedy* (Washington, D.C.: Government Printing Office, 1896), 11–12, 15, 22.
2. James Belford to Teller, March 26, 1896, Earl Coe to Teller, May 18, 1896, E. Ammons to Dawson, May 15, 1896, all in Teller Papers, Colorado Historical Society; Teller letter in Thomas Dawson, *Senator Teller* (Washington, D.C.: Judd and Detiveiler, 1898), 9–10; William L. Hewitt, "The Election of 1896," *Colorado Magazine* (winter 1977), 49–51.
3. James Belford to Teller, March 26, 1896, Teller Papers, Colorado Historical Society; *Rocky Mountain News,* June 19, 1896; unidentified articles, 1896, "Teller Scrapbook," Chris Buys private collection; Paul F. Gerhard, "The Colorado Delegation in the Fifty-fifth Congress, 1897–1899," unpublished M.A. thesis, University of Colorado, 1948, 37–38, 41.
4. Telegram to Teller, July 1, 1896, Teller Papers, Colorado Historical Society; Teller to Dubois, June 24, 1896, "Teller Scrapbook," Chris Buys private collection; *Weekly Republican,* June 25, July 2, 1896; *New York Times,* July 2, 1896; *Rocky Mountain News,* June 19, July 2, 1896; *Argus,* June 27, 1896.
5. *Ouray Herald,* June 25, July 2, 1896; *Silverton Standard,* June 27, 1896; *Weekly Republican,* June 25, 1896; three unidentified articles, 1896, Ezra Kendall letter, July 1?, 1896, all in "Teller Scrapbook," Chris Buys private collection; *Rocky Mountain News,* July 3, 1896; *Chaffee County Record,* June 26, 1896; John Shafroth to Teller, July 3, 1896, Charles Towne to Teller, July ?, 1896, Fred Dubois to Teller, July 1, 2, 1896, R. L. Pettigrew to Teller, July 6, 1896, Dubois and others to Teller, July 7, 1896, Francis Newlands to Teller, July 8, 1896, all in Teller Papers, Colorado Historical Society; Paolo E. Coletta, *William Jennings Bryan* (Lincoln: University of Nebraska Press, 1964), 119.
6. *Ouray Herald,* June 11, 25, 1896; *Rocky Mountain News,* June 9, 1896; William Jennings Bryan, *The Cross of Gold* (Lincoln: University of Nebraska Press, 1990), Introduction, 1–13, and the speech, 18–28. William J. Bryan, *The First Battle* (Chicago: W. B. Conkey, 1896), discusses the events leading up to the speech. *New York Times* and *Rocky Mountain News,* July 7–11, 1896.
7. Dubois to Teller, July 10, 1896, Pettigrew to Teller, July 10, 1896, Frederick Horton to Teller, July 12, 1896, Teller to H. E. Taubeneck, July 13, 1896, Charles Thomas to Teller, July 14, 1896, Dubois to Taubeneck, July 15, 1896, all in Teller Papers, Colorado Historical Society; Louis Koenig, *Bryan* (New York: G. P. Putnam's Sons, 1971), 163–164; *Seattle Interview,* August 1, 1876; unidentified article, "Teller Scrapbook," Chris Buys private collection.
8. Thomas Dawson, *Edward Oliver Wolcott* (New York: Knickerbocker, 1911), vol. 1, 232–240, vol. 2, 339–342; *Rocky Mountain News,* August 1, October 26, 1896; *Ouray Herald,*

June 18, August 6, 1896; *Denver Republican,* August 2, October 23, 1896; *Silverite-Plaindealer* (Ouray), January 31, 1896; Hewitt, "The Election of 1896," 45, 48, 55, 57; *Democrat, Eagle County Times,* and *Montrose Times* cited in Gerhard, "Colorado Delegation," 39–43; Thomas Dawson, "Teller and Wolcott," Colorado Historical Society, 16–17.

9.   Irving Howbert, *Memories of a Lifetime in the Pike's Peak Region* (New York: G. P. Putnam's Sons, 1925), 276–277; *St. Louis Globe-Democrat,* June 20, 1896; Wolcott speech in *Ouray Herald,* June 25, July 30, 1896; H. Wayne Morgan, *William McKinley* (Syracuse: Syracuse University Press, 1963), 214.

10.   Teller to A. J. Jackson, July 27, 1896, Teller to James Teller, July 27, 1896, Teller to J. K. Jones, July 27, 1896, Teller to Bryan, July 22, 1896, John Shafroth to Teller, July 3, 1896, Irving Howbert to Teller, July 16, 1896, all in Teller Papers, Colorado Historical Society; *Ouray Herald,* July 30, 1896; *Salida Mail,* July 14, 1896; *Chaffee County Record,* July 17, 1896.

11.   Teller to Dunham Wright, ?, 1896, Tabor to Teller, August 29, 1896, Teller to Brooks Adams, September 3, 1896, Teller to Lars Gunderson, September 3, 1896, Teller to Joseph Hutchinson, ?, 1896, all in Teller Papers, Colorado Historical Society; Gerhard, "Colorado Delegation," 55.

12.   George Dorr to Teller, September 8, 1896, Willard Teller to Dorr, September 9?, 1896, Teller to William Van Nostrand, September 3, 1896, Teller to Joseph Sheldon, September 3, 1896, Teller to Bryan, September 2, 1896, Teller to George Cannon, September 1, 1896, "Speech," "Campaign Speech 1896," all in Teller Papers, Colorado Historical Society; James Hague to Mary Hague, November 9, 1896, James Hague Collection, Henry E. Huntington Library, San Marino, California; Vachel Lindsay, *Collected Poems* (New York: Macmilllan, 1967), 96–105; unidentified article, July 25, 1896, newspaper clippings from Ashland, Kentucky, September 16, 1896, Adrian, Michigan, October 5, 1896, Lansing, Michigan, October 6, 1896, Kalamazoo, Michigan, October 7, 1896, Fort Wayne, Indiana, October 21, 1896, La Porte, Indiana, October 22, 1896, all in "Teller Scrapbook," Chris Buys private collection; William W. Davis, *History of Whiteside County, Illinois* (Chicago: Pioneer, 1908), 307, 327; *Denver Times,* September 8, 1898; *New York Times,* September 27, 1896; *News-Tribune,* October 4, 1896.

13.   *Rocky Mountain News,* November 1–7, 1896; *Avalanche,* November 6–9, 1896; *Ouray Herald,* November 17, 1896; Teller to R. Pettigrew, August 1, September ?, 1896, Teller Papers, Colorado Historical Society; *World* quote, Thomas Dawson, "Scrapbooks," Colorado Historical Society, vol. 61. The Stratton story is found in Marshall Sprague, *Money Mountain* (Boston: Little, Brown, 1957), 131, 209–210; Vachel Lindsay, *Collected Poems* (New York: Macmillan Company, 1967), 102–103.

14.   Bryan, *First Battle,* 23, 25; Hague to Mary, November 9, 1896, James Hague Collection, Henry E. Huntington Library, San Marino, California; Thomas Dawson, "The Personal Side of Senator Teller," Colorado Historical Society, 3; *Pagosa Springs News,* January 15, 22, 1896; Chas. Newman to Teller, January 29, 1897, undated note, both in Teller Papers, Colorado Historical Society.

15.   Coletta, *William Jennings Bryan,* 199–203, 205–206; Gene Clanton, *Populism* (Boston: Twayne, 1991), 160–162; William A. White, *Autobiography* (New York: Macmillan, 1946), 278–280; Nell Painter, *Standing at Armageddon* (New York: Norton, 1989), 139–140; Robert D. Marcus, *Grand Old Party* (New York: Oxford University Press, 1971), 230–

232; Arthur Schlesinger Jr. (ed.), *History of U.S. Political Parties* (New York: Chelsea House, 1973), vol. 2, 1724, 1795–98; Stephen Kneeshaw and John M. Linngren, "The Republican Comeback, 1902," *Colorado Magazine* (winter 1971), 28–29; Edward Keating, *The Gentlemen from Colorado* (Denver: Sage, 1964), 138–139; Koenig, *Bryan*, 175–176.

16. See George H. Mayer, *The Republican Party* (New York: Oxford University Press, 1967), 171–173, 215, 255–256; Marcus, *Grand Old Party*, 199, 251–258; Stanley L. Jones, *The Presidential Election of 1896* (Madison: University of Wisconsin Press, 1964), 64–67, 247–248, 331, 348–350, 366; Schlesinger, *History of U.S. Political Parties*, vol. 2, 1721–25, 1729; Thomas Cronin and Robert Loevy, *Colorado Politics and Government* (Lincoln: University of Nebraska Press, 1993), 62; Coletta, *William Jennings Bryan*, 146–147, 206; White, *Autobiography*, 275–276; Kneeshaw and Linngren, "Republican Comeback," 19–20.

Colorado's Grand Old Man

Nearly sixty-seven years old and exhausted from the strenuous campaigning and pressures of 1896, Teller started his nineteenth year
in the Senate in March 1897. His health showed signs of the trials and
tribulations Henry had faced in the past decade. Yet he had decided to
stand for his fourth full term. "Colorado's Grand Old Man," as the *Montrose
Press* (September 29, 1898) hailed him, stood alone among the state's leaders.

Harriet and Henry had sold their Central City home to Gilpin County
and moved to Denver. Their son Harrison packed up their belongings and
cleaned out the old law office. The Tellers lived with their daughter most of
the time when they were not in Washington. In the summer they often
stayed with Harrison at the family farm in Grand Junction. Henry had
purchased 230 acres, which his son operated.

Henry made another choice: he officially left the Republican Party.
Because of the party's position on gold, he had become a silver Republican. His old allies John Jones, Fred Dubois, Frank Cannon, John Shafroth,
and others joined him.

Teller's adamant silver stand and support of Bryan alienated many
party leaders, some of whom took revenge by placing him on committees
as a non-Republican. The party had not consulted him on patronage
matters since 1893. Henry was bitter about what he considered the Republicans' betrayal of silver and other matters, plus his own treatment. The
disgruntled senator clearly stated his view of the current Republican Party

on the Senate floor in January 1898: "I will destroy it if I can. I hope to see it go down in defeat in 1900, and, if living, I pledge you my word I will do everything I can to bring it to grief."

By 1900, maintaining a separate Silver Republican Party did not seem reasonable. Some folks drifted back to the GOP, others joined the Democrats. Teller, who had gotten along well with Colorado Democratic leaders since the mid-1890s, changed parties. He also valued the efforts of William Jennings Bryan, who praised Teller: "I appreciate your friendship and value your opinion."

Officially, he made the announcement in March 1901—when Congress reassembled he would take a seat on the Democratic side. The *Washington Star* speculated: "He will look a little out of place there for a while." After all, he had delivered "many a scathing arraignment of the democratic party" from his old seat. Now when "he fires back on his old friends the spectacle will be interesting."[1]

No future existed for a Silver Republican Party. Created as a home for the bolters of 1896, it and the issue faded into yesteryear. Teller and the other silverites, however, did not concede silver's demise. As one of the organizers of the national Silver Republican Party, Teller hoped to continue the fight. The silverites vowed, "We must rally to rescue the Republic." Through the rest of the decade he talked about silver and rallied the troops within Colorado. Henry traveled through the San Juans in October 1898 giving talks in Durango, Silverton, and Ouray earnestly advocating silver. Bryan obviously did not give up, either. He sent Teller a check for $500 from the royalties of his book *The First Battle* to promote the cause.

As late as 1900, Teller gave a vintage free silver speech in the Senate. "We cannot get rid of the monetary question," Henry argued. It alone offered the "ability to settle the other problems." Defiantly, he stated, "I took my position when I came here, and I have not had occasion to doubt the correctness of my judgment at that time." His speech failed to convert his listeners.[2]

The country and Colorado had changed even in the few years since the 1896 election. Prosperity had returned generally to midwestern urban and rural areas, for which McKinley and the Republicans took full credit. Even farmers in the South and West enjoyed better times.

For Colorado, the pure silver districts lay comatose, deserted by investors and residents alike, and the ones with more silver than gold production continued to suffer. Nevertheless, times had improved from the dark days of 1893. An increase in the price of silver to more than 60 cents an ounce helped a little, but as the *Engineering and Mining Journal* reported, few mines were worked for silver alone. Gold production soared to all-time highs at the turn of the twentieth century. More than Cripple Creek sparked the revival; other districts, especially the San Juans, switched to gold with silver as a by-product. By 1900 the state production of gold, silver, copper, lead, and zinc topped $50 million.

Ed Wolcott, meanwhile, forlornly chased the illusionary international bimetallism dream. McKinley did carry out a campaign pledge and appoint members to the

International Bimetallic Commission, among them Ed. Teller predicted England would never budge, and it did not. Wolcott worked diligently but gained little. His stock sank further in Colorado, and he faced a reelection campaign in 1900. It would take a mighty Republican resurgence to save him.[3]

Teller loyally supported Bryan when he was renominated in 1900: "I say Bryanism is Americanism, and if we could have less Hannaism and more Bryanism we should be better off." Silver, he hoped, would remain the paramount issue. During the campaign Teller and the silver Republicans fused with the state Democrats. Henry appeared before the latter's convention and spoke for fusion. With him was Thomas Patterson, candidate for the U.S. Senate. Henry predicted the Republicans would not carry the state or the legislature.

It would not be another 1896. Bryan was no longer a new, exciting personality; the silver cause had died in most of the country; and the Republican slogan of "a full dinner pail" was in tune with the times. A host of western states returned to the Republican column. Colorado was not one of them, although McKinley's vote total increased dramatically to 41 percent. Bryan's national vote total dipped below what it had been four years before.

How dead was silver? Back in March, the Gold Standard Act had become law, declaring the gold dollar the standard for U.S. currency. The United States had officially adopted the gold standard.

Teller's prediction proved correct on all counts. Bryan and the Democrats swept Colorado, including returning Henry's friend John Shafroth, also now a Democrat, to Congress. Wolcott's Senate career ended the following January when the victorious Democrats elected Thomas Patterson senator. Two years later, Teller's term would end.

Writing to Teller on February 1, 1901, Bryan felt they had done the best they could. He would gladly have given way to someone else "if there had been anyone with a better prospect of winning." There was not. Never one to quit, Bryan concluded, "We must keep up the fight in the hope that the people will yet realize the dangerous tendencies of republican politics." He hoped further that the senatorial contest had not left any bitterness to interfere "with future success there."[4]

Bryan's hope for the future rested not with silver but with some of the other reforms the Populists had advocated and the Democrats had "borrowed" in 1896. America had changed in the past four years. The United States had become a world power with colonies. Imperialism, not silver, caught political attention with the coming of the new century.

Teller had unexpectedly played a role in this new America. During his Senate career he had not been the author of what might be termed national impact legislation. He had worked more on state and regional issues. In the 1870s he had been the junior senator, in the late 1880s he had allowed Wolcott to author state documents, and in the 1890s silver had taken his time. Now, however, the "Teller Amendment" gained him a place in U.S. diplomatic and foreign affairs history.

Teller, until the mid-1890s, had never taken much interest in foreign affairs except on the silver issue and concern over the "yellow peril," the threat Chinese laborers posed to U.S. workers. Since the Civil War, few Americans had shown much interest in diplomacy until the country started to develop a case of "Manifest Destiny" in the late 1880s. This can be briefly defined as the idea that Americans anointed themselves as God's chosen people whose destiny pointed to becoming a world power with a mission. To do that, America needed colonies for trade, profit, empire, mission, and glory. After all, the sun never set on the empire of the world's superpower, England. The celebration of Queen Victoria's diamond jubilee in 1897 showed the world everything England and the British Empire had achieved in terms of power and prestige. Press coverage of this event was strongest in the United States.

Expansionism had long been a central tradition for Americans; after all, Colorado and the West had been settled because of it. Now in the 1890s it carried world implications of trade and a mission. The mission called Americans to carry their cherished institutions—democracy, education, government—to more "backward" peoples. Add Christianity, and off they went. The British termed this the White Man's Burden. It produced a mixture of high motives, profit, racism, and a national feeling of power and prestige. All told, it gave the United States a license to get involved in international affairs and business and to scramble for colonies. The United States had the technology to do so, which it did under the guise of a self-proclaimed, self-assumed mission.[5]

The renewed U.S. interest in diplomacy appeared in several ways: interest in a harbor at Pago Pago, excitement over Hawaii, potential world business markets, and President Cleveland becoming involved in a boundary dispute between Venezuela and British Guiana. Henry had always been a firm believer in the Monroe Doctrine; however, he thought Cleveland went too far in his demands because of England's involvement in the boundary question.

What really stirred Americans into an uproar were events in Cuba, only 90 miles off their coastline. In the 1890s Spain struggled desperately to maintain its hold on the last valuable piece of its American empire. The Cubans, yearning for independence, rose up in revolt. Thanks to propaganda, business interests (American-owned Cuban sugar plantations), renewed attention to Manifest Destiny, a New York city newspaper war, and natural sympathy for the underdog, their belligerency caught the attention of their Yankee neighbors. Much to their pleasure, they found more and more Americans supporting them. By mid-decade Americans intensely followed developments on this war-torn island. They overwhelmingly favored the patriots against the "evil, decadent" European monarchy. When the battleship *Maine* exploded and sank in Havana Harbor in February 1898, believed to have been caused by an "infernal machine"—perhaps a floating mine?—Spain naturally received the blame. The slogan became: "Remember the *Maine*, to Hell with Spain."

The publication of the De Lome letter came just before the *Maine* tragedy. In a purloined letter, Spain's ambassador had criticized McKinley as weak and vacillating. The public raged, in no mood for any condemnation from any Spaniard about the president or anything else American.

President McKinley wanted peace, but he did not stand up to the war hawks and the expansionists in his own party. Among them was wayward Republican Henry Teller. The *Washington Post* (February 26, 1898) stated that his "pro-Cuban sentiments" were so strong that he was one of five senators who voted to recognize "the belligerence of Cuba." Teller swore, "I would recognize these people as belligerents if it brought war tomorrow because it is one of the rights we have." It had been, Colorado's senator declared, a great mistake three years earlier "that we did not declare, what everybody on the face of God's green earth knew": a state of war on Cuba existed.

By April the United States teetered on the threshold of war. It all came together: Manifest Destiny, sympathy for the Cuban patriots, profit, and the desire for colonies so the United States could assume the "role" of a world power.

Henry wanted Spain to withdraw from Cuba, and if it refused to "disclaim any sovereignty over that island, then I want to answer with the shotted guns of the American Army and American Navy." No warmonger, Teller explained on April 15, "I am not warlike. I have said on the floor of the Senate again and again that I do not like war. I have said, though, that there are infinite[ly] worse things than war." He still hoped the United States would not have to intervene. Although he did not always approve of McKinley's actions, he did not criticize the administration. The American people had to be united; war could not be waged "under the Republican flag and by a Republican Administration."

Teller was concerned about the growing interest in making the island an American colony. That imperialist impulse alarmed Teller, compounded by the fact that Colorado had started raising sugar beets. Duty-free Cuban sugar threatened a growing Colorado industry. Yet Henry was sincerely worried about colonies, obligations, and naive assumptions about the wonderful benefits of being a world power.

On April 11 McKinley sent a message of war to Congress requesting the use of army and naval forces to end the Cuban hostilities. Americans assumed this heralded a call to arms. In the days that followed, Congress debated the message. Teller introduced an amendment that passed without a dissenting vote: "That the United States hereby disclaims any disposition or intention to exercise sovereignty, jurisdiction, or control over said island [Cuba] except for the pacification thereof." When that was accomplished, the United States would "leave the government and control of the island to its people." The *Chicago Tribune* (April 23) hailed Teller, noting that "such a disclaimer is eminently proper. It expresses the present intentions and feeling of the people of the United States." The *Pueblo Chieftain* agreed: "Glory is not sought, conquest is not the prize to be gained." On April 19, 1898, Congress approved a joint resolution declaring Cuba free and authorized the use of force to liberate the island. On April 25 McKinley formerly declared war as having existed since April 21.[6]

The Teller Amendment, a "self-denying" statement unusual in world affairs, epitomized the idealist spirit with which many Americans jauntily undertook the war with Spain. As one of his admirers proclaimed proudly, the amendment "set up a new standard for nations, pulling them like men on golden rule footing." It appeased the Cuban rebels who had become apprehensive that they might be about to exchange Spanish masters for American ones.

Meanwhile, the war had become a crusade to liberate Cuba from a decadent and oppressive European power—Americans had found their neighborly Manifest Destiny. The Teller Amendment would place it on a higher moral plain. Even as the amendment was approved, however, some people began having second thoughts. Eventually, Cuba would be "freed," but it would be tied to the United States by intervention strings.

Amid the crashing chords of Sousa's "Stars and Stripes Forever" and the popular hit tune "There'll be a Hot Time in the Old Town Tonight," Americans marched off to war. In three months the "splendid little war," as John Hay called it, was over. With the conclusion of peace negotiations, the United States had freed Cuba, obtained Puerto Rico and Guam, and by capturing Manila assumed it had gained the Philippine Islands. Hawaii had fallen into U.S. hands (July 1898) as well. An enthusiastic Teller had favored the acquisition of Hawaii: "These islands are necessary to our safety, they are necessary to our commerce, and we can give to those people the blessings of a free government."

Congress and the president had made no declaration of independence and self-government for any territory except Cuba. The United States had gained an empire and therefore must be a world power. Imperialism ran rampant. Teller opposed the treaty, but he could not influence the outcome and finally voted for it.

He had been an expansionist when it came to Hawaii and during the early days of the war. Sounding like an ardent Manifest Destiny advocate, during a September 1898 Colorado Springs speech, he asked: "What are we going to do with Puerto Rico, the Asiatic Islands, and even Cuba?" He answered by pleading that the United States cannot escape its responsibility: "God puts on us as a nation our responsibility, and we must interest ourselves in the interest of mankind." Henry retained his faith; he knew he could depend on the American people to "do the right thing." The right thing might be to institute a territorial government controlled by the United States. Seemingly, he backed off from his amendment, only to again support the concept when he realized what was happening in the Philippines.[7]

THE PHILIPPINES MESS TESTED TELLER'S IDEAS ON IMPERIALISM, confirming some of his worst fears. The Filipinos had been fighting their own civil war against Spain before the U.S. fleet destroyed the Spanish Pacific fleet in Manila Bay. At first they thought liberation appeared at hand, only to find out they had exchanged one overlord for another, no matter how well intended the latter might be. As a result, a revolt broke out against the Americans in 1899 and lasted nearly four years.

Christianizing and civilizing "our little brown brother" proved more of a task than Americans had expected. The war shattered American innocence. It turned out to be a brutal, savage, dehumanizing struggle—jungle warfare at its worst, with Americans acting like the Spanish had in Cuba. They burned villages, destroyed crops, tortured prisoners, and killed Filipinos (probably around 20,000). Disease and pestilence swept across the land. The American cost was huge—embarrassment, money, and more than 4,000 soldiers killed in action or by disease. Some of Teller's neighbors were among those fighting. The First Colorado had been organized to fight Spain but went to the Philippine Islands instead. The troops' feelings are revealed clearly in this ditty:

> Damn, damn, damn the Filipinos!
> Cutthroat Khakiac ladrones [bandits]!
> Underneath the starry flag,
> Civilize them with a Krag,
> And return us to our beloved home.

The 30-caliber Krag rifle, standard issue to U.S. troops, failed to advance Manifest Destiny in the way Americans had planned. Nor did the war do much for the troops' morale.

The conflict dragged on and on with no end in sight, despite the efforts of McKinley, his successor President Theodore Roosevelt, and the generals. An increasing number of people opposed the war, including Teller's Senate colleague Thomas Patterson, old antagonist Carl Schurz, labor leader Samuel Gompers, industrialist Andrew Carnegie, reformer Jane Addams, author Mark Twain, and others.

Teller's initial reaction to the Philippines was simple. In an interview in the Lewiston, Idaho, *Tribune* (July 3, 1899), he concluded: "We ought not to rule them, all we want is to commercially control the islands." Teller thought he saw business opportunities in the early imperialist days. With the Philippine war, however, Teller's view shifted; there seemed, he warned, no way to pacify them except by the sword. Even then, the Filipinos' rights would have to be maintained. The press besieged Henry about the challenging diplomatic problems of the day. Regarding the Philippines situation, he observed: "We are in an exceedingly unfortunate position. It is an ugly question to handle."

Colorado's senior senator opposed bills dealing with various Philippine matters and army appropriations. Teller presented a petition signed by 2,000 of Manila's "most prominent citizens" asking for the same degree of autonomy enjoyed by Canada. The petition further praised Filipino resistance hero Emilio Aguinaldo "as a worthy leader." The imperialists promptly accused Henry of "flat treason" for this attack on the United States, its authority, and its troops.[8]

In a lengthy speech, "The Problem in the Philippines," delivered February 11–13, 1902, Teller thoroughly discussed his views, hopes, and concerns. As usual, he framed his arguments with historical precedents, starting with the American colonies' relations

with England and tracing colonial development elsewhere in the world. His conclusions were revealing. The racism, killing, and horror relating to the war that so many
Americans had wrestled with in recent years was nothing new and was likely to
continue for years to come. Like the Old Testament prophet Jeremiah, Henry had
"no desire to make political capital out of American misfortunes"; he simply warned
the American people to understand what they had drifted into in the Philippines.

The Filipinos were a "tropical people" whose ideas of government differed from
those of Americans: "They do not want us there." Teller did not want to make the
Philippines a territory or give them statehood. The U.S. interest does "not demand
our presence in the Philippines on our present footing." He concluded, trade will not
compensate the country for "what we have already sacrificed and suffered." Although
he did not want a U.S. defeat, he believed the war in the islands "to be damnable. I
believe it to be a disgrace to us. I believe it is unnecessary on any line of conduct that
we are justified in pursuing." Henry feared this "devastating war will go on" until we
"have devastated the land." The United States should create government institutions
and an educational system, "that I approve," and "if we should withdraw from the
islands tomorrow [those are the things] that would still be left." He added, however,
"It will be a thousand years before the Asiatic mind will stand before the world
representing those great fundamental truths of free government for which the Teu-
tonic branches of the human race stand."

Teller continued: "Does anyone here believe that we can force a civilization and
a culture upon them contrary to their desires? Has that result ever been accomplished
in the history of the world?" Teller scoffed at those who thought it was our Christian
duty to "our little brown brother." He did not "hear the directing voice of the al-
mighty in this matter."[9]

The anti-imperialists cheered the speech; those supporting the administration's
policy did not. Teller's speech clearly showed the anguish of the times and his personal
dismay about developments that had seemed so hopeful back in 1898. In addition, it
showed some racism and arrogance on the senator's part. Despite his best intentions,
Henry was not free from the prejudices that affected so many of his contemporaries.

Although sincere, the anti-imperialists proved unable to swing administration or
public opinion. Fear that another country might "gobble up" the Philippines, dreams
of the potential Asian trade market, Manifest Destiny, moral obligations, and visions
of world power undermined their cause. Many naive Americans enjoyed being a
world power and relished the country's seemingly unburdened acclaim. Anti-
imperialists were hurt as well because few prominent Republicans joined them, the
Democratic Party lacked unity and boldness, and President Roosevelt branded his
hated Democrats as equal to the traitorous copperheads during the Civil War. He
held similar feelings toward all those who opposed "my policies."

The Philippine-American war displayed, as had Teller's comments, the ambiva-
lence of Americans in the new century. There existed patriotism and racism,
confusion and optimism, and Americans who worried about their future and others

convinced of their national superiority. Involvement in a war as far away as Asia worried many, although others thought it must be part of their Manifest Destiny.

Teller had been right; it was an "ugly" question to handle. The United States found itself in an "exceedingly unfortunate position." Obviously, the questions raised by the anti-imperialists were not resolved. What was the true mission of the United States? What did we owe the rest of mankind overseas? Does the flag follow U.S. business into foreign lands? Americans throughout the twentieth century would try to answer these questions with various degrees of unanimity and success. The anti-imperialists had played a role by questioning the actions of the majority as unjust and unwise. The debate would continue.[10]

President Roosevelt declared that the war was over in 1902, but it lingered on beyond that self-imposed date. The responsibilities that came with "victory" were just beginning. It took several generations before Americans really learned what transpired when the United States captured Manila, fought a brutal war, and assumed control over its colonial empire.

Henry Teller had alienated Roosevelt by questioning and even opposing his pet project, the Panama Canal. The Spanish–American War had shown the necessity of shortening the distance between America's West and East Coasts, its widespread empire, and world trade markets. Since the California gold rush, Americans had dreamed of opening a water route through Central America. Although some favored a Nicaraguan route, the most economical and logical canal route lay across the isthmus of Columbia.

Theodore Roosevelt was not one to wait. Would Columbia give us a lease? When the country balked at U.S. terms, a revolution took place in 1903 that gave birth to Panama. Canal construction started. Members of Congress questioned the legality of some actions, but that did not deter Roosevelt, who kept on building and let them debate.

Teller initially did not oppose the canal idea, but with the "secession" of Panama from Columbia, both he and Patterson attacked this "imperialistic" adventure. In January 1904 a spirited debate over the canal occurred. Henry called it an act of aggression. With no chance of winning, the opponents fought on. They were unable to stop ratification of the treaty giving the United States the canal zone.

Distressed about the cost, cost overruns, and other matters, Teller fought against Roosevelt's canal. On his last day in the Senate, March 3, 1909, he gave a two-hour speech on the issue. He bitterly criticized the Panama Canal as unsafe for ships, adding that the lock system would not work, and the whole project was "far, far too costly." Henry scolded that the misadventures with Columbia and the canal project had brought disgrace on the United States throughout the world.[11]

Teller faced another reelection campaign in 1902. Fewer parties were factors now. Colorado's Populist Party was on its last legs and disappeared after the election. The silver Republicans no longer existed. The Republicans, who had made a steady comeback since the 1890s debacle, captured the governor's chair. The Democrats hung onto a slim majority in the legislature, although the Republicans edged them out in the House. This set the stage for the first in a series of Colorado political fights and embarrassments.

His reelection received national attention, which showed Teller's stature. The ardent gold voice, observed the *Washington Post* (November 13, 1902), "has so much respect for one of the conspicuous advocates of that folly [silver] that it desires his reelection to the Senate." The newspaper chided Colorado Democrats and Republicans for even thinking of turning "a cold shoulder" on "Colorado's grand old man."

The Democrats backed Teller; the Republicans supported Ed Wolcott, who was seeking vindication and reinvigorating his political career. If he lost, there would be no resurrection. The increasingly morose and disagreeable Wolcott had been living in New York, a fact the press did not overlook. Even some of the Republican press took him to task, asking, "The Republican Party or the Wolcott Gang?" Meantime, Teller's opponents accused him of lying and treachery.

The backroom deals, frauds, and corruption that increasingly symbolized Colorado politics came into evidence with both parties. The first days of the legislative session could best be described as a comic opera. The fifty-five Democrats (forty-five Republicans) had the right to select their candidate, but the thirty-four Republicans in the House planned to unseat enough Democrats by various devious means to give them the overall majority.

On January 19–20 the Republicans in the House unseated six Democrats, and the Democrats responded by replacing two Republicans in the Senate with Democrats. That restored their majority. Amid increasing charges of corrupt bargains, graft, and other desperate shenanigans, each party refused to recognize the other's action. Eventually, even the conservative Republican governor, James Peabody, balked at accepting his cohorts' legislative actions.

The Senate split into two rump factions, one for each party. The Democrats met in the Senate chamber, the Republicans in the lieutenant governor's chamber. They locked the doors, and "toughs" and policemen guarded one or the other group. Democrats refused to leave the Senate and stayed there day and night. Republicans in the House tried to conduct business as usual and got nowhere. The governor refused to recognize either Senate. "Blackmailers and Falsifiers," charged the *Rocky Mountain News*. Ouray's *Plaindealer* agreed. Party leaders had used disreputable tactics "that would put a blush of shame on a Tammany hall leader." All they had succeeded in doing was to bring "shame and disgrace upon the fair name of our state."

The Republicans splintered into two factions best described by their slogans: "Anything to beat Wolcott!" and "Wolcott or nobody!" Some Democrats bolted to support Wolcott.

In the end, while the Republicans were absent, the Democrats elected Teller. Republicans talked of a challenge, then Wolcott, realizing the inevitable, withdrew. The whole scenario embarrassed Henry Teller, Coloradans, and the state of Colorado throughout the West and across the nation. Watching from afar in Montana, the editor of the *Anaconda Standard* wrote: "To have defeated Henry M. Teller would have been to Colorado's lasting shame. He is a splendid American, a noble man and an ideal senator, every inch of him." Chicago's *Inter-Ocean* summarized the affair as a "scandalous struggle in the Colorado legislature."

Henry stayed above it all. An observer wrote Dawson that Teller's conduct "through the struggle was perfectly admirable." He refused "to entertain stories of bad faith and present criticism." Wolcott, in a statement to the Republican Party, graciously, although a little bitterly, said, "Senator Teller is in no sense a party to the frauds, while he is the beneficiary of them." Patterson presented Teller's credentials to the Senate amid an ovation that "was remarkable in its cordiality." The seventy-two-year-old Henry Teller entered his last term as senator.[12]

The failed election bid ended Ed's Colorado career. Wolcott died while vacationing in Monte Carlo in March 1905. Some of his friends surmised a broken heart had caused his death, largely because of his "disagreement" with his own party in Colorado. Teller paid a gracious tribute to his former colleague, speaking of the high respect he held for him. They had served twelve years together in Washington, Henry recalled, and "not an unkind word passed between us."

The dynamic reelection came as Colorado politics once again stormed into turmoil. Questions about illegal voting in 1902 had led John Shafroth to voluntarily resign. "Honest John" refused to serve when it looked as if Denver's Democratic machine's fraud had put him into the victory column. A few calls surfaced for Teller to resign, although his election was not an issue. Shafroth defended his friend, deploring anyone who would question his election.

The depth of Colorado's woes had yet to be plumbed. The contested governor's election in 1904–1905, which resulted in three governors in twenty-four hours, topped the drama in 1902. Robert Speer's Democratic machine in Denver voted early and often. Not to be outdone, the Republicans counted ballots without votes being cast in some rotten borough coal districts, and they intimidated voters at the polls. The *Denver Post* called these "stupendous frauds." Teller commented, "I am disgusted at some democrats and more so at the republicans. If all the men who ought to be in the penitentiary could be sent there we would need a dozen new ones." Colorado needed reform, as did other parts of the country.[13]

ADDED TO THE POLITICAL WOES, labor disturbances blasted both hard rock and coal mining. These strikes dated from 1894, and Colorado emerged as a pariah among the states. Violence and hatred became almost the norm in some mining districts. For the hard rock miners, the final struggle took place in 1903–1904.

From Cripple Creek to Telluride, the Western Federation of Miners called its miners out in a decisive showdown with owners, backed by reactionary, antilabor governor James Peabody, the courts, and the Colorado National Guard. Before the struggle ended, the state declared martial law, civil rights were trampled by militia and special deputies, strikers and innocent people were injured and killed, reputations were ruined, boycotts were staged, and union members were deported.

As a result, Colorado gained the image of an antilabor, violent state. It cost well over a million dollars to maintain the guard in the strike districts; add to this the lost wages and profits and the disruption of the economy Colorado suffered. A generation would pass before the aftereffects died away.

An appalled Senator Teller watched from Washington. In a letter to the *Rocky Mountain News* (July 24, 1904), he outlined his views on the rights of the laboring man, unions, and the role of the state in labor disputes. He stated emphatically:

> The acts of the military authorities, not less than their utterances, show conclusively that they do not recognize the fact that their true and only function is to protect the rights of both parties.
>
> On the contrary, they act upon the theory that they are employed to disrupt the union.
>
> The gross injustice of such a position is evident to all the world, and has brought our state into undeserved disrepute.
>
> These unions of labor for mutual benefit are as old as history. . . . They have been useful in encouraging a laudable ambition among workers, and have been a distinct and immediate agency in the elevating of the world's labor.

He clearly stressed that unions, with their advantages for the laboring man, still could not justify forcing laborers to join or to commit crimes.

Scathingly, Henry summarized Peabody's actions: "I do not believe the governor has the authority to declare martial law. The calling out of the militia by the governor does not create martial law, and does not suspend the writ of habeas corpus, although I understand the governor holds that it does." Henry was not pleased that the governor had declared three counties to be in a state of insurrection: "He has not acted as a support to the authorities, but, on the contrary, as independent of and in some cases in opposition thereto." Finally, Teller cut to the heart of the issue: "In all free governments the protection of the person—securing to the citizen his political and civil rights—has always been considered more important than the protection of property rights."

Peabody could not have been pleased with Teller's views. What was the result of Peabody and the owners crushing the union? The state incurred great debt, but of greater importance "is the disgrace inflicted upon our state."[14]

Peabody's actions eventually led to a crisis in Colorado politics, and for years the state's reputation suffered. Trapped in Washington, Teller could do frustrating little to resolve the labor-owner war. He and Senator Patterson petitioned President Roosevelt to investigate the situation, but Roosevelt saw no need for federal intervention. Back in Colorado, the war dragged on until finally ending in 1904 with a complete owner victory.

The exciting years 1893–1896, 1898–1899, and 1903–1904 obscured the routine of life in the U.S. Senate. Teller slipped back into the pattern of political life. A glimpse of some of the problems, concerns, and issues he handled during the second session of the Fifty-fifth Congress in 1898 showed that times had evolved yet, at the same time, remained hauntingly similar to his first years in Washington.

He presented petitions on a variety of subjects—restricting immigration; creating a military park at Vicksburg; placing an assay office in Juneau, Alaska; purchasing Fort Ticonderoga; and advocating anticigarette legislation. Interestingly, he spoke against the concept of rural free delivery of mail. It would, he reasoned, be too costly, doubling post office expenses. It seemed no "hardship" occasionally to wait for mail. Expanding the Civil Service gained his support, as it had earlier.

The Homestead Act, which had helped settle Colorado's eastern plains, attracted Henry's attention once more. Some new method of payment for land was needed, he maintained. Teller admired the concept for all it had done for the West: "I myself have great faith in the conservative influence of a home for every man." Without question, he still favored the income tax: "I believe the time has come when the great expenses of this country necessitate an income tax."

Colorado had been racked by costly labor strikes starting in 1894 at Cripple Creek. Henry thought the federal government should offer assistance. There needed to be a mechanism, he affirmed, to resolve such disputes before damage and expenses mounted. Colorado's senior senator suggested the government should offer voluntary arbitration for labor strikes. The long-term economic and social benefits of federal mediation would more than pay for whatever expenses were initially incurred. His idea failed to gain acceptance.[15]

One old issue recaptured Henry's attention: the Utes in southwestern Colorado. Teller and Wolcott both worked to settle the ongoing dispute over the Ute Reservation. To their neighbors, the Ute land still seemed underutilized and unappreciated by its inhabitants. It sounded like the 1870s all over again! In a speech in January 1895, Teller had argued for breaking up the reservation. "Savagery and solitude" would give way to homes, farms, and prosperity. Teller visited Durango in July 1895 to discuss the removal and investigate the conduct of their agent, former newspaperman Dave Day. Much to locals' approval, he supported their contentions about the agent and about giving the Utes a choice of land or moving.

In 1895 Congress passed a bill that gave the Utes the right to choose individual allotments or move to a reservation at the western end of their land. Those who chose allotments became the Southern Ute community. The rest of their eastern reservation land was opened for settlement on May 4, 1899. The people who chose a reservation became the Ute Mountain Ute.

In the twentieth century Teller continued to insist that the government should protect Ute lands and honoring their treaty agreements. Henry also wanted more help for the Utes in Colorado and Utah.

Teller had been involved in investigating the aftermath of the Oklahoma land rush. Whites had monopolized much of the land reserved for the tribes. A Senate committee investigated, found what it considered the cause, and reported that intermarriage had given the whites the "largest and best part of the lands."[16]

Teller had always strongly supported education. Two Indian boarding schools, Teller Institute and Fort Lewis, continued operating in his state. He fought to get more funding, bragging about Fort Lewis to his colleagues in 1900: "It is a very successful school, one of the most successful in the United States." It succeeded in doing, he proudly observed, what it was intended to do—put "education within reach of Indian children." Both schools needed all the help they could get. Underfunded, understaffed, and, in Fort Lewis's case, with the buildings nearly falling down around them, they still carried out the dream of the former secretary of the interior.

Teller also pushed for more schools in Indian Territory (Oklahoma in 1907) for both whites and native peoples. The shortage was abominable. By the time he retired in 1909, the Indian Bureau had decided boarding schools were not achieving what it had hoped and gone back to reservation schools. Fort Lewis, Teller Institute, and all the others would soon close.

His involvement in southwestern Colorado also included the state's first national park, Mesa Verde. The classic prehistoric ruins had been "discovered" in 1888 and in the years following had gathered increased attention. Their significance and spectacular nature, plus damage and looting by visitors and "pot hunters," inspired a group of dedicated women to work to preserve them by creating a park. Virginia McClurg and Lucy Peabody, joined by others throughout the state and country, led the fight. They wanted a national park to preserve these treasures or, at the least, a state park.

The irrepressible McClurg lobbied both Colorado senators. In April 1898, for instance, she wrote to ask Henry to help her save the ruins. They needed to be protected from "miners, cowboys and relic-hunters." She also wanted information about whether they sat on Ute Reservation land, which they did in part. Would it be possible to buy the land and, if nothing else, donate it to the state for a park? Nothing came of the idea, but the women pushed ahead.

Teller initially exhibited some reservations about a national park. His uneasiness focused on more government encroachment and exactly where and on whose land the ruins were found, reflecting his worry about federal "seizure" of forestlands. One of McClurg's supporters, Ella McNeil, visited Henry in Washington, and her appeal must have helped change his mind. He did insist, however, that an accurate map of the Mesa Verde area would be "indispensable" to save the ruins.

McClurg also wrote to Mrs. William McKinley, asking her to raise the issue with her husband. A reply from an "assistant" secretary told her not to bother either of them. Representative John Shafroth showed the most interest initially about a national park, whereas Teller grew more agreeable to the idea. Shafroth introduced several bills without success, the last just before he resigned. Wolcott had no better success. Teller helped sponsor a park bill in 1904; it passed in the Senate and died in the House.

Finally, after a decade of effort, the women neared success. In 1906 Congress created Mesa Verde National Park.[17]

Both Shafroth and Teller reflected the typical western attitude when it came to national forests. They did not want westerners' "rights" circumscribed and denied. The movement to establish national forests increased dramatically when Theodore Roosevelt became president after McKinley was assassinated in September 1901. Roosevelt brought with him Gifford Pinchot, a trained forester who proposed what needed to be accomplished. Forests represented a legacy for all Americans to enjoy, not just for neighboring settlers to exploit.

Horrified westerners watched as Pinchot and Roosevelt, who also signed the bill for Mesa Verde and other national parks and monuments, raced about creating national forests. For example, the fight to set aside Roosevelt National Forest in Larimer and Boulder Counties lasted six years. Both Teller and Shafroth opposed it, supported by the Larimer County commissioners, petitions, and the local Democratic Party.

Teller harangued the Roosevelt administration. In 1905 Henry protested declaring forests to exist where trees do not: "I will venture to say that any two-horse team could cart off every stick that ever grew or ever will grow on hundreds and hundreds of acres." In 1908 he declared that this foolish idea deprived the states of taxation and the people of their rights.

He also defended state's rights and attacked the mushrooming federal government: "I am disgusted and irritated when a man comes in and says 'the State cannot do it as well as the General Government.' Why not abolish State lines if that is the fact?" Teller continued:

> But you are willing, some of you, at least to shear the States, or if you are not here, in some of the other branches of the Government they are anxious to shear the States of all power and gather in the hands of the Executive of the nation the powers that belong to the people of the states by the very words and letters of the Constitution and by every principle that underlies a free government.

He concluded, "I am one of those who believe a man who does not help himself does not deserve being helped. If the State cannot take care of its own forests and take care of everything that belongs to it, it ought not to be a State."

In a 1908 speech Colorado's senior senator carefully explained for the last time his views on the issue of the states versus the federal government. The rights of the states, in his estimation, rested on "the foundation of this government, and it will be maintained just as long as you can maintain the separate states in their statehood, and no longer." The right of each and every state to control its own domestic institutions "is essential to that balance of power on which the perfection and endurance of our political fabric depends."

Willing to admit that the government might have "authority to reserve land for sale," Teller would go no further. Now Washington was taking care of the forests, hiring more "special agents than any other country in the world," and planting trees. Henry was appalled. He also did not like to be told that the United States would run out of timber in "twenty-eight years" if it continued its present cutting course. Teller doubted it, but nevertheless he suggested that if it did occur, we could look to Canada and its forests.[18]

Teller and his fellow westerners would lose the fight. Despite threats of violence, political maneuvering, and protests, federal control over the forests had come to stay. They accused "czar" Pinchot of being an "impractical dreamer, a petty despot, rapacious and venal"; it did no good. Even Theodore Roosevelt—outdoorsman and former Dakota rancher—did not escape unscratched. Pinchot and Roosevelt had used the divide and conquer method. Ruralites versus urbanites, big lumber companies versus small companies, and large versus small ranchers each had a different agenda. Eventually, much of the opposition dwindled, but the rhetoric did not.

All this led to a fight with conservationist Theodore Roosevelt, the most activist president Teller encountered during his Senate career. Roosevelt, as mentioned, did not like Democrats, and he also became unhappy with westerners who fought his ideas. In addition, Roosevelt fumed about the treatment he had received in 1900 while campaigning in Colorado as the vice presidential nominee. At a riotous political meeting in Victor, he and Wolcott had nearly had to run for their lives. Colorado miners did not like goldbugs: "Governor Roosevelt was hit and narrowly escaped a crowd of angry men."

Although Teller had introduced Roosevelt at a July 1901 meeting in a most "appropriate and felicitous" manner, Roosevelt expressed this opinion in November 1902: "I most earnestly hope that Teller will not under any circumstances be put in [the Senate]. It would be far better to have a vacancy than to have Teller." All this transpired while Henry opposed the administration's Philippine policy and stated his incipient objections to the Panama Canal.

The president could not understand why Colorado preferred Teller to Wolcott and thought the retention of Teller was "a great misfortune." The frustrated activist, though, could do nothing. He wrote to his friend Philip Stewart in Colorado Springs: "Of course now I can take no part of any shape or kind in the senatorial contest. The President has no business to interfere." His dislike of Teller went so deep that he hoped the Republicans would contest Teller's victory. Additionally, Roosevelt did not trust Henry because of his "bitter party prejudices" and because he had been one of the most "mischievous opponents of the Republican Party and of general decency for the last six years."[19]

Unfortunately for Henry, Roosevelt occupied the White House throughout the remaining years of his last term. As he complained to Dawson in 1904, "The President is now the party and what he wants to do his party will do." Teller at least reached a partial understanding: "I can stand Roosevelt if we can get rid of Peabody here." The state did get rid of Peabody, who had caused so much grief during the 1903–1904 strikes and in the contested 1905 governor's election.

Not all matters with which the senator became involved had such profound ramifications. The christening of the new battleship *Colorado* caused a minor flap that seems comical today. In 1902 Teller selected the daughter of Thomas Walsh, millionaire owner of the famous Camp Bird Mine, for the honor. This caused a tempest among some Denver "busybodies" who thought he should have chosen newly elected governor Peabody's daughter. The *Denver Post* fueled the fire, criticizing Walsh for pushing his daughter's candidacy. The incident became so heated that Walsh "cheerfully, willingly, and of my own volition" withdrew his daughter. Teller initially refused to accept the withdrawal; he had chosen Evelyn "because of the appropriateness of the selection." The Walshes insisted, however, so Henry yielded. The battleship *Colorado* was finally christened in 1903 by Cora Peabody.[20]

Momentum was building toward national women's suffrage. With Henry's known support of the idea, plus the fact that his state was the first to grant it by ballot, he received letters regarding the consequences women had on Colorado politics. He proudly responded in 1907 to one inquiry about women voting and about women as elected officials: "I am satisfied that it has been in every way beneficial to the best interests of the State." Henry also gave women "the greater share of credit" for the efforts to reform Colorado politics, a movement that had gained momentum since the 1904–1905 fiasco. He went on to explain that he supported suffrage because he had watched closely what had happened in neighboring Wyoming: "I was satisfied that if the women of that territory were capable of exercising the right of franchise, our women of Colorado were equally so." Moreover, suffrage "will stay because it is based on the principle of human equality, and because the women themselves have demonstrated their ability to maintain the privilege."

From far back in his past, the Meekers reappeared. This time they were squabbling over Arvilla Meeker's pension, family property, and the treatment she had received from one of her daughters. They pleaded with Teller for government relief, and he did sponsor a bill on her behalf. His involvement did not end until Mrs. Meeker died in 1905.[21]

Water, or the need for it, also never seemed to go away. On March 31 and April 2, 1908, Teller strongly defended western water rights. Part of the reason for the timing reflected growing federal water control in the West and what he had seen happening with the forest situation. Liberally supported by water case decisions, Henry argued that to take away water "is equivalent to taking away your life."

He hammered ardently for state's rights. The forty-six sovereignties (two territories) were closer to the people and "are better calculated and better qualified to maintain order and peace" within their boundaries. He was particularly disturbed by federal dam building and the government claiming irrigation rights over water. Teller denied that the U.S. government had any control over the water of Colorado: "Our safety lies, and we intend to stand by it, in holding that the water belongs to the State and that we mean to keep it." He could not resist talking again about federal forest policies: "I would rather see people living on land than to see timber on it, no matter how beautiful it is or how fine. We have destroyed some timber in Colorado, but we have added to the sum happiness by so doing."[22]

Before the speech concluded, Henry had covered all of his major concerns about Washington and the West. He put his finger on two very significant issues that are still being debated. States were already arguing over water issues in court; water, as he insisted, was, is, and will be the lifeblood of the West. The question of growth and development versus the environment and natural resources had taken on added meaning since his earlier days. His reaction to the issue was typical for his era when the "grow or die" mentality held sway. Henry cannot be chastised too severely for reflecting his own and his constituents' views. Coloradans even a generation removed from the frontier still clung to the ideas, or perceived ideas, that guided the pioneers.

With Roosevelt, reformers finally found a supporter in the White House. Because of a host of national problems, the attention called to these issues by muckraking journalists, and the public's confidence that the ills could be resolved, the nation launched into what has been called the progressive era. It lasted beyond Teller's last term. Henry's moderate involvement with the progressives included backing suffrage, trying to curb corporation donations to favored candidates, limiting the working hours of railroad men, and supporting the 1906 Hepburn Act that regulated railroads. Despite some problems with the press, he wanted the United States to maintain a free press: "No one can overestimate the importance of an untrammeled press to the general welfare."

Some of the other matters that concerned Henry in his last term reflected what once had been and what loomed ahead. Kit Carson's heirs asked him to sponsor a bill to help them with claims against the government "due their father." Teller ardently supported increased pensions for veterans, but he did not back a memorial highway for Lincoln to be built between Washington and Gettysburg. A highway, in his estimation, did not seem the proper way of "recognizing the distinguished services of Lincoln." The longtime backer of giving women the vote was asked to support women's suffrage in Oklahoma and nationally: "Your faithful championship is one of the richest treasures possessed by the women of Colorado." Teller, as usual, presented petitions on a variety of topics.

The boundary line between New Mexico and Colorado again gained his attention. It had never been accurately surveyed. He jokingly teased, "We will not try to take any part of Texas!" Mining matters, the Colorado School of Mines, and government buildings in various communities ranked high on his agenda. He championed the admittance of both Arizona and New Mexico as states, whereas some of his colleagues wanted one large state. Teller disagreed, believing the two territories' widely separated population centers, among other things, handicapped such an effort. The senator also downplayed the idea that the "babble" of languages spoken in the two territories would cause problems: "There may always be a little friction between people who speak different languages," but that was nothing serious.

On a more minor issue, when asked whether the University of Colorado or the University of Denver should have a chapter of Phi Beta Kappa, Henry apparently supported the state institution. That year the national chapter initiated the one chapter allotted to each state at the University of Colorado.

A brief Teller presidential boomlet for 1908 quickly died. Henry had no interest in being a candidate; age, among other things, dissuaded him. Bryan received the Democratic nomination in 1908 and lost once again, carrying Colorado, only two other western states, and the solid Democratic South.[23]

The Tellers, as mentioned, stayed with their daughter or son when in Colorado. When they stayed with Harrison in Grand Junction, Henry liked to dabble in farming. A reporter caught up with the "Colorado Cincinnatus" in his blue overalls and "farmer's garb." Teller, who was helping prepare a field for alfalfa, told the reporter he "thoroughly enjoyed this sort of thing." His "hearty laugh and cheerful face bore abundant evidence of that fact." Grateful for the rest from politics and public life, Henry even talked longingly about making Grand Junction his permanent home. The peace and quiet of country life "would be a pleasant change."

Teller approached retirement with relief, and no appeals could get him to change his mind. He would be seventy-nine in May 1909; nearly thirty-three of those years had been spent in Washington in the Senate and the cabinet. He announced: "I think that is sufficient time for me to spend in public service, and will retire."[24]

NOTES

1. Harrison Teller Diary, March 1897, Chris Buys private collection; *Congressional Record,* January 7, 1898, 426; *Grand Junction Sentinel,* February 23, 1914; James Wright, *The Politics of Populism: Dissent in Colorado* (New Haven: Yale University Press, 1974), 218; Bryan to Teller, December 5, 1900, Teller Papers, Colorado Historical Society; Henry Teller, *The Gold Standard Bill* (Washington, D.C.: Government Printing Office, 1900), 4–5; Elmer Ellis, *Henry Moore Teller* (Caldwell, Idaho: Caxton, 1941), 333–334; H. Wayne Morgan, *William McKinley* (Syracuse: Syracuse University Press, 1963), 2909; *Star,* March 9, 1901. For Teller's health problems, see, for example, the *Congressional Record* for 1905.

2. Teller, *Gold Standard,* 1, 3–4, 10; William J. Bryan, *The First Battle* (Chicago: W. B. Conkey, 1896), 153–155; unidentified newspaper articles, "Teller Scrapbook," Chris Buys private collection; *Congressional Record,* January 7, 1898, 424–425; Henry Teller, *The Financial Bill* (Washington, D.C.: Government Printing Office, 1900), 1–16; Bryan to Teller, March 22, 1897, "Silver Republicans," both in Teller Papers, Colorado Historical Society; *Durango Evening Herald,* October 1, 1898; *Denver Times,* September 8, 1898.

3. Page to Dear Grandpa, September 6, 1897, Richard Page Whittle letters, author's possession; undated 1898 clipping, *Engineering and Mining Journal,* unidentified February 23, 1897, clipping, both in "Teller Scrapbook," Chris Buys private collection; *Denver Republican,* April 20, 1899; *Herald* (Omaha), January 21, 1897; Louis Koenig, *Bryan* (New York: G. P. Putnam's Sons, 1971), 267; Henry Teller, "Silver Coinage Speech, January 2, 1898," Teller Papers, University of Colorado; James Teller, *The Battle of the Standards* (Chicago: Schulte, 1896), 9, 14–15. For Colorado production, see Charles Henderson, *Mining in Colorado* (Washington, D.C.: Government Printing Office, 1926).

4. *The World,* December 31, 1899?, "Teller Scrapbook," Chris Buys private collection; *Weekly Republican,* April 13, 1899; *Denver Times,* July 30, 1902; Teller cited in Koenig, *Bryan,* 329; Teller to Dawson, September 13, 1900, Bryan to Teller, February 1, 1901, both in Teller Papers, Colorado Historical Society.

5. Thomas Dawson, "Scrapbooks," Colorado Historical Society, vol. 61; David Healy, *United States Expansionism* (Madison: University of Wisconsin Press, 1970), 9, 11, 35; Henry Graff, *American Imperialism and the Philippine Insurrection* (Boston: Little, Brown, 1969), vii; H. Wayne Morgan, *America's Road to Empire* (New York: John Wiley and Sons, 1965), 113.

6. Teller to Robert Cameron, December 23, 1895, Teller Papers, Colorado Historical Society; Henry Teller, *Cuban Resolution* (Washington, D.C.: Government Printing Office, 1902), 3, 5, 8; Philip Foner, *The Spanish-Cuban-American War and the Birth of American Imperialism* (New York: Monthly Review Press, 1972), 271, 279; Paul F. Gerhard, "The Colorado Delegation in the Fifty-fifth Congress, 1897–1899" unpublished M.A. thesis, University of Colorado, 1948, 141, 144, 146, 254; *Congressional Record,* April 15, 1898, 3898–99, April 20, 1898, 4091, 4093–95.

7. *Congressional Record,* January 5, 1895, 626; *Washington Post,* February 7, 1899; Gerhard, "Colorado Delegation," 173–175; Foner, *Spanish-Cuban-American War,* 419–420, 527; John Corry, *1898: Prelude to a Century* (Bronx: Fordham University Press, 1998), 211; *Denver Times,* September 8, 1898; Edward Taylor, *Senator Henry M. Teller* (Washington, D.C.: Government Printing Office, 1923), 14–15. See also, Teller *Cuban Resolution.*

8. Unidentified clipping, August 1, 1898, "Teller Scrapbook," Chris Buys private collection; Geoffrey R. Hunt, "The First Colorado Regiment in the Philippine Wars," unpublished Ph.D. diss., University of Colorado, 1997, iii–iv, 272; Graff, *American Imperialism,* xv–xvii, 171–172; William Pomeroy, *American Neo-Colonialism* (New York: International, 1970), 9–105, 109–111, 117; Robert Smith, "Antiimperialist Crusade," *Colorado Magazine* (winter 1974), 33–38; Stuart Miller, *Benevolent Assimilation* (New Haven: Yale University Press, 1982), 144; Daniel Schirmer, *Republic or Empire* (Cambridge, Mass.: Schenkman, 1972), 3, 127, 235, 259–260; Corry, *1898,* 327–328. See also, Brian Linn, *The Philippine War, 1899–1902* (Lawrence: University Press of Kansas, 2000).

9. Henry Teller, *The Problem in the Philippines* (Washington, D.C.: Government Printing Office, 1902), selections from 80 pages; *Tribune* (Lewiston, Idaho), July 3, 1899; *Congressional Record,* January 30, 1900, 1315–16; "Remarks, February 11, 1902," Teller Papers, Colorado Historical Society.

10. Richard E. Welch Jr., *Response to Imperialism* (Chapel Hill: University of North Carolina Press, 1979), 60, 67, 73, 159; Corry, *1898,* 327–328; Miller, *Benevolent Assimilation,* 21–22; *New York Times,* January 14, 1899; Schirmer, *Republic,* 257; Healy, *Expansionism,* 257.

11. Dawson, "Scrapbooks," vol. 61; *Congressional Record,* January 1904, February 4, 1908, 1518, February 9, 1909, 2076–77; *New York Times,* March 3, 1909; S. F. Tappen to Dawson, January 9, 1905, Edwin Berthoud to Teller, February 10, 1908, both in Teller Papers, Colorado Historical Society; Smith, "Antiimperialist," 39, 42.

12. *Washington Post,* November 13, 1902; *Rocky Mountain News,* January 18–25, 1903; *Plaindealer,* January 30, 1903; *Anaconda Standard,* January 25, 1903; *Inter-Ocean,* January 27, 1903; *Denver Republican,* January 28, 1903; Dawson, "Scrapbooks," vol. 61; Charles Bayard, "Theodore Roosevelt and Colorado Politics," *Colorado Magazine* (fall 1965): 317–318;

Denver Republican, January 20, 28, 1903; *Denver News,* January 23–24, 1903; *Denver Post,* January 25, 1903; Thomas Dawson, "Teller and Wolcott," Colorado Historical Society, 17; E. M. Ammons to Dawson, January 29, 1903, Teller Papers, Colorado Historical Society; five unidentified articles, 1903, "Teller Scrapbook," Chris Buys private collection.

13. Dawson to *Post,* February 16, 1904, Shafroth to Dawson, June 30, 1903, Teller to Dawson, December 6, 8, 1904, all in Teller Papers, Colorado Historical Society; *Denver Post,* February 16, 1904; *Denver Republican,* February 29, 1904.

14. *Rocky Mountain News,* July 24, 1904; Thomas Noel, "William D. Hanwood," *Colorado Heritage* 2 (1984): 7–8.

15. See *Congressional Record* for the Fifty-fifth Congress, 2d sess., especially May 4, 1898, 4569, May 5, 1895, 4616–17, May 6, 1898, 4799, June 22, 1898, 6228.

16. *Congressional Record,* January 28, 1895, 1444–54, January 10, 1905, 45, March 28, 1908, 4089, February 20, 1909, 2776; Teller to Dawson, September 20, 1884, Teller Papers, Colorado Historical Society; Thomas Dawson, *Wolcott* (New York: Knickerbocker, 1911), vol. 2, 98, 101–102; 1895 Ute Commission Record, Southwest Center, Fort Lewis College; Francis Prucha, *American Indian Policy in Crisis* (Norman: University of Oklahoma Press, 1976), 392–393.

17. *Congressional Record,* March 24, 1900, 5937, January 10, 1905, 45, January 27, 1905, 1468; *Denver Times,* June 12, 1904; Virginia McClurg, "Scrapbooks," Pioneer Museum, Colorado Springs; Park Records, Mesa Verde National Park; *Durango Democrat,* May 31, 1899; *Denver Republican,* October 13, 1898; *Rocky Mountain News,* October 29, 1899; *Denver Times,* June 12, 1904; *Mancos Times,* October 13, 1899.

18. W. J. Morrill, "Birth of the Roosevelt National Forest," *Colorado Magazine* (September 1943): 179–180; *Congressional Record,* February 4, 1905, 186, February 4, 1908, 1869, April 7, 1908, 4476 and 4478; Henry Teller, *Rights of the States* (Washington, D.C.: Government Printing Office, 1908), 2, 7, 11, 19, 24.

19. *Rocky Mountain News,* September 27, 1900; John M. Blum, *The Republican Roosevelt* (Cambridge: Harvard University Press, 1977), 40–41; Richard White, *It's Your Misfortune and None of My Own* (Norman: University of Oklahoma Press, 1991), 408–409; Richard Lamm and Michael McCarthy, *The Angry West* (Boston: Houghton Mifflin, 1982), 216–217; Bayard, "Theodore Roosevelt and Colorado Politics," 312–313; Roosevelt to Philip Stewart, October 25, November 4, 1901, August 3, November 24, 1902, in Elting E. Morison, *The Letters of Theodore Roosevelt* (Cambridge: Harvard University Press, 1951), vol. 3, 42, 412.

20. Charles Thomas to Teller, April 4, 1902, Thomas Walsh to Teller, February 20, 23, March 2, 1903, Teller to Walsh, February 23, 1903, James Peabody to Teller, 1903, Teller to Charles Cramp, March 5, 1903, Teller to Peabody, 1903, Thomas to Dawson, February 23, 1903, *Denver Post* cited in Teller to Dawson, December 8, 1904, all in Teller Papers, Colorado Historical Society.

21. Susan B. Anthony to Teller, May 26, 1900, Teller to Mary C. Bradford, January 8, 1907, Lillian Whiting to Teller, November 13, 29, 1901, Charles Tew to Teller, March 6, 8, 1905, Bill for Relief of Mrs. Meeker, all in Teller Papers, Colorado Historical Society; Marshall Sprague, *Massacre: The Tragedy at White River* (Boston: Little, Brown, 1957), 319.

22. Henry M. Teller, *The State's Control Over Its Water* (Washington, D.C.: Government Printing Office, 1908), 2, 5–8, 9, 14, 16, 31–32, 34–35.

23. G. M. Dameron to Teller, December 9, 1907, Teller to Dawson, October 31, November 6, 1905, Mary Bradford to Teller, January 2, 1907, Ed Hale to Teller, February 29, 1904, all in Teller Papers, Colorado Historical Society; *Congressional Record,* January 31, 1905, 1638, January 15, 1906, 1667, December 5, 1907, 172, April 13, 1908, 7108, May 28, 1908, 4663, December 18, 1908, 440, January 22, 1909, 1282, February 19, 1909, 2668–69. See also index for 1908–1909 sessions, *Congressional Record.* Robert Smith, "Progressive Senators," *Colorado Magazine* (winter 1968), 28, 32–33, 38–39.

24. Undated, unidentified newspaper clipping, "Teller Scrapbook," Chris Buys private collection; Dawson, "Scrapbooks," vol. 61; Teller to Dawson, December 5, 1904, Teller Papers, Colorado Historical Society; *Denver News,* January 1, 1905; William W. Davis, *History of Whiteside County, Illinois* (Chicago: Pioneer, 1908), 327.

Epilogue: "My Record Is My Life"

Teller traveled home from the Senate with many honors and tributes from his colleagues. As he neared his seventy-ninth birthday he, along with other pioneers of Clear Creek and Gilpin Counties, went to Idaho Springs on May 7, 1909, to participate in the fifty-year celebration of the gold discovery and gold rush. In July he spoke at the Pioneers Annual Reunion and gave a "characteristic speech, full of thought and feeling."

Teller had also gone to a pioneer reunion in 1908 at Elitch Gardens to celebrate the anniversary of the arrival of the Russell party, who found the gold that started the rush. Henry gave a "very neat five minute speech." To a new generation, the fifty-niners were relics of a long vanished past. Airplanes, automobiles, electricity, movies, telephones, ragtime melodies had all come into existence since those exciting days.

The Tellers stayed with their daughter Emma in Denver. They were not in the best of health, although they suffered more from old age than from anything debilitating. Henry would no longer farm; nor did he return to a law practice. Willard had died in 1905, and Henry had been in Washington too long to sustain a successful law practice. He did maintain an office in the Boston block and rode a streetcar to his office every day, staying until noon. His mining properties produced little income. The Tellers had not found great mining wealth in Colorado like most of their contemporaries. They did live comfortably, however.

Henry stayed in close touch with current events. He spoke at the 1909 University of Colorado graduation on "The Duties of Citizenship in a Representative Government" and received an honorary doctor of law degree. He called upon the graduates to take the "politics of this state out of the low condition in which it is found." He implored them to demand of the men and women in public office a "devotion to public duty and a fidelity to public trust." You have, Henry reminded them, the right to demand of public officials "their entire energy, entire zeal, and entire intellect." In conclusion, he challenged the graduates: "We owe it to ourselves, we owe it to our children, we owe it to our ancestors to make this the greatest nation in the world."

Proud Harriet heard her husband summarize his creed to public service, a creed his political life had exemplified. In 1911 he returned to Washington for five months, attending meetings of the National Monetary Commission. When he came back to Denver, he urged the legislature to provide funds for the construction of the Moffat Tunnel through the Continental Divide, a project long dreamed about by his longtime friend David Moffat.

He could look with pride on the work of his old congressional and silverite colleague John Shafroth, now governor. Between 1909 and 1913 Shafroth put in place a sweeping reform program in Colorado, including many of the ideas the Populists and Teller had advocated twenty years before. Colorado went from a political backwater to one of the nation's most progressive states thanks to Shafroth.

Teller offered his opinions on topics that had bedeviled him while in the Senate. Federal land ownership received top priority. Before he spoke on the subject, he jokingly remarked that senators were allowed to speak as long as they wanted with no one to tell them when to stop. "My good wife asked me this morning not to tire you out," and I "assure [you] I shall be brief." He was brief, but he still hit point after point. The federal government had no right to exploit the West for its benefit: "We must not become tenants of the government." All the national government should do is "to protect the states against foreign invasion and encroachments."

Teller continued his fight against federal control of Colorado's waters, although he did not believe people should blame the government per se. Henry lamented to a reporter, it was "some cheap one-horse fellow gotten into office." He blasted one of his pet peeves at a speech at a public lands convention: "Forest rangers now move prospectors off reserves. My friends, if that had happened when I first came to this state there would have been one less ranger."

The conservation movement was also a victim of Teller's wrath:

> I haven't heard that the government claims the air yet, but I expect that some of these gentlemen who favor conservation will claim it and try to get revenue from this air for the government.

> We could not have settled Colorado if we had this new-fangled notion of conservation. It is the theory that the people don't know enough to take care of their resources.

The old pioneer seemed a bit curmudgeonly in his old age.[1]

Henry exhibited some reservations about college-trained youth, interesting because he had long championed education. Although pleased to find more college graduates in Denver than in any other city of its size in the United States, he sputtered to a reporter, "College men and women are supposed to be the educated people, though of course they are not always so."

Reporters liked to interview Teller around the time of his birthday. Henry obliged and gave them his opinions on a sweeping array of subjects. Like many old-timers he provided his recipe for a long life: "Don't drink, don't smoke, and marry early."

> Don't drink. Whisky is the curse of the nation.
> Don't smoke, it is costly to health and pocketbook.
> Marry early if you can, but late if not early. Bachelors are an abomination.
> They are of no real good to the community.

Henry had not married until he was past thirty because, he remarked, of his inability to support a wife and family.

Among his other advice: eat moderately, rise early, follow a daily routine, and get lots of sleep starting at 8 P.M. Parties and society had never interested him. In an interview while he was still in the Senate, Henry had laid out his views: "Society does not appeal to me. It is very shallow and silly and I never go to a dinner or a reception in Washington unless it is impossible for me to send my regrets. There are too many other important things to think about." He did enjoy working in the garden, reading, and writing letters.

On politics, he ventured his views to a new generation. Reflecting back, he commented on the presidency: "It doesn't take much brains to be president judging from the men who got away with it." In his time, Chester Arthur was "the best man and most loyal friend that ever sat in the White House." He took one last crack at Roosevelt during his run for the presidency in 1912: "Roosevelt is a clown!" Henry voted for Wilson in what would be his last political act. Regarding his retirement, Teller said he stayed in the Senate until he believed he "could no longer do full justice for the people."

For his beloved Colorado, Teller saw nothing but a bright future: "Colorado is a great state. It is growing greater, better every day." He did not forget his roots. Praise for Colorado's success should go to the people who came here to make it home and built it into what it "is today." Teller expected a "true awakening of mining" that would bring such prosperity that Colorado would move into the forefront of the "industrial and prosperous commonwealths of the nation."

Regarding himself, he said he had never expected to live much over seventy, but "right living" had gotten him into his eighties. With a bit of wry humor he concluded, "It is hard to grow old. I hate to be old. I wish I could roll the years back and be 70 again."[2]

His contemporary Mark Twain reflected thoughts along the same vein: "I was young then, marvelously young then, wonderfully young, younger than I'll ever be again by several hundred years." It had been an exciting, heartbreaking, adventure-some, at times tragic, and legendary generation in which to have been alive.

He and Harriet were almost alone now. The friends and colleagues of their youth and political career were gone. Evans, Chaffee, Wolcott, Gilpin, Routt, Byers, Hill, Moffat, Tabor, all the presidents he had served with except Theodore Roosevelt, and most of their neighbors from Central City were dead.

Henry Moore Teller caught up with his past just after midnight Monday, February 23, 1914. He had been in ill health for the past two years, and his death was not unexpected. His beloved Harriet lived until December 29, 1924, dying also at the home of her daughter Emma.

How does one measure a man's life and contributions? Teller himself gave insights into the subject. When asked to compile notes for his biography, he declined: "No, my record is my life; I must stand or fall by that before posterity."

Geographically, the memory of Henry Teller is preserved in several Colorado locations, with Teller County, which covers the rich Cripple Creek district, the most prominent. The county was organized in March 1899 when the legislature carved it out of El Paso and Fremont Counties. Fittingly, Teller County ranked as Colorado's number-one gold and silver producer during Teller's lifetime. Teller Mountain, near the headwaters of the Platte and Swan Rivers, once had mining prospects. So did Teller City, located in North Park. A silver camp of several hundred inhabitants with a "bright future in 1881," it was nearly deserted within two or three years. Teller City never had the predicted boom "that will surprise some of the older and more talked of camps."

Teller, who when he served in the Senate advocated the development of Alaska—including introducing reindeer—was honored with two place-names in that state. Teller Harbor is the most northerly harbor on the American side of the Bering Sea. The village of Teller, about 60 miles northwest of Nome, had a transitory population of reportedly near 1,000 during the 1900 gold rush. Today it hovers around 200.[3]

Central City's Teller House still stands, as does his law office—visible reminders of the man who once lived and worked there. One is used by the Central City Opera House Association; the other, retired from gambling and the hotel business, offers a restaurant for visitors. The opera house Henry helped support presents operas now. A few communities have Teller streets or avenues.

In the days following Teller's death, Colorado newspapers and Coloradans paid tribute to the "grand old man of Colorado." Governor Elias Ammons lauded Teller as "easily the first citizen of the state." Colorado's pioneer newspaper, the *Rocky Mountain News*, eulogized: "In every hour of his public and private life, he was the American of towering strength, of exalted principles, a devotee of exemplar ideals." The *Silverton Miner* called him one of the best-known men in the West. The Christ Methodist Episcopal Church remembered its member: "His coming in and going out of our services in the years past has been so quiet, modest, and unobtrusive that many were not aware that so eminent and distinguished a man was a lowly member of our beloved church."

His friend Irving Stanton said Henry embodied "an important part of the history of Colorado Territory and State." A contemporary newspaperman stressed, "He stands before the country as the tongue of Colorado, but he speaks not for Colorado alone, nor alone for the United States, but the humbler three-fourths of all humanity." No one knew him better than Thomas Dawson, who observed: "He endeared himself to the people of his own State of Colorado by his untiring devotion to and championship of their interests in the many problems which came up for adjustment between the new State and the National Government." He described Senator Teller as always thoughtful:

> Not thoughtful only, but reasonable, patient and forebearing, good-natured, agreeable and often even mirthful. All this without flurry or pretense or ostentation, without an effort to make the recipient of the kindness feel that he had been. He often seemed most indifferent to the thanks of beneficiaries—so indifferent, indeed, as to create the impression that he was cold.

Montana representative Thomas Carter admired him greatly: "I venture to say that no Senator in the history of the country has been more punctual and constant in attending the sessions of the Senate or more vigilant in scrutinizing legislative proceedings." Old-time Populist and South Carolina senator Benjamin Tillman recognized his colleague "as the embodiment of honesty, high moral purpose, and sincerity. In my fourteen years' association with him I have frequently had occasion to admire his manliness and intense Americanism or patriotism."[4]

These tributes are as true today as they were when written and uttered. Teller was a dedicated, conscientious, knowledgeable, and forthright public servant. Even his opponents granted him that. Colorado was fortunate to have him in Washington from 1876 to 1909 during the state's formative years.

Victory did not crown his every effort; principle and dedication did. It took courage to take some of the positions Teller espoused. From his opposition to statehood in the 1860s through his opposition to the Republican Party and the Panama Canal, he boldly took his stand regardless of the consequences. It took mettle to support the Mormons in the 1880s, to speak out for women's suffrage and fight for the silver cause. His ideas on the education of natives, imperialism, and the rights of laborers looked accurately into the future. In Washington during his tenure no one better represented Colorado's and westerners' opinions and desires.

Henry Teller was a transitional leader with roots in the nineteenth century and views that looked into the twentieth. His career reflected much of what had been and foreshadowed much of what would come. Henry saw the old West and he saw the new West. Like Moses, he led his people—sometimes stumbling, sometimes marching—to their "new" promised land.

Henry's concern for the people reflected Lincoln and heralded Wilson and Franklin Roosevelt. Teller was wrong on occasion, too, as in his support of statehood in 1864, for example, and his opinions on the Panama Canal and national forests. He clearly reflected western attitudes that were less progressive about Ute removal, forests, and conservation. For his era, however, he generally embraced his constituents' views. Many westerners have continued to sympathize with his position on states' rights.

Henry Teller has been sharply criticized by Yellowstone Park historians for his role involving the park during his term as secretary of the interior. He has been described as "the weakest secretary" in terms of the park's interests, a "negative force," and "antipark." The fact that he appreciated the park and its wonders cannot be denied, but whether he tried his best to run the park without tradition or specified policy depends on one's interpretation. His stated ideas and recommendations to Congress were sound, especially in the political climate of the 1880s. Congress often did not act on his or other secretaries' recommendations. His administration—the first to wrestle with railroad-produced publicity, crowds of tourists, increasing popularity, and mounting damage to the park's treasures—had few guidelines. Teller handled the situation as well as he could from Washington and with having to face new problems every year.[5]

Before going to Washington, however, Teller depicted the easterner who came West to find fame and fortune. Although the lawyer-turned-entrepreneur had a better education and starting point in life than many of his contemporaries, they held aspirations in common in this, their promised land. The lawyer became a mining man, railroad official, investor, businessman, military officer, and politician. Like most of his neighbors, Teller never made a great fortune from his profession and investments. In that, Henry was more typical than the Tabors and Strattons in Colorado's and the West's saga. Teller did help develop, promote, economically strengthen, and settle his beloved Colorado. Politically, he gave the state respectability and honor.

He was actively involved in the American scene in one of its great transitional eras. The United States had gone from an agricultural/rural/continental outlook to an industrial/urban/world power view. The silver issue he so ardently championed reflected deeper yearnings than merely a higher price for the metal. It spoke about concerns for something fundamental in the American character—anxiety about changes in economic foundations, lifestyles, traditional values, America's role in the world, political power, and the "common people." That new world seemed a fearsome place for those whose roots were buried deep in the past.

Despite all this, optimism underlay much that occurred in Teller's lifetime—optimism that beckoned from the promised land for those fortunate enough to take advantage of the opportunity, optimism that the darkest situation would prove reversible, optimism that against all odds the cause would triumph.

To be sure, there had been bumps and detours along the way, and not all people had participated equally. Some had been pushed aside in the rush to open and develop the West. The natural resources had been ruthlessly developed, and in the stampede for profit and pleasure, a mess remained for another generation to resolve. Most folks were certainly aware of all this, but they had come West to develop and exploit, to make a new life for themselves, and perhaps to build a greater America. They asked nothing more than to be judged by the standards of their own day.

The family man, church member, and civic leader assisted in making Central City a "civilized" settlement with all the attributes of the home he left behind. That goal was shared by his generation. The Central Cities of the West transplanted culture, education, religion, commerce, personal values, and society from back East or any other homeland to urbanize their new home in proper Victorian style. Henry helped bring investment and investors to Gilpin County and the entire territory in the formulative years in the 1860s and into the late 1870s. The fact that Central City failed to continue to grow and develop was not his or his neighbors' fault. Mining created the community, and mining and its economic hinterland generally had a calculable life expectancy. Towns have a life cycle from birth to decline; mining often only speeded the process.

The contrast, though, between Colorado of 1861 and that of 1914 was startling. In fifty-three years the state had been transformed. Colorado's population had soared from 34,000 to over 799,000, Denver's from 4,756 to 213,381. Wagons, stagecoaches, and pack trains had been replaced by railroads, automobiles, and the airplane. The telephone and movies opened a new world. The electric light had taken the place of the kerosene lamp in urban Colorado, and indoor plumbing had replaced the outhouse. Rural Coloradans, though, often failed to notice a change in their lives. Nonetheless, mining and early Coloradans had succeeded better than they may have realized as they and their descendants—and all Americans—neared World War I. Henry Teller could take pride in being a part of making that success possible.

Thomas Hornsby Ferril's poem "Judging From the Tracks" offers a yardstick to measure Henry Moore Teller and his career.

Man and his watchful spirit lately walked
This misty road . . . at least the man is sure.
Because he made his tracks so visible,
As if he must have felt they would endure.

There was no lovely demon at his side,
A demon's tracks are beautiful and old,
Nor is it plausible a genius walked
Beside him here, because the prints are cold.

And judging from the tracks, it's doubtful if
A guardian angel moved above his head,
For even thru the mist it can be seen
That he was leading and not being led.

NOTES

1. *The Trail,* July 1908, 27, May 1909, 25, July 1909, 16; Thomas Dawson, "Scrapbooks," Colorado Historical Society, vol. 61; *Denver Republican,* April 7, 1911; *Denver Times,* September 29, 1911. On some of his health problems, see Teller to Dawson, September 22, 1890, July 24, 1892, Teller Papers, Colorado Historical Society; *Denver Republican,* April 13, 1899; *Denver News,* May 23, 1913.

2. *Denver Republican,* April 13, 1899, May 24, 1912; *Denver News,* May 23, 1913; unidentified newspaper article, "Teller Scrapbook," Chris Buys private collection; *Denver Times,* September 29, 1922, February 23, 1914.

3. Unidentified newspaper articles, "Teller Scrapbook," Chris Buys private collection; Charles Henderson, *Mining in Colorado* (Washington, D.C.: Government Printing Office, 1926), 27, 247; *Weekly Republican,* March 16, 1882; *Denver Post,* May 10, 1916; *Rocky Mountain News,* April 29, 1881.

4. Undated, unidentified article, "Teller Scrapbook," Chris Buys personal collection; *Denver Times,* February 23, 1914; *Grand Junction Sentinel,* February 23, 1914; *Rocky Mountain News,* February 24, 1914; *Silverton Miner,* February 27, 1914; Christ Methodist Episcopal Church, "Bulletin," March 1, 1914; Irving Stanton, *Sixty Years in Colorado* (Denver: State Historical Society, 1922), 60; Thomas Dawson, *Senator Henry M. Teller* (Washington, D.C.: Government Printing Office, 1923), 4; Carter cited in Edward Taylor, *Senator Henry M. Teller* (Washington, D.C.: Government Printing Office, 1923), 30–33; Thomas Dawson, "The Personal Side of Senator Teller," Colorado Historical Society, 4; *Portrait and Biographical Record of Denver and Vicinity, Colorado* (Chicago: Chapman, 1898), 127.

5. For criticism, see Aubrey L. Haines, *The Yellowstone Story* (Yellowstone, Wyo: Yellowstone Library and Museum Association, 1977), vol. 1, 324; Richard Bartlett, *Yellowstone: A Wilderness Besieged* (Tucson: University of Arizona Press, 1985), 215, 250.

Bibliographical Essay

Henry Teller has been the subject of a variety of nineteenth- and twentieth-century articles and a book. Elmer Ellis wrote a detailed biography, *Henry Moore Teller: Defender of the West* (1941), but since that date no others have appeared. This short essay is intended to give interested readers information on where to look for further material. Everyone is encouraged to check the notes for specific references and an array of secondary books and articles on individuals and subjects.

Three archives contain the majority of Teller's original material—University Archives (University of Colorado), Western History Department of the Denver Public Library, and the Colorado Historical Society. Thomas Dawson material is found at the Colorado Historical Society. Colorado College's Special Collections contain some Teller items. Other Teller letters and primary documents are scattered throughout a variety of collections, and some are in private hands, as indicated in the notes.

Colorado newspapers provide a wealth of information and are well worth looking through. A small number oppose Teller on various issues; more support him, especially beginning in the 1890s. The *Whiteside Sentinel* (Morrison, Illinois) provides background for the early years. A few out-of-state newspapers add a small share of information; the *New York Times*, with its index, is the best of these—particularly during his Department of the Interior period and the later silver issue. The *Congressional Record* is a gold mine of information on Teller's congressional career and his time as secretary of the interior. Federal records in a variety of categories add help and enlightenment for the researcher.

The search for information on Henry and Harriet Teller and their era is fascinating and abounds with historical adventure. The rewards will far outweigh the time and effort spent. As Sherlock Holmes exclaimed, "Come, Watson, come! The game is afoot."

Index

Page numbers in italics indicate illustrations.